HUDSON BAY
NTARIO
QUÉBEC
NEWFOUNDLAND
NEW BRUNSWICK
P.E.I.
NOVA SCOTIA
ATLANTIC OCEAN

HANDBOOK OF CANADIAN MAMMALS

1 Marsupials and Insectivores

HANDBOOK OF CANADIAN MAMMALS

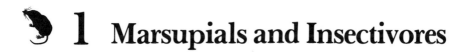 **1** Marsupials and Insectivores

C.G. van Zyll de Jong

Coloured Illustrations
Brenda Carter

Drawings
C.H. Douglas and E. van Ingen

National Museum of Natural Sciences
National Museums of Canada

© National Museums of Canada 1983

National Museum of Natural Sciences
National Museums of Canada
Ottawa, Canada K1A 0M8

Catalogue No. NM92-80/1-1983E

ISBN 0-660-10328-1

Printed in Canada

Édition française
Traité des mammifères du Canada
ISBN 0-660-90271-0

Published by the
National Museums of Canada

Editor
Bonnie Livingstone

Design/Production
James MacLeod

Design Layout
Gregory Gregory Limited

Typesetter
PGTA Ltd.

Printer
Ateliers des Sourds Montréal (1978) Inc.

CONTENTS

LIST OF COLOUR PLATES

LIST OF FIGURES

18. Snout of (a) *Parascalops*, (b) *Scapanus*, and (c) *Scalopus*

19. Skull of *Sorex arcticus*

20. Skull of *Sorex cinereus*

21. Skull of *Sorex fumeus*

22. Skull of *Sorex gaspensis*

23. Skull of *Sorex monticolus*

24. Skull of *Sorex trowbridgii*

25. Skull of *Sorex palustris*

26. Skull of *Sorex bendirii*

27. Skull of *Sorex hoyi*

28. Skull of *Blarina brevicauda*

29. Skull of *Cryptotis parva*

30. Skull of *Neurotrichus gibbsii*

31. Skull of *Scalopus aquaticus*

32. Skull of *Parascalops breweri*

33. Skull of *Scapanus townsendii*

34. Skull of *Scapanus orarius*

35. Skull of *Condylura cristata*

LIST OF DISTRIBUTION MAPS

ACKNOWLEDGEMENTS

The writing of this handbook would have been impossible without the accumulated wealth of information published by many individuals over the years. Their names are listed in the appropriate reference section.

I was fortunate in being able to draw on the artistic skills of Brenda Carter, Charles Douglas, and Egbert van Ingen, whose illustrations enhance this book. David Campbell, staff member of the Mammalogy Section, assisted with the compilation of mensural and distributional data and the literature search. Donna Naughton prepared the final distribution maps. I am indebted to Henri Ouellet for help in coining new French common names.

For typing the manuscript I thank Mrs. J. McConnell, Head of Word Processing and her staff, and I am grateful to the staff of the Publishing Division for their part in bringing about the production of this book.

Eleanor Fenton and Chuck Gruchy nursed the book through its early stages of development and did much to speed up its eventual production. Finally I owe a debt of gratitude to the following colleagues and their institutions across the country for providing information and access to their collections: S. Gorham, New Brunswick Museum; C.J. Guiguet, British Columbia Provincial Museum; R.L. Peterson, The Royal Ontario Museum; W.E. Roberts, University of Alberta; F. Scott, Nova Scotia Museum; H.C. Smith, Alberta Provincial Museum; J.E. Storer, Saskatchewan Natural History Museum; M.E. Taylor, University of British Columbia; and R.E. Wrigley, Manitoba Museum of Man and Nature.

PREFACE

The first major scientific work devoted to Canadian mammals was John Richardson's *Fauna boreali–americana* (1828). Although the late nineteenth and early twentieth centuries witnessed a steadily increasing interest in mammalogy in North America, it was not until 1946 that a taxonomic and distributional synopsis of the mammal fauna of Canada appeared, with R.M. Anderson's *Catalogue of Canadian Mammals*. A number of publications dealing with the mammals of provinces or regions of Canada have appeared over the years. One of the earliest of these is Seton's (1909) *Life Histories of Northern Animals*, an account of the mammals of Manitoba, which was popular and widely read. Since then various publications have followed in its wake, so that there are now one or more titles devoted to the mammals of every province and territory in Canada (e.g. Anderson 1938, Beck 1958, Cameron 1958, Cowan and Guiguet 1956, Dionne 1902, Harper 1956, Morris 1948, Northcott 1974, R.W. Smith 1940, Soper 1961 and 1965, and Youngman 1975, to mention a few). Peterson's (1966) *The Mammals of eastern Canada* is broader in scope, encompassing all provinces and their offshore waters east of the Manitoba border, including the islands in James Bay and eastern Hudson Bay. A popular account of the mammals of all of Canada, *The Mammals of Canada* by A.W.F. Banfield, was finally published in 1974 as a companion volume to W.E. Godfrey's (1966) *The Birds of Canada*.

The present work seeks to fill the need for a treatment in greater depth of all Canadian mammals for use as a basic reference by students, professional biologists and naturalists. The aim of this handbook is to provide an up-to-date summary of the systematics, distribution and life history of all free-living species of mammals, other than man, that occur in Canada, or that occured in this country in the historic past.

It goes without saying that a work of such scope is of necessity based on the observations and research of numerous individuals. This first volume of the handbook, and the others that will follow, is thus to a large extent a compilation and synthesis, although I hope a critical one, of information widely scattered in the literature. Wherever possible only primary sources of information were used.

The majority of mammals that share the land with us lead secretive, hidden lives and are rarely seen; when seen they are glimpsed only fleetingly by most people. Because of this elusiveness, mammals have never attained the same popularity among naturalists that birds have enjoyed. To the persistent and patient naturalist, however, the study and observation of mammals in the field offers much intellectual stimulation and aesthetic enjoyment.

In view of the difficulty of observing most mammals, it is not surprising that much remains to be learned about our native species. It is not only the professional mammalogists, relatively few in number, who can fill the gaps in our knowledge. The amateur mammalogist can make a significant contribution to our store of knowledge, particularly with respect to details of life histories, and distribution, by careful observations and by submitting specimens of uncommon or rare species found dead, to provincial natural history museums or to the National Museum of Natural Sciences in Ottawa.

It is hoped that this volume and the other volumes of the handbook will be useful to all those with a serious interest in our wild mammals. If these volumes contribute to a wider appreciation and understanding of our mammal fauna, and stimulate its study by a greater number of people, they will have achieved their objective.

THE AUTHOR

Constantinus G. van Zyll de Jong was born in Bandung, Java, and, as a young man, came to Canada from the Netherlands. He attended the universities of Guelph and Alberta and obtained his Ph.D. degree in Zoology in 1968 from the University of Toronto, where he was associated with the Royal Ontario Museum. After graduation he worked for the Manitoba Government in furbearer management and wildlife research. Since 1972 he has been Curator of Mammals at the National Museum of Natural Sciences in Ottawa. His research on the systematics and distribution of mammals has taken him from coast to coast and has included studies on a number of species ranging from shrews to bison.

External and skull measurements and skeletal characteristics of Soricids. 1) total length (TL); 2) tail length (T); 3) hind foot length (HF); 4) skull length (SL); 5) cranial breadth (CB); 6) maxillary width (MW); 7) interorbital width (IOW); 8) incisor width; 9) width across M2–M2; 10) length of the upper unicuspid tooth row; 11) P4–M3 length; 12) glenoid width; 13) length of mandible; 14) height of coronoid process; 15) coronoid process-condyle length; 16) length of mandibular toothrow; 17) occlusal view of upper left toothrow of *Sorex* from bottom to top upper incisor, five unicuspids, P4 and M1–M3: me = metacone; ms = mesostyle; mts = metastyle; pa = paracone; ps = parastyle; hy = hypocone; pr = protocone; 18) occusal view of left lower toothrow of *Sorex* from bottom to top lower incisor: c, p4 and m1–m3: end = endoconid; med = metaconid; pad = paraconid; hyd = hypoconid; prd = protoconid; 19) skeleton of a soricid (*Blarina*): c = cranium; ca = carpals; cav = caudal vertebrae; cv = cervical vertebrae; f = femur; fi = fibula; h = humerus; lv = lumbar vertebrae; m = mandible; mca = metacarpals; mta = metatarsals; p = patella; pe = pelvis; ph = phalanges; r = ribs; ra = radius; s = sacrum; sc = scapula; t = tibia; ta = tarsals; tv = thoracic vertebrae; u = ulna.

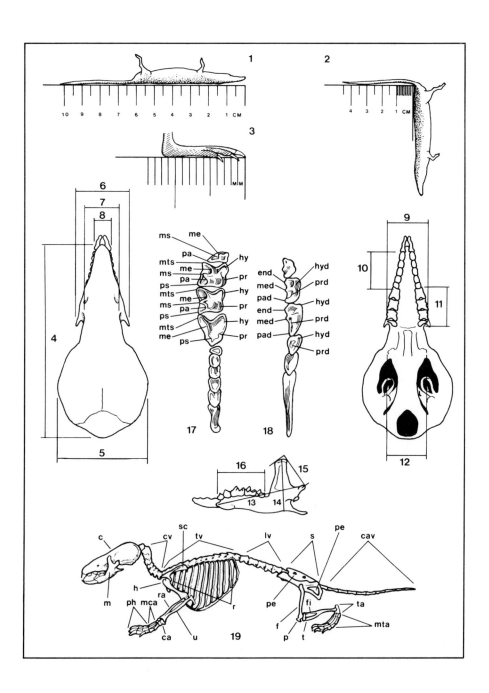

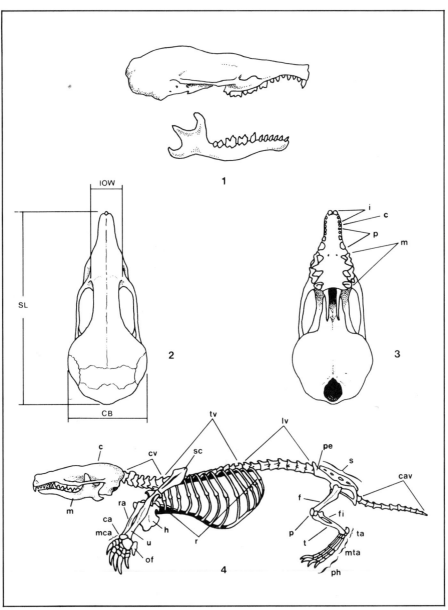

Skeletal characteristics of talpids (1) lateral (2) dorsal and
(3) ventral aspect of the skull (*Scapanus*); SL = skull length;
CB = cranial breadth; IOW = interorbital width; c = canine;
i = incisors; m = molars; p = premolars. (4) Skeleton of a talpid
(*Parascalops*): c = cranium; ca = carpals; cav = caudal vertebrae;
cv = cervical vertebrae; f = femur; fi = fibula; h = humerus;
lv = lumbar vertebrae; m = mandible; mca = metacarpals; mta =
metatarsals; of = os falciforme; p = patella; pe = pelvis; ph = phalanges;
r = ribs; ra = radius; s = sacrum; sc = scapula; t = tibia; ta = tarsals; tv =
thoracic vertebrae; u = ulna.

INTRODUCTION TO VOLUME 1

The basic format followed in this book is taxonomic, with sections on orders, families, genera, and species in hierarchical sequence forming the bulk of the text. The main body of the text is preceded by a brief synoptic classification of the mammals and a summary of the composition of the Canadian mammal fauna.

The sections on the higher taxa deal mainly with their morphology, systematics and worldwide distribution.

To aid in the correct identification of the insectivores, many of which are somewhat difficult to identify for those not familiar with them, an illustrated key has been provided. External as well as internal diagnostic characters have been included to allow where possible for the identification of the animal in the flesh, as well as of well prepared specimens. For the identification of most smaller shrews, a magnifying glass or dissecting microscope is needed.

The species accounts contain detailed information on morphology, including measurements and weight; distribution; and systematics and biology; presented in a standardized manner for each species. Bibliographic references follow each species account. The information presented in the species accounts includes the following.

Name   The scientific and English and French common names of each species are given. A brief synonymy of scientific names is included giving the name changes that reflect changes in our understanding of the taxonomy of a species. Etymological information is given in brackets immediately below the name. Greek words are written with equivalent English letters. Where more than one English name has been used in the literature, preference is given to those that are morphologically, ecologically or geographically descriptive; the other names are listed in brackets. French names, with some exceptions, follow Bernard et al. 1967.

Measurements and Weight   Measurements and weights (in millimetres and grams respectively, unless indicated otherwise) are presented in tabular form. The following measurements are listed: total length (TL), tail length (T), hind-foot length (HF), weight (W), skull length not including the incisors (SL), cranial breadth (CB), interorbital width (IOW) and maxillary width (MW). For definitions of these measurements see the glossary. Sample size (N), mean ($\bar{x}$), standard deviation (SD), coefficient of variation (CV), and observed range (OR) are given for all the variates listed. If original data could not be obtained, observed range and mean values were extracted from the literature.

Description   The description of individual species is brief and concentrates on essential points. Most descriptions are supplemented by illustrations of the whole animal, the skull, and diagnostic characters. Differential diagnoses of a species and other species with which it can be confused are also given to assist in identification. In discussing individual teeth, those in upper and lower jaws are denoted by upper and lower case respectively.

Distribution   The geographic range of each species is outlined briefly in words and depicted on range maps showing the Canadian and world distribution. The distribution in Canada is shown in some detail, including peripheral localities, which are also listed in the text. Full documentation of the distributional data on which the maps are based has been omitted for the sake of brevity. This information is available at the National Museum of Natural Sciences, Ottawa. The North American or Holarctic distribution is shown in less detail on small insets.

Systematics   Under this heading are discussed relationship to other species, unresolved systematic problems, occurrence in the fossil record, evolutionary and zoogeographic information where appropriate, and geographic variation and subspecies.

Classification is the ordering of organisms into groups on the basis of their relationship in a system of hierarchic categories. The most important of these categories is the species, which exists in nature and can be determined with some degree of objectivity. The biological species concept followed here is defined as groups of actually or potentially interbreeding natural populations, which are reproductively isolated from other such groups. This definition cannot be directly applied to populations that are separated in space or time, the so-called allopatric or allochronic populations. In practice the evidence of specific identity is usually largely morphological and the presence or absence of interbreeding is inferred from it. Assignment of taxa to categories above or below the level of species, such as family, genus or subspecies, is much more subjective.

Subspecies, sometimes referred to as geographic races, are phenotypically similar populations of a species, which occupy a subdivision of the species range, and which are phenotypically distinct from other such populations. Recognition of subspecies usually requires that they are not connected by clinal variation, but by steps (zones of intergradation) or that they are separated by barriers that inhibit gene flow.

The majority of subspecies of Canadian mammals were described a long time ago, often on the basis of inadequate samples and without basic statistical evaluation. The often subtle differences in colour or in size or proportion of the skull, which formed the basis for recognition of many of these subspecies, make identification of an individual to subspecies next to impossible in many cases. Critical analysis of geographic variation and a re-evaluation of the subspecies of many of our species are needed, but lie outside the scope of this book.

Although I would prefer to recognize as subspecies only distinct isolated populations of a species or those that are contiguous and connected by a narrow zone of intergradation, I have for the sake of completeness listed all nominal subspecies occurring in Canada with a summary of their distinguishing characters as reported in the literature. Measurements have been included where size or proportion are alleged to be important in distinguishing between subspecies. Where possible, the distinctness of a subspecies or the lack of it, is commented upon. Most contiguous subspecies appear to be linked by continuous or clinal variation, which makes their objective delineation impossible. For this reason and the lack of reliable information on distribution of subspecies no boundaries between subspecific ranges are shown on the distribution maps, and published subspecific distributions are merely indicated in the text.

Biology   Ecology, behaviour, reproduction, and ontogeny of the species are discussed under this heading. The discussion of the ecology of the species includes information on habitats, places in which to live, food, interaction with other animals, and population structure and dynamics. Where possible this information has been drawn from studies done in Canada, but if such studies were not available, information from neighboring parts of the United States, likely to be applicable to the Canadian part of the range, was used.

References   Instead of following the practice used in technical papers of citing author and date in the text, the references are numbered and listed by author and date at the end of a section for the sake of brevity. Full citation is given in the terminal bibliography. The references listed generally serve as an indicator of the amount of information available for each species, as well as the geographic origin of the information and its applicability to parts of the Canadian range. Emphasis is on primary sources and purely distributional literature has not been included.

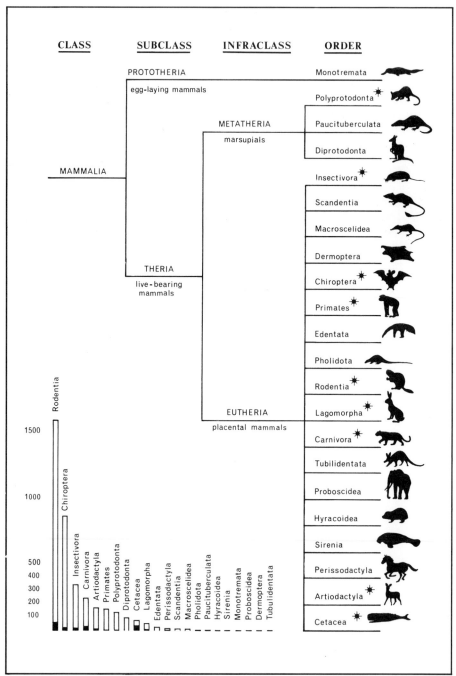

Figure 1.   Classification of the Recent mammals of the world to order.
The orders indigenous in Canada are marked with an asterisk. The
histogram represents the approximate numbers of living species in
each order. The black portion of a bar represents the number of
species native to Canada. Only a small fraction of the world fauna is
represented in Canada.

SYNOPTIC CLASSIFICATION OF THE CLASS MAMMALIA AND THE COMPOSITION OF THE CANADIAN MAMMAL FAUNA.

The simplified classification presented here follows that of G.G. Simpson (1945) with minor modifications. It shows the 22 extant orders of mammals of which 9 (41%), marked with an asterisk, are indigenous to Canada. The Rodentia, the largest order, has 64 living species in Canada, representing approximately 4% of the world's rodents. Similar figures for the other orders represented in Canada in order of the number of species are: Carnivora, 38 species (27 fissipeds, 11 pinnipeds), 16%; Cetacea, 34 species, 45%; Insectivora, 22 species, 6%; Chiroptera, 19 species, 2%; Artiodactyla, 11 species, 6%; Lagomorpha, 7 species, 13%; Primates, 1 species, 0.6%; Polyprotodonta, 1 species, 0.7%.

The above figures do not include a small number of introduced species that has become established, as wild or commensal populations in Canada, comprising 4 rodents, 2 lagomorphs, 1 perissodactyl and 1 artiodactyl.

The total number of species recorded for Canada including introduced species is 205 (about 5% of the world fauna) of which 159 are terrestrial and 46 marine.

Although Canada's mammal fauna therefore represents only a small fraction of the total world fauna, relatively few species have been lost in historical times and good populations of many of the larger mammals fortunately remain.

Four species, all carnivores, have been extirpated on Canadian territory — the swift fox (*Vulpes velox*), the sea mink (*Mustela macrodon*), the black-footed ferret (*M. nigripes*), and the sea otter (*Enhydra lutris*). The last-named has recently been reintroduced to its former range in British Columbia and attempts to re-establish the swift fox are underway. The outlook for the eventual re-establishment of the black-footed ferret is less optimistic. The species still occurs in the United States although at a much reduced level. Under the impact of human settlement and exploitation of natural resources a few distinct geographical forms (e.g. eastern wapiti, *Cervus elaphus canadensis*) vanished completely, some species were driven close to the edge of extinction, and many more, especially the larger mammals and furbearing carnivores, were reduced in numbers and distribution. On the other hand a small number of species (e.g. white-tail deer, *Odocoileus virginianus*, red fox, *Vulpes vulpes*, and coyote, *Canis latrans*) not only survived but benefitted from the changes brought about by man, by increasing in number and extending their ranges.

Didelphis virginiana

Colour Plate I

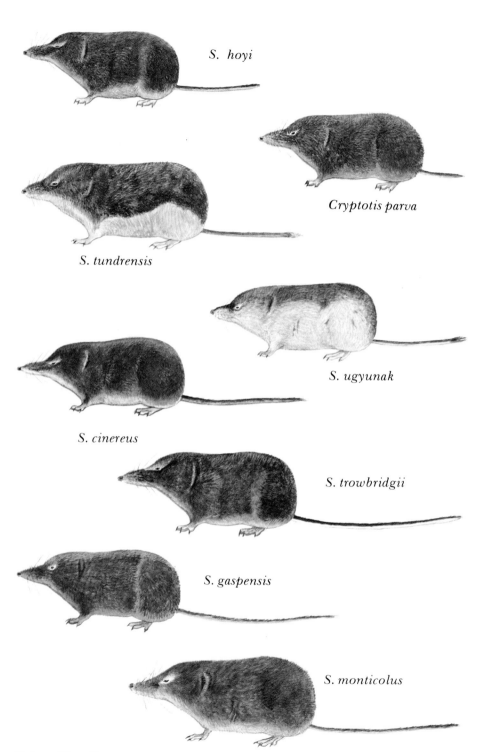

S. hoyi

Cryptotis parva

S. tundrensis

S. ugyunak

S. cinereus

S. trowbridgii

S. gaspensis

S. monticolus

Colour Plate II

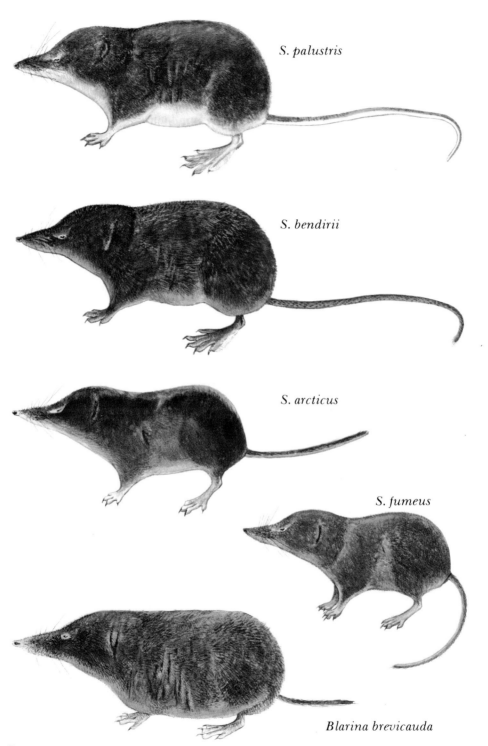

S. palustris

S. bendirii

S. arcticus

S. fumeus

Blarina brevicauda

Colour Plate III

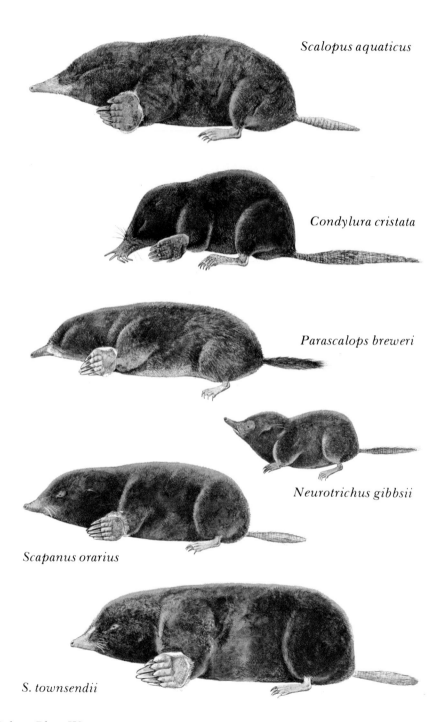

Scalopus aquaticus

Condylura cristata

Parascalops breweri

Neurotrichus gibbsii

Scapanus orarius

S. townsendii

Colour Plate IV

ORDER **POLYPROTODONTA** OWEN, 1866

(f. Gk *pollus* many + Gk *protos* first, primary
+ Gk *odous* genit. *odontos* tooth,
referring to the number of incisors)

Carnivorous and insectivorous marsupials	Polyprotodontes

This order includes the carnivorous and insectivorous marsupials, usually characterized by an elongated snout and a large number of teeth. As a rule there are four upper incisors on each side; upper and lower canines are present; and the molars are of a tuberculo-sectorial type, adapted for crushing and cutting. In most members of this order the feet are not greatly modified and the second and third toes are usually not reduced, although the first toe may be reduced or missing. Syndactyly is absent except in the Peramelidae (bandicoots). The stomach is simple and the intestinal tract short.

With other marsupials, the Polyprotodonta share many characters that distinguish them from placental mammals [2, 11]. The skull is characterized by a small braincase; the orbit and temporal fossa are always confluent; a postorbital bar is always lacking; the palate has large fenestrae; and the jugal process of the zygomatic arch extends posteriorly to form part of the glenoid fossa. The angular process of the mandible is well developed and is turned inward. There is no separate optic foramen, the optic nerve sharing a foramen with the trigeminal, ophthalmic, and oculomotor nerves. The auditory bulla, in forms that possess one, consists of a wing of the alisphenoid and not, as in most eutherian mammals, of the tympanic bone. Marsupials have a heterodont dentition, of which only the last upper premolar is deciduous in Recent forms. Incisors are usually more numerous than in eutherian mammals. Attached to the pubic bone is a pair of epipubic bones. The brain is generally smaller than in eutherian mammals. The cerebral hemispheres are relatively smooth and there is no *corpus callosum*. In the eye, the retina has some cones containing oil droplets, a reptilian character.

However, the most fundamental difference between the Metatheria and Eutheria lies in the urogenital system [10]. In marsupials the scrotum is situated in front of the penis, which is often bifid (e.g. *Didelphis*). The female reproductive tract consists of two vaginae and two uteri. The two passages come together forming a *cul-de-sac* (median vagina), which acquires an opening to the urogenital sinus before the birth of the young (Figure 4). The birth canal thus formed is transient in most marsupials, disappearing again after parturition, but persisting in kangaroos, wallabies and the honey possum (*Tarsipes*). No placenta is formed, except in *Perameles*, and to a lesser extent in *Dasyurus* and *Philander*, where the alantois and yolk sac respectively form attachments with maternal tissue. The young are born in a premature state after a brief gestation. Development is often completed in a marsupium or pouch where the young attaches itself to a nipple. Marsupials and eutherian mammals probably evolved at about the same time from Jurassic pantotheres, a group of primitive mammals with a tri-tubercular molar cusp-pattern similar to that found in early marsupials and eutherians [1].

The oldest known marsupials from the Upper Cretaceous (70–80 million years B.P.) of North America were polyprotodonts, which were contemporaneous with primitive eutherian mammals [8, 9]. The dichotomy of the Eutheria and Metatheria probably occurred during the mid-Cretaceous. Differentiation in the Upper Cretaceous led to major adaptive radiation with several lineages. By the end of the Cretaceous all these lines appear to have become extinct with the exception of the Didelphidae (*Alphadon*), which survive to this day. During the Upper Cretaceous or early Cenozoic, didelphids probably colonized South America and, probably via Antarctica, Australia. Much uncertainty still surrounds the question of marsupial origins and migrations. Didelphids reinvaded North America from South America in the late Pliocene or early Pleistocene when the two continents were joined by the Panamanian land bridge.

All marsupials were formerly combined in a single order. A recent classification, based on new evidence, proposes a division into three orders: the Polyprotodonta, comprising the New World opossums and the Australian dasyurids and peramelids; the Paucituberculata, containing the South American caenolestids; and the Diprotodonta, consisting of phalangers, koalas, wombats and kangaroos [5, 6]. The Polyprotodonta are the most primitive and most widely distributed marsupials, occurring in the Americas and Australia. Known fossil forms of this order are also confined to these continents with the exception of the North American didelphid *Peratherium*, which is also known to have lived in Europe from the Eocene to the Miocene.

References

[1] Clemens, W.A., 1968
[2] Grassé, P.P., 1955
[3] Hunsaker, D., 1977
[4] Keast, A., F.C. Erk, and B. Glass, 1972
[5] Kirsch, J.A.W., 1968, [6] 1977
[7] Ride, W.D.L., 1970
[8] Slaughter, R.H., 1968
[9] Stonehouse, B., and D. Gilmore, 1977
[10] Tyndale-Biscoe, H., 1973
[11] Weber, M., 1928

Family DIDELPHIDAE Gray, 1821

The Didelphidae comprise a group of small to medium-sized, unguiculate, pentadactyl, plantigrade marsupials with a well-developed clawless, opposable hallux and a more or less prehensile and partially naked, scaly tail. They have a large number of teeth; the dental formula is i 5/4, c 1/1, p 3/3, m 4/4, total 50. The dentition is characterized by well-developed canines and tuberculo-sectorial premolars and molars. A pouch may be present or absent. The skull shows the typical marsupial characters discussed under the order. Epipubic bones are present. Didelphids are for the most part insectivorous or omnivorous and generally arboreal and terrestrial, although one species, the Neotropical yapok (*Chironectes minimus*), is semi-aquatic.

The family represents a very old lineage going back to the Upper Cretaceous. There are 11 Recent genera with 70 species, which are mostly Neotropical in distribution. Only one species occurs in Canada.

Genus *Didelphis* Linnaeus, 1758
(f. Gk *di*, prefix meaning two, double
+ Gk *delphus* womb)

Cat-sized didelphids are characterized by a long pointed snout, prominent naked ears, dense underfur, long coarse guard-hair and a well-developed pouch in the female. The genus contains three living species: *D. virginiana* in North America; *D. marsupialis*, a tropical species distributed from southern Mexico to northern Argentina; and *D. albiventris*, which is restricted to the subtropical highlands and temperate areas of South America. The genus probably evolved in South America from an *Alphadon*-like ancestor during the Pliocene.

Didelphis virginiana Kerr
(Named after type locality)

North American Opossum
(Virginia, Common or
American Opossum)

Opossum d'Amérique du Nord

(Of Algonquian origin, f. a Virginian
language of that group, *apasum*, rel. to
Ojibwa *wabassim* white animal)

1792 *Didelphis virginiana* Kerr, Anim. Kingdom, p. 193.
1885 *Didelphis virginiana* True, Proc. U.S. N. Mus., vol. 7 (1884,
p. 587), (1885).
1952 *Didelphis marsupialis* Hall and Kelson, Univ. Kans. Mus.
Nat. Hist. Publ. 5:322.
1973 *Didelphis virginiana* Gardner, Spec. Publ., The Museum,
Texas Tech Univ. 4:28.
Type locality: Virginia
TL 650–850; T 220–400; HF 60–80; W 2–5.5 kg.

Description (Colour Plate I)

A medium-sized marsupial; nose long, pointed, rhinarium pink and
hairless; ears naked, black, tipped with white or pink; tail prehensile,
furred at base, scaly, proximal third black, remainder light; eyes
prominent, black; fur, guard hairs long, coarse, white, medium-
length hairs black-tipped; wool hairs fine, white; overall colour
varies from black to white, mostly grey; face lighter than body,
usually white, but dusky colour of black continues between eyes
in tapering stripe, often dusky around eyes, lower legs black, distal
portion of front feet and toes of hind feet white; vibrissae, mystacial,
genal, mental, supercilliary and carpal, well developed; feet plantigrade, pentadactyl, clawed, except the opposable hallux; throat
gland with yellow secretion in males. This species cannot be easily
confused with any other Canadian mammal.

Distribution

Distribution in Canada is confined to southern Ontario and southwestern British Columbia. In Ontario most records are from a
broad band along Lake Erie. The most northerly records in this part
of Ontario are from Goderich Township, Huron County, in 1955
and Toronto, 1858. It has also been reported from west of the
St. Lawrence River in eastern Ontario (near Morrisburg, Lansdowne
near Gananoque, and Lanark County). Occurrence in Ontario is
sporadic and appears to represent successive invasions from Michigan
and New York. Between 1892 and 1906 at least nine opossums were
reported, one in 1934 and approximately 29 known reports between
1947 and the present. The records from eastern Ontario are more
recent (1952, 1960 to 1962) and coincide with the expansion of the
species into northern New York State. In British Columbia, opossums

have been known since 1949 when two specimens were taken at Crescent Beach. The species probably invaded from Washington, where they were introduced around 1925. The opossum has increased and extended its range south and east of the Fraser River as far as Spuzzum, B.C. It has also been recorded north of the river at Point Grey [2, 3].

Peripheral localities: *British Columbia*: (**1**) Spuzzum; (**2**) Maple Bay; (**3**) Point Grey. *Ontario*: (**4**) Lanark County; (**5**) near Morrisburg; (**6**) 10 km west of Gananoque; (**7**) Toronto; (**8**) Port Colborne; (**9**) Goderich Township.

Outside Canada *D. virginiana* is found over a large area of North America from southern New Hampshire, northern Vermont, New York State, central Michigan, Wisconsin and southern South Dakota south to the Gulf States, Mexico and outside the Nearctic Region in Middle America as far as Costa Rica. The species was introduced to several western localities and is now established along the Pacific from Baja California to southern British Columbia.

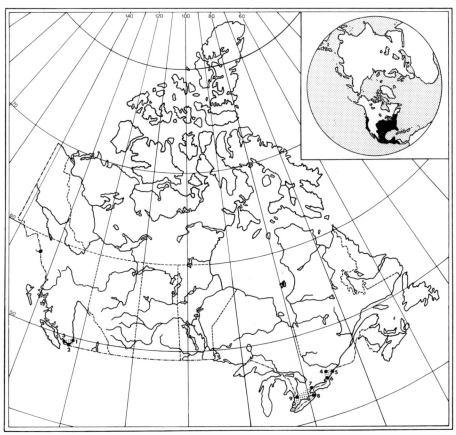

Map 1.   Distribution of *Didelphis virginiana*

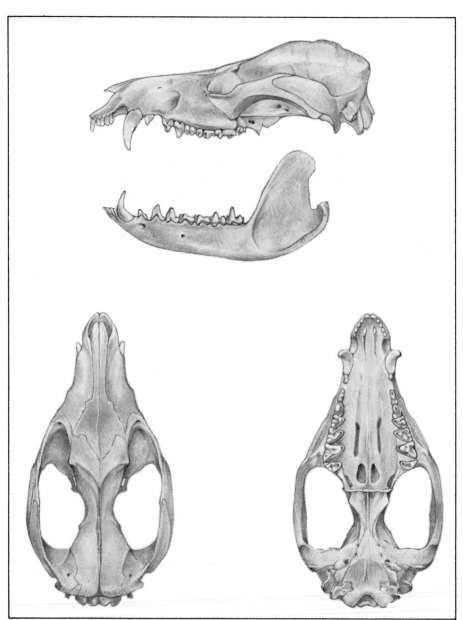

Figure 2.   Skull of *Didelphis virginiana*

Systematics

Four subspecies of *D. virginiana* are recognized on the basis of geographic variation in size, relative length of the tail, and coloration [9]. Only the subspecies *D. v. virginiana* occurs in Canada. It differs from the southern subspecies in its larger size, relatively smaller ears, shorter tail, and lighter colour.

The oldest known *Didelphis* fossil from North America dates from the Sangamon Interglacial [20]. The temperate *D. virginiana* probably evolved from the tropical *D. marsupialis* during the Pleistocene [9]. The two species are quite similar morphologically, differing only in minor skull characters, coloration, and hair pattern. The karyotype of *D. virginiana*, however, differs greatly from all other species in the genus in having subtelocentric and submetacentric chromosomes, probably resulting from pericentric inversions, giving the species a fundamental number (FN) of 32 compared to 20 in *D. albiventris* and *D. marsupialis*. The diploid number in all species is 22 [9].

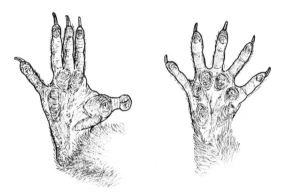

Figure 3.   Manus (a) and pes (b) of *D. virginiana*

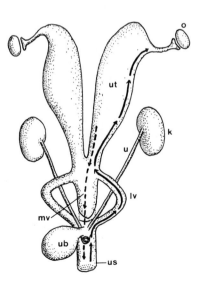

Figure 4.   Diagram of the uro-genital tract of *D. virginiana*: k = kidney; lv = lateral vagina; mv = median vagina; o = ovary; u = ureter; ub = urinary bladder; us = urogenital sinus; ut = uterus; solid arrows show the route followed by the spermatozoa; stippled arrows show the route through which the young are expelled during birth through the transient opening between the median vagina and the urogenital sinus.

Biology

Although opposums occur in a variety of habitats over most of their range, they prefer woods, especially those in the vicinity of streams. They are also found on agricultural land with sufficient cover. Shelter in the form of underground cavities is required for denning purposes. Hollow trees and old buildings are used to a lesser extent.

Opossums are omnivorous, exploiting both the arboreal and terrestrial resources of their environment. Relatively unselective feeders, they take a wide variety of animal and plant foods [11, 19, 25]. Food of animal origin is more important in terms of volume and includes invertebrates (insects, earthworms), frogs, snakes, birds, eggs, and mammals. Plant foods comprise mainly fruits such as wild grapes and apples. Because of their broad feeding habits and adaptability to different habitats, opossums have no serious competitors. Opossums themselves are probably preyed upon by a number of mammalian and avian predators [6], but no detailed information is available.

The opossum does not hibernate and winter is a time of stress for the animal. In fact the severity of the winter climate sets a northern limit to its distribution, which does not exceed the –7°C January isotherm. In Michigan the northern limits of the opossum's geographical range coincide with the limits of the pine–hemlock ecotone between deciduous and coniferous forest [1]. In Ontario most records are from the Deciduous Forest Region, with a few from the southern parts of the Great Lakes–St. Lawrence Forest Region. In British Columbia the species is confined to the southern part of the Coast Forest Region. There is evidence that opossums leave their dens in winter when air temperatures are below freezing, but they are seldom active at temperatures below –7°C and never at temperatures below –12°C. The critical limits for survival are reached in areas where the temperature forces the animal to remain in its den for 70 consecutive days. At the northern periphery of its range the species frequently suffers frost damage to the naked parts of ears and tail [12]. Opossums are able to maintain their normal body temperature of approximately 35°C at ambient temperatures down to 0°C [17]. At lower ambient temperatures a drop in body temperature occurs, and at –10°C the animal is unable to maintain its body temperature. The animal responds to cold by curling up, piloerection, vasoconstriction and denning. When the temperature rises above 35°C the animal's body temperature rises rapidly and above 37°C apparent heat stress occurs. Lacking sweat glands, the opossum thermoregulates by licking its forefeet, hind limbs, and tail, applying copious amounts of saliva. The evaporative heat loss from the salivated parts, coupled with vasodilation, results in lowering of the body temperature.

Nothing is known about opossum populations in Canada, but studies elsewhere suggest a rapid turnover. The average life-span has been estimated at 1.3 years, and longevity rarely exceeds 4 years [20]. The major causes of mortality are unknown. The heavy mortality is offset by the greater fecundity of the species. Females mature at 6 months and 80 per cent produce young. Each female may have 26 young in a year.

Habitat

Food

Predators

Climate

Population

Opossums are predominantly nocturnal with a peak activity period
between 21:00 and 02:00 hours [19]. During the day the animal rests
in a den. Several dens are used during the year. During one night,
adults may forage over an area with a radius of 620 m [6]. Average
nightly foraging distance from the den was determined at 946 m and
413 m for males and females respectively in Wisconsin [10]. Young
animals stay in a relatively small area at first, gradually extending
the range of their activities. The home range is not rigid and during
a year it covers an average of 108 ha for males and 51 ha for females.
Sudden dispersal movements over long distances by some females
with pouch young provide a mechanism by which the species can
move into new areas or reoccupy areas formerly inhabited. Adult
males do not undertake long-distance dispersal movements, but
change their home range through gradual shifts.

Behaviour patterns in the opossum are generalized [18]. There are
two modes of terrestrial locomotion: a slow plantigrade walk and a
faster running gait. In the walk, three feet are on the ground, while
the fourth is moved forward. The animal progresses at a speed of 0.4
to 1.8 km per hour. In running, the animal balances on diagonally
opposed limbs, while the other two limbs move forward. A running
opossum attains speeds of approximately 7.5 km/h.

Opossums climb in a slow methodical manner. On stems and
larger branches, the legs are extended laterally from the body and
moved in the same sequence as that of the walk. Climbing along
thin branches of 3 cm in diameter or less, a "hand-over-hand"
method is used, with the opposable hallux providing a firm grip.
The prehensile tail is used for balance and support during climbing;
it may be coiled about the branch, alternately constricting and
relaxing as the animal moves along. In descending a vertical surface
the animal usually moves head first.

Opossums enter the water readily and are strong but slow swimmers [18]. The legs move as in the walking gait or, more commonly,
the legs on one side move in unison as in pacing while the tail performs
lateral sculling movements. The body is submerged, with only the
upper part of the head appearing above the surface.

Grooming is a frequent activity. It almost always follows feeding
and is particularly thorough after precipitation. The animal proceeds from the head to other parts of the body. One or both forefeet
are licked and then wiped over the snout and the sides of the head.
The haunches, hind legs, and ventral parts are licked directly. The
backs and sides of the body are usually scratched with the hind feet
in a combing action, but sometimes they are also licked. After a
series of scratches, the plantar surface is licked to remove dirt and
hair. Shaking dog-fashion is common in rain or snow.

Nest building consists of lining pre-existing dens with dry leaves
or grass. The litter is picked up with the mouth, passed between the
forelimbs and placed on the tail, which is curved forward between
the hind legs. The hind legs pack the bedding while the tail wraps
around it. This sequence is repeated several times before the nesting
material is carried to the den in the coiled tail, held straight out from
the body [15, 23, 25, 28]. At the den site the material is then arranged
using the forefeet and the mouth. Nest building behaviour has been
observed in animals as young as an estimated 88 to 97 days of age [14].

Vocalization is limited to a graded series of sounds, uttered in agonistic encounters. In order of intensity, they are the hiss, growl, screech, and click. The click is also used by males in sexual encounters and by females in the presence of their young [19].

Saliva rubbing has been observed in males and, to a lesser extent, in females. It consists of rubbing both sides of the head against an object that has previously been licked. This type of behaviour occurs more frequently during the breeding season [20].

The opossum is a solitary animal and social behaviour is predominantly agonistic. Encounters between males are usually accompanied by threats or fighting. Females behave similarly but less intensely. In male–female encounters, the female's behaviour is agonistic if she is not sexually responsive, but the male does not respond agonistically to her. When the female is in heat, she tolerates the male, who approaches her while making clicking sounds. Copulation follows. The male mounts the female from the rear, clasping her thorax with his forelegs and grasping her nape with his jaws. Holding the female's hind legs with his hind feet, the male then shifts his weight to one side, causing the pair to topple. Insertion of the penis follows and pelvic thrusting commences. Copulation last 15 to 20 minutes, directly after which the female resumes her usual agonistic behaviour toward the male [17, 24, 28].

Maternal behaviour in females with pouch young is poorly developed, judging from the lack of interest they show in their young. The young do not interact much with one another and play is apparently absent.

The best-known behaviour pattern of the opossum is feigning death or "playing possum". This stereotyped behaviour pattern is characterized by immobility and ventral flexure of the body while the animal is lying on its side. The eyes remain open or are partly closed. The mouth is usually open with the tongue slightly extended. Death feigning is part of the animal's defensive behaviour, which consists of a series of intimidation displays including crouching, baring of teeth, hissing, growling, screeching, and possible emission of anal-gland secretion. If intimidation fails and escape is not possible, death feigning may occur, usually as a result of sudden tactile stimulation such as grabbing or biting by the aggressor. Responsiveness to external stimuli is much reduced while the opossum is in a cataplectic state. Some responses to external stimuli still occur; for example, sharp noises produce twitching in the ears, prodding causes the lips to retract, etc. Brain activity continues normally as encephalograms of animals feigning death do not differ from those of animals not in that state [7, 8, 21].

In the northern part of the opossum's range (New York State), the breeding season is from late January to mid-March and from mid-May to early July [12]. Heat lasts from one to two days and if fertilization does not take place, heat recurs at intervals of about 28 days. The egg, which measures up to 0.75 mm in diameter, is relatively large for a mammal. It consists of a yolk covered with an albumin-like acid mucopolysaccharide layer and a keratinous shell membrane. The developing embryos do not attach to the wall of the uterus and derive nutrients from the uterine secretion surrounding them. After a brief gestation of 12 days and 18 hours the young are born in a

Reproduction and Ontogeny

premature state, being blind and naked with well-developed clawed forelimbs and relatively underdeveloped hind parts. Litter size varies from 4 to 13 young, each weighing approximately 0.16 g and measuring 14 mm in length. The young are born enveloped in amnionic and chorionic membranes, which the mother removes by licking. She also licks the fur of her abdomen, which presumably aids the young in getting to the pouch. The young reach the pouch on their own, using their well-developed forelimbs. The mechanism by which the neonate finds its way to the pouch is an interesting one. While giving birth the mother sits up and a young invariably travels up until it reaches the pouch. As the newborn opossum has not developed an inner ear at this stage, and therefore cannot distinguish up from down, it cannot use gravity to guide it. The reason it always moves up has a simple mechanical explanation. The body pivots on the well-developed forelimbs while the hind end is pulled down by gravity. As a result a movement can only take place in one direction, up [13].

Once in the pouch, the young immediately attaches itself to one of the thirteen nipples, where it will remain for 50 to 65 days. After that period the young leave the pouch, but suckle for another month before leaving the mother. Approximately 97 days after the birth of the first litter, a second heat period follows and a second litter may be produced. Young animals are themselves capable of reproducing during the breeding season following their birth.

References

[1] Brocke, R.H., 1970
[2] Carl, G.C., and C.J. Guiguet, 1972
[3] Cowan, I. Mct., and C.J. Guiguet, 1965
[4] de Vos, A., 1964
[5] Doutt, J.K., 1954
[6] Fitch, H.S, and H.W. Shirer, 1970
[7] Francq, E.N., 1969, [8] 1970
[9] Gardner, A.L., 1973
[10] Gillette, L.N., 1980
[11] Hamilton, W.J., Jr., 1953, [12] 1958
[13] Hartman, C.G., 1952
[14] Hopkins, D., 1977
[15] Layne, J.M., 1951
[16] McManus, J.J., 1967, [17] 1969, [18] 1970, [19] 1971, [20] 1974
[21] Norton, A.C., A.V. Beran, and J.A. Misrahy, 1964
[22] Peterson, R.L., and S.C. Downing, 1956
[23] Pray, L., 1921
[24] Reynolds, H.C., 1952
[25] Smith, L., 1941
[26] Taube, C.M., 1947
[27] Verts, B.J., 1963
[28] Yates, A.T., and T.G. Newell, 1969

ORDER **INSECTIVORA** BOWDICH, 1821
(f. L *insectum* notched animal = insect +
L *voro* to devour)

Insectivores are generally small, unguiculate, pentadactyl, planti-grade, or semi-plantigrade mammals. Pollex and hallux are not opposable. The nose tends to be pointed and tubular. Eyes and ears are usually small. The dentition is diphyodont and heterodont. The canine, which is in many forms double rooted, usually resembles the adjacent incisor or premolar, but may be caniniform. The pre-molars and molars are of the tubercular or tuberculo-sectorial type. In some forms the deciduous teeth are lost early or fail to erupt. The skull has many primitive characters. The cranial cavity is generally small, the tympanic is ring-shaped and free or fused to varying degrees with surrounding bones, forming a complete bulla in some forms. The mandible usually has a well-developed angular process, which unlike the homologous structure in marsupials, is not bent inward. A clavicle is present except in the African genus *Potamogale*. The radius and ulna are free, but the tibia and fibula are often fused distally. The stomach is simple and the intestine short, reflecting the insectivorous and carnivorous feeding habits. The brain has smooth and short cerebral hemispheres, which leave the cerebellum exposed. The uterus is bicornate and the placenta diffuse or discoidal and of the epitheliochorial, endotheliochorial, or haemochorial type. The testes are abdominal or inguinal; there is no true scrotum [3].

The insectivores are an ancient and diversified group dating back to the Middle Cretaceous of Asia and North America. Their classifi-cation presents many difficulties [1, 2, 5, 6]. The characters they share are generally those of primitive eutherians; on the other hand, living forms are often highly specialized in different directions. The order has long been considered as an unnatural grouping of several lines of descent. The tree shrews (Tupaiidae) and the elephant shrews (Macroscelidae), traditionally included in the Insectivora, are now placed in separate orders, the Scandentia and the Macroscelidea.

Recent insectivores comprise the following families: 1) tenrecs (Tenrecidae), 2) otter shrews (Potamogalidae), 3) golden moles (Chrysochloridae), 4) solenodons (Solenodontidae), 5) hedgehogs (Erinaceidae), 6) moles (Talpidae), and 7) shrews (Soricidae). Insectivores are found on all continents except Australia and Antarctica. Africa has five families (1, 2, 3, 5, 7), Europe and Asia three (5, 6, 7), North America three (4, 6, 7) and South America one (7). The occurrence of one genus (*Cryptotis*) in northern South America represents a relatively recent invasion from North America. Only the Talpidae and Soricidae are represented in Canada with a total of 22 species.

The species density in the major vegetation zones of Canada (Rowe 1972) is as follows: Deciduous Forest Region, nine species (three talpids, six soricids), Acadian Forest Region, nine species (one talpid, eight soricids), Coast Forest, nine species, most in the extreme south (three talpids, six soricids), Boreal Forest Region, eight species (one talpid, seven soricids), Great Lakes–St. Lawrence Forest Region, seven species (two talpids, five soricids), Subalpine,

Montane and Columbia Forest Region have four species of shrews each. The Tundra has at least two species of shrews, and the prairie grasslands proper has one species of shrew. Transition zones between the major vegetation zones usually support somewhat fewer species than the richest neighboring zone, e.g. Forest–grassland transition has seven species, Forest–tundra transition has five.

References

[1] Butler, P.N., 1956
[2] Cabrera, A., 1925
[3] Grassé, P.P., 1955
[4] Hall, E.R., and K.R. Kelson, 1959
[5] McDowell, S.B., Jr., 1958
[6] Van Valen, L., 1967

Key to the Canadian Insectivores

1   Front feet with small claws, not modified for digging, pinna present, skull without zygomatic arches, lower incisors greatly elongated and projecting forward along the long axis of the mandible, upper incisors large projecting forward, two cusped and falciform .... Soricidae 2

      Front feet with large claws, modified for digging, no pinna, skull with slender zygomatic arches, lower incisors not enlarged or projecting forward, upper incisors not falciform .... Talpidae 16

2   (1) Tail length > 40% of head–body length, pinna relatively well developed; articular condyles of the mandible only slightly separated, interarticular area relatively narrow, lower condyle not enlarged, coronoid process not deflected labially (Figure 5a), proximal end of lower incisor at alveolus not extending beyond p4, mental foramen located at level of protoconid of m1, or anterior to it (Figure 6a), postglenoid process separated medially, foramen ovale not enclosed (Figure 7a) ...... (Long tailed shrews, Soricini) 3

      Tail length < 40% of head–body length, pinna relatively small; articular condyles of the mandible widely separated, interarticular area broad, lower condyle enlarged, coronoid process deflected labially (Figure 5b); proximal end of lower incisor (at alveolus) extending back to m1, mental foramen at the level of hypoconid of m1 (Figure 6b), postglenoid process fused medially, foramen ovale enclosed (Figure 7b) .... (Short-tailed shrews, Blarini) 16

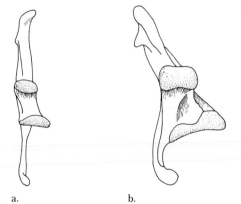

Figure 5.   Interarticular area of the mandible in the Soricini (a) and Blarini (b).

a.   b.

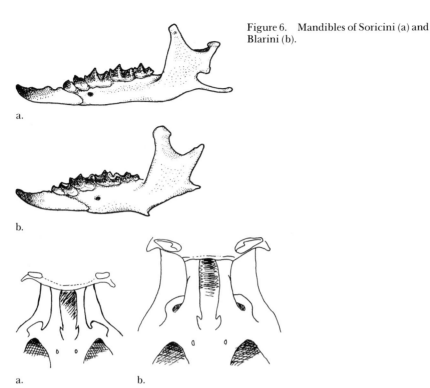

Figure 6.   Mandibles of Soricini (a) and Blarini (b).

a.

b.

a.   b.

Figure 7.   Postglenoid process in the Soricini (a) and Blarini (b).

3   (2) TL usually > 104 mm, but if 104 mm or less the length of
         the nose from the rhinarium to upper incisors approximately 3 ×
         the width of the rhinarium (Figure 8a), 4 or 5 unicuspids in
         upper jaw easily visible in lateral view .... (*Sorex*) 4

         TL < 104 mm, length of the nose from the rhinarium to upper
         incisors approximately 2 × the width of rhinarium (Figure 8b),
         only 3 unicuspids in upper jaw easily visible in lateral view (3rd
         and 5th unicuspids vestigial) .... *Sorex hoyi*, p. 119

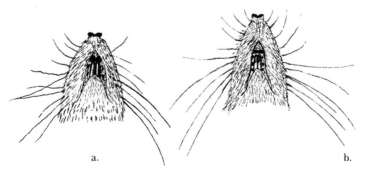

a.   b.

Figure 8.   Ventral view of the snout of *Sorex hoyi* (a) and other similar-sized *Sorex* species (b).

4 (3) Large shrews, TL usually > 130 mm, large HF (> 18 mm) with fringe of stiff hairs (Figure 9a), skull large, SL usually > 19 mm and MW > 5.5 mm 5

Medium or small shrews, TL usually < 130 mm, HF < 18 mm, without conspicuous fringe of stiff hairs (Figure 9b), SL usually < 19 mm, MW < 5.5 mm 6

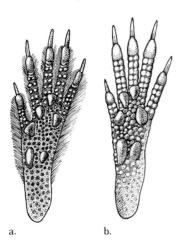

Figure 9.   The hind foot of water shrews (*Sorex palustris*) (a) and other species of *Sorex* (b).

a.   b.

5 (4) Back dark grey to black, underparts and feet much lighter, usually whitish or grey, tail bicoloured, skull with rostrum comparatively short and not curved ventrally; length of the unicuspid row < 70% of the premolar–molar length ..... *S. palustris*, p. 108

Back very dark greyish-brown to black, underparts dark, feet brownish; skull with rostrum comparatively long and curved ventrally; length of the unicuspid row > 70% of the premolar–molar length (Figure 26) .... *S. bendirii*, p. 115

6 (4) Clearly tricoloured or in winter bicoloured, back much darker than sides, with a distinct line of demarcation between back and sides, sides darker than underparts but demarcation less distinct; hind foot approximately 3 mm wide, 3rd uniscuspid > 4th, outline of anterior margin of 1st unicuspid rounded (Figure 10a), lingual ridge from apex does not reach cingulum and is separated from it by a rounded groove; skull with broad bony bridge over infraorbital canal, its posterior margin (orbit) at a point between metastyle and mesostyle of M2, its anterior margin approximately above mesostyle or M1 (Figure 11a); mandible with postmandibular canal (Figure 12a) 7

Not tricoloured, or if tricoloured hind foot < 3 mm wide; 3rd unicuspid > or < 4th, outline of anterior margin of 1st uni- cuspid with one or two concavities (Figure 10b), lingual ridge from apex reaches cingulum and may end in a cuspule; skull with a relatively narrow bony bridge over infraorbital canal (Figure 11b), unlike the one described above; mandible usually without postmandibular canal (Figure 12b), but where present (Figure 12c), 3rd unicuspid < 4th 8

7 (6) Back brown, underparts greyish; T < 36 mm,
SL < 18.5 mm .... *S. tundrensis*, p. 61

Back very dark brown or black, underparts brownish; T > 36 mm,
SL > 18.5 mm .... *S. arcticus*, p. 54

8 (6) Third unicuspid < 4th 9

Third unicuspid > 4th or subequal 11

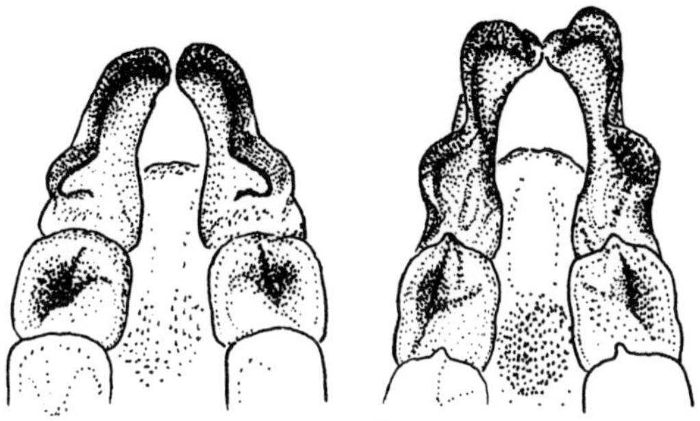

Figure 10. Occusal view of the first upper unicuspid in the *S. arcticus* group (a) and other species of *Sorex* (b).

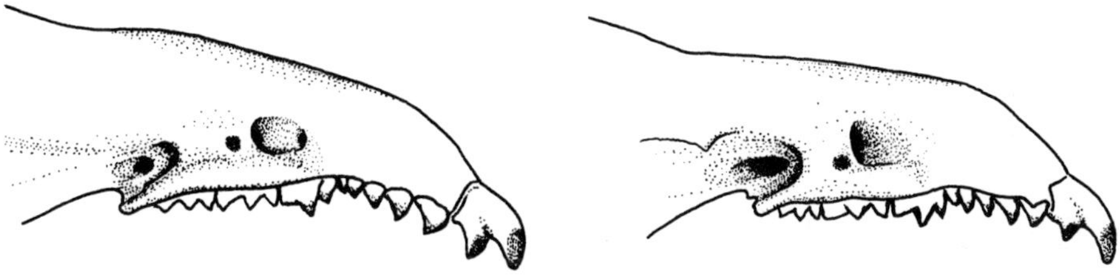

a.   b.

a.   b.

Figure 11. Lateral view of the infraorbital canal in the *S. arcticus* group (a) and that of other Canadian species of *Sorex* (b).

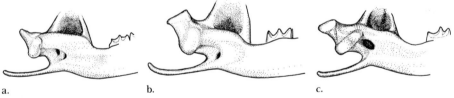

a.   b.   c.

Figure 12. Posterior part of the mandible showing the usual condition in (a) the *S. arcticus* group, inferior dentary foramen and postmandibular foramen usually distinct; (b) other Canadian species of *Sorex*, postmandibular foramen usually absent; and (c) *S. trowbridgii*, inferior dentary foramen and postmandibular foramen usually confluent.

9 (8) Pelage dark grey (in subadults slightly brownish), tail
distinctly bicolour, dark dorsally, white below, feet whitish;
unicuspids narrow with lingual ridge not ending in a cusplet,
postmandibular canal present (Figure 12c) .... *S. trowbridgii*, p. 103

Pelage brownish, maybe dark grey or blackish in winter, tail
brown, dark above, paler below, but not distinctly bicolour;
feet pale brownish; unicuspids with well-developed lingual
ridges usually heavily pigmented and ending in a cusplet,
mandible without postmandibular canal (Figure 12b) 10

10 (9) Accessory medial cuspule on upper incisor at or above
pigmented area (Figure 13a), digits of hind foot relatively short,
digits 2 to 5 usually with no more than 4 paired friction pads
(Figure 14a) .... *S. vagrans*, p. 99

Accessory medial cuspule on upper incisor below the line of the
pigmented area (Figure 13b), digits of hind foot relatively long,
digits 2 to 5 with more than 4 paired friction pads
(Figure 14b) .... *S. monticolus*, p. 92

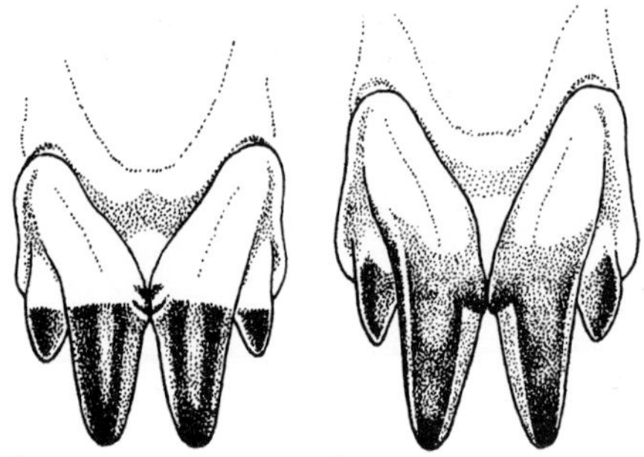

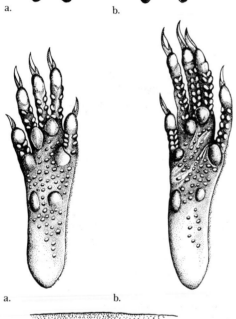

Figure 13.   Frontal view of the upper incisors
of (a) *S. vagrans* and (b) *S. monticolus* showing
medial accessory cuspules and their position
relative to pigmentation.

a.   b.

Figure 14.   Feet of (a) *S. vagrans,* and
(b) *S. monticolus.*

a.   b.

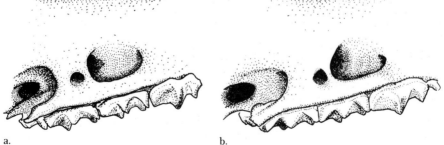

a.   b.

Figure 15.   Position of the posterior border of the infraorbital foramen and lacrimal
foramen in (a) *S. gaspensis* and (b) in other similar species of *Sorex.*

11   (8) Pelage dark grey, tail dark grey above, only slightly paler
     below, skull long and narrow, braincase flattened, posterior
     border of infraorbital foramen situated at or posterior to the
     space between M1 and M2 (Figure 15a), mandible slender
     (height of mandible < height of unworn M1), mental foramen
     at the level of space between p4 and m1 (Figure 16a) 12

     Pelage brownish, may be dark grey to blackish in winter, but
     then with bicoloured tail, yellowish below, brownish above;
     skull has posterior border of infraorbital foramen anterior to
     space between M1 and M2, mandible not as above (height of
     mandible approximately equal to height of unworn M1) and
     mental foramen approximately at the level of the protoconid
     of m1 (Figure 16b) 13

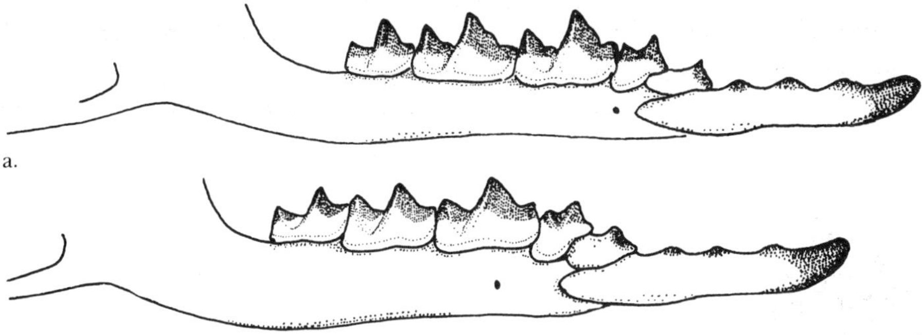

Figure 16.   Depth of mandible and position
of mental foramen in (a) *S. gaspensis* and
S. dispar and (b) in other similar species
of *Sorex*.

12   (11) Size small, TL usually < 120 mm, SL < 16.4 mm, P4–M3
     length < 3.7 mm .... *S. gaspensis*, p. 85

     Larger, TL usually > 120 mm, SL > 16.4 mm; P4–M3 length
     > 3.7 mm .... *S. dispar*, p. 89

13   (11) Small, TL averages 93 mm, brownish to dark brown on
     back, winter pelage similar but slightly greyish; underparts
     greyish white, much lighter than sides or back, hind foot 2 mm
     or less wide at base of toes, SL < 17 mm 14

     Larger, TL averages 114 mm, brown in summer, dark grey in
     winter, underparts brownish, only slightly paler than back
     and sides, hind foot > 2 mm wide at base of toes;
     SL > 17 mm .... *S. fumeus*, p. 80

14   (13) Unicuspid row < 2.2 mm, unicuspid usually wider than
     long, ventral side of tail usually with pale-brownish terminal
     tuft 15

     Unicuspid row > 2.2 mm, unicuspids longer than wide, ventral
     side of tail usually with contrasting blackish terminal
     tuft .... *S. cinereus*, p. 65

a.

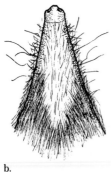

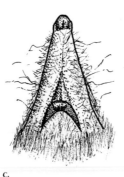

b.   c.

Figure 17. Snout of (a) *Condylura*, frontal
view, and *Neurotrichus* (b) dorsal, (c) ventral
view.

19 (17) Tail covered with long coarse hair, nostrils lateral, crescent-shaped with concavity dorsad (Figure 18a). Skull with incomplete auditory bulla. .... *Parascalops breweri*, p. 157

Tail thinly haired or naked, nostrils superior (Figures 18b, c), skull with complete auditory bulla 20

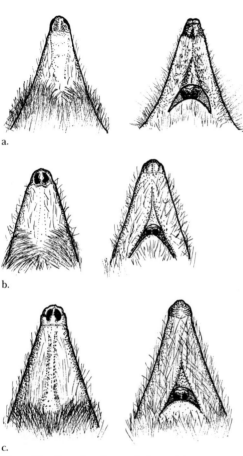

a.

b.

c.

Figure 18. Dorsal and ventral views of the snout of (a) *Parascalops*; (b) *Scapanus*; and (c) *Scalopus*.

20 (19) Toes webbed, 36 teeth .... *Scalopus aquaticus*, p. 151

Toes not webbed, 44 teeth 21

21 (20) Large (TL > 175 mm, HF > 24 mm, SL > 37 mm) ....
.... *Scapanus townsendii*, p. 166

Smaller (TL < 175 mm, HF < 24 mm, SL < 37 mm) .... *S. orarius*, p. 171

Family SORICIDAE Gray, 1821

Shrews are small insectivores (head–body length from 35 to 180 mm), with short legs, long pointed nose, small eyes, and naked or thinly furred pinnae that are usually partially hidden in the fur, with three lobes or valves. There are five claw-bearing toes on each foot. The tail is well developed. The fur is soft and often velvet-like. Cutaneous glands with distinct odour are often present. The most conspicuous of these, the side glands, are present in all shrews. They are particularly well developed in breeding males and their function appears to be predominantly sexual.

The skull is generally long and narrow; zygomatic arches are absent and there are no postorbital processes or auditory bullae. The tympanic bone is ring-shaped and not fused to the skull. The mandible has a slender angular process pointing posteriad. The manidbular condyle has upper and lower articular facets, which articulate with the glenoid fossa and postglenoid apophysis respectively. The tibia and fibula are fused distally. The dentition is diagnostic. There is one pair of lower incisors, laterally compressed, greatly lengthened, with a number of cusps along its dorsal edge and pointing horizontally forward. Together with the enlarged, double pronged, hook-like, upper incisors, they form a shearing pincer-like organ for grasping and cutting insect prey. The enlarged incisors are followed by a series of smaller teeth referred to as unicuspids. There is no agreement on the identity of the unicuspids. According to some researchers, the canine is absent and the unicuspids represent incisors and premolars. Molars have a dilambdodont (W) cusp pattern. The milk dentition does not calcify and erupt, but is resorbed before birth. Soricids are therefore functionally monophyodont. The permanent teeth are present at birth.

The digestive tract is short, the stomach simple and there is no caecum. There is no scrotum. During the breeding season, the testicles lie in a peritoneal evagination under the skin. The brain is small with smooth cerebral hemispheres and large olfactory lobes. The eyes are small, and vision is generally believed to be poor. The sense of smell and hearing are well developed.

Most soricids are terrestrial, some are semi-fossorial (*Cryptotis, Blarina*), and others are adapted to a semi-aquatic way of life (e.g. *Sorex palustris*). None of our native soricids are arboreal, although a few observations suggest that long-tailed forms do occasionally climb low bushes. Shrews are active day and night and in all seasons. They are chiefly insectivorous; the large species, to some extent, are also carnivorous and some are known to eat seeds seasonally. The semiaquatic forms are more or less piscivorous. Their small size makes shrews vulnerable to the effects of low temperatures and suitable microclimate undoubtedly plays an important role in determining their local distribution and abundance. The insulation of adequate snow cover is essential to their survival in winter when they lead a largely subnivean existence.

The Recent Soricidae comprise some 23 genera with approximately 300 species. The family is divided into two subfamilies, the Crocidurinae and the Soricinae. The Crocidurinae are characterized by non-pigmented teeth, p4 with a single triangular cusp, and articular facets of the mandibular condyle that are not widely separated and with a labial articular depression. Externally, many members of this subfamily tend to have more prominent ears than the Soricinae. The Soricinae usually possess reddish-pigmented teeth because of the presence of iron in the outer enamel layer [1], a p4 with a crown forming an oblique blade, and articular facets of the mandibular condyle, which are widely separated, and a lingual depression in the interarticular area. The distal portion of the guard hair in the Soricinae has a longitudinal groove on either side, which gives it an H-shaped cross section [2, 5]. In species adapted to an aquatic mode of life this groove has a greater or lesser number of ridges, varying with the degree of adaptation. These ridges are thought to improve the ability of the fur to retain air under water, thereby increasing its insulating quality.

The ancestry of the Soricidae can be traced to the Oligocene of Europe and North America. The origin of the family is unknown but as they share a number of characters with talpids and the Chiroptera, it has been suggested that shrews, moles, and bats evolved from an unknown soricoid well before the Eocene [4].

The distribution of the Recent Soricidae encompasses Eurasia, Africa, North America, and the northwestern part of South America. Only the Soricinae occur in the New World. There are 16 species belonging to the three genera native to Canada. Three species, *Sorex merriami, S. nanus,* and *S. preblei,* have been collected not far from the international boundary in Montana and it is not impossible that they may some day be found in Canada. Shrews are a taxonomically difficult group. Recent studies have revealed a number of cryptic species that were unrecognized for many years.

References

[1] Dötsch, C., and W. von Koenigswald, 1978
[2] Hutterer, R., and T. Hürter, 1981
[3] Pruitt, W.O., Jr., 1957
[4] Repenning, C.A., 1967
[5] Vogel, P., and B. Köpchen, 1978

Genus *Sorex* Linnaeus, 1758
(f. L *sorex* genit. *soricis* shrew, rel. to Gk *hurax* shrew)

Small, mouse-like insectivores, with pointed snouts extending well beyond the upper incisors; small ears often hidden in the fur, which is soft and velvet-like; tail relatively long (> 1/3 of total length); mammae six (one pair abdominal, two pairs inguinal). Side glands present. Penis varies in shape from attenuated to blunt and club-shaped. Skull cone-like, possessing all the characters described under the family, with 32 teeth, five unicuspids in upper jaw, of which four are usually easily visible in lateral view. The genus is Holarctic and is in many respects the most primitive of the living soricids. There are approximately 30 Nearctic species, distributed from the Arctic Ocean south to Guatemala, of which 14 are found in Canada. The earliest fossil evidence of *Sorex* dates back to the late Pliocene.

Classification within the genus presents many difficulties, and the exact number of species (now estimated at around 60) remains uncertain. The genus is now subdivided into three subgenera, *Sorex*, *Otisorex*, and *Microsorex* [4].

Sorex, a predominantly Palearctic group, which probably arose there, is characterized by the presence of a postmandibular canal, the third unicuspid being larger than the fourth and the absence of a pigmented lingual ridge connected to the cingulum and accessory cusps on the upper unicuspids.

Otisorex is predominantly Nearctic and is characterized by lack of a postmandibular canal (although it is present in some), the third unicuspid often being smaller than the fourth and by the presence of usually pigmented lingual ridges connected to the cingulum of the upper unicuspids, which often have accessory cuspules.

Microsorex is restricted to the Nearctic and shares the characters listed for *Otisorex*, from which it differs in the more pronounced expression of these characters, in particular the extreme reduction of the third and fifth unicuspids and the well-developed pigmented lingual ridges and secondary cuspules on the other upper unicuspids. *Microsorex* was until recently regarded as a genus, but it is almost certainly derived from *Otisorex* and it is better treated as a subgenus of *Sorex*. Reassessment of the above characters and consideration of certain other skull characters (see Figures 10, 11, 12) as well as the thoracico-lumbar vertebral formulae of our native species (14, 6 in *Sorex* and 13, 6 in *Otisorex* and *Microsorex*) has led to a somewhat different tentative arrangement here than that proposed by Findley [2] or more recently that by Junge and Hoffmann [4].

Sorex fumeus, S. dispar, S. gaspensis, and *S. trowbridgii* assigned to *Sorex* by Findley [2] are here placed in *Otisorex.* The arrangement used here is as follows:

Subgenus *Sorex*
              S. arcticus
              S. tundrensis
Subgenus *Otisorex*
              S. cinereus
              S. haydeni
              S. ugyunak
              S. fumeus
              S. gaspensis
              S. dispar
              S. vagrans
              S. monticolus
              S. trowbridgii
              S. palustris
              S. bendirii
Subgenus *Microsorex*
              S. hoyi

References

[1] Diersing, V.E., 1980
[2] Findley, J.S., 1955
[3] Jackson, H.H.T., 1928
[4] Junge, J.A. and R.S. Hoffmann, 1981

Sorex arcticus Kerr

(f. Gk. *arktos* genit. *arktikos* of the bear, land of
the bear; in reference to constellations of
Greater and Lesser Bear, i.e. the North, Northern)

Black-backed Shrew   **Musaraigne nordique**
(Saddle-back Shrew, Arctic Shrew)

1792 *Sorex arcticus* Kerr, Anim. Kingdom, p. 203
1837 *Sorex richardsonii* Bachman, J. Acad. Nat. Sci. Phila. 7(2):383
1925 *Sorex arcticus arcticus* Jackson, Proc. Biol. Soc. Wash. 28:127.
Type locality: Fort Severn, mouth of Severn River, Ontario.

External Measurements and Weight

	TL	T	HF	W
N	25	25	25	10
X̄	111.8	40.6	14.0	7.0
SD	4.70	3.01	0.70	1.31
CV	4.20	7.41	5.01	18.82
OR	97–122	36–48	12–15	5.1–9.3

Cranial Measurements

	SL	CB	IOW	MW
N	48	46	48	44
X̄	19.0	9.3	3.5	5.2
SD	0.38	0.30	0.17	0.14
CV	2.00	3.22	4.86	2.69
OR	18.5–19.7	8.9–10.4	3.0–4.0	4.8–5.5

Description (Colour Plate III)

A medium-sized tricolour shrew, the back very dark brown to nearly
black, sides lighter brown, underparts greyish brown, the most
colourful of our native shrews; demarcation between colours of
back, sides, and underparts distinct. Tail indistinctly bicolour,
brown to brownish black above, lighter below. Summer pelage less
distinctly tricolour than winter pelage, paler above, darker and more
brownish below. Juveniles and subadults are browner and less
distinctly tricoloured than adults. Feet dark buffy-brown above,
large and broad. Moults in June over most of its range; some moult
until August, and again in last half of September and first half of
October. Skull with anterior margin of orbit between metastyle and
mesostyle of M2, margin of infraorbital foramen and lacrimal
foramen approximately at level of mesostyle of M1. Mandible possesses
a postmandibular foramen. Unicuspids evenly graded with the third

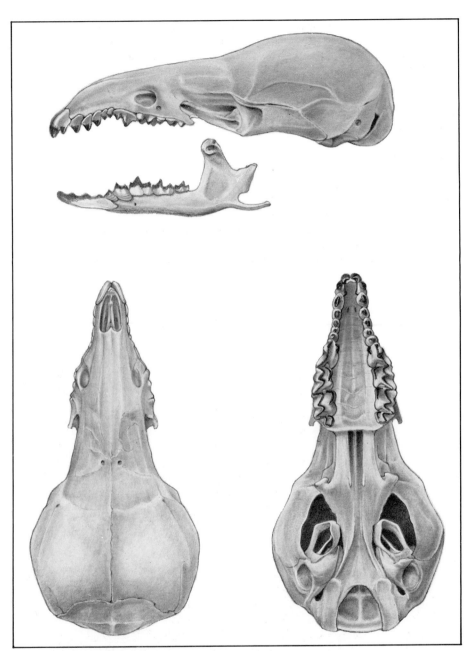

Figure 19.   Skull of *Sorex arcticus*

larger than the fourth; lingual ridge from apex does not reach the cingulum from which it is separated by a groove. Similar species: *S. tundrensis* has shorter tail (22–36 mm), lighter colour, back never blackish, sides and underparts greyish, skull smaller (SL < 18.4 mm). *S. cinereus*: tricoloured forms have been confused with *S. arcticus* but *S. cinereus* is smaller, has a smaller and narrower hind foot (< 2.5 mm wide), smaller skull (SL < 18 mm), and lacks a postmandibular foramen.

Distribution

S. arcticus is a predominantly boreal species, whose distribution coincides largely with that of the Boreal Forest Region. It is distributed over an area from the southern Yukon and the Mackenzie Valley east to Quebec and the Maritimes and south to the north-central United States (Minnesota, Michigan, Wisconsin). In the eastern part of its range, the distribution appears to be discontinu-

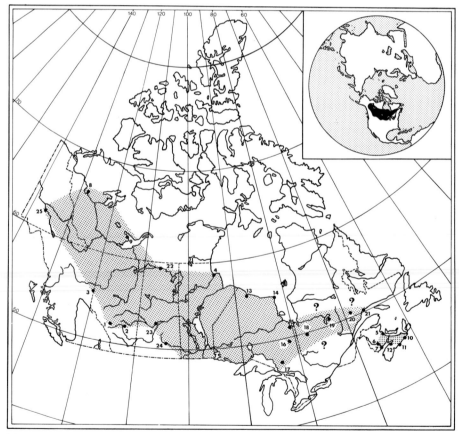

Map 2.   Distribution of *Sorex arcticus*

ous. There are a good number of records from northern Ontario, but it has been recorded from only four localities in Quebec. Specimens were recently collected near Matagami (1976) and Einer Lake and Manicouagan (1980), and there is an older record (1937) from the Moisie River, to the east. Although documentation is as yet lacking, it is highly probable that the species is found throughout the boreal forest of Quebec and Labrador. The populations in Nova Scotia and eastern New Brunswick appear to be true relict populations, suggesting a wider distribution of this species in the past.

Peripheral localities: *Alberta:* (**1**) south Ram River; (**2**) Stettler. *British Columbia:* (**3**) Tupper Creek. *Manitoba:* (**4**) Churchill. *New Brunswick:* (**5**) Kouchibouguac; (**6**) Maugerville; (**7**) Saint John. *Northwest Territories:* (**8**) Chick Lake; (**9**) 40 km south to Old Fort Rae. *Nova Scotia:* (**10**) Sherbrooke; (**11**) Chezzetcook Inlet; (**12**) Wolfville, *Ontario:* (**13**) Fort Severn; (**14**) Cape Henrietta Maria; (**15**) Moosonee; (**16**) Fraserdale; (**17**) Ridout. *Quebec:* (**18**) 1 km west of Matagami airport; (**19**) Einer Lake; (**20**) 4 km east of Manicouagan; (**21**) mouth of Moisie River. *Saskatchewan:* (**22**) Stony Rapids; (**23**) Wingard; (**24**) Indian Head. *Yukon:* (**25**) Yukon Crossing.

Systematics

Geographic variation in the black-backed shrew is relatively slight and consists of small differences in cranial characters and colour. Re-evaluation of these differences is desirable. Three subspecies have been described; of these, *S. a. maritimensis* is the most differentiated.

S. a. arcticus Kerr, 1792, Anim. Kingdom, p. 206
Winter pelage somewhat darker on the back and sides than that of the next subspecies, skull higher. Distribution: central Canada.

S. a. laricorum Jackson, 1925, Proc. Biol. Soc. Wash. 28:127.
Winter pelage lighter than that of preceding subspecies, skull flatter, interorbital width somewhat greater. Distribution: extreme southern Manitoba and southwestern Ontario, and Michigan, Minnesota, Wisconsin, and the Dakotas.

S. a. maritimensis Smith, 1939, J. Mamm. 20(2):244–45.
Colour lighter than that of preceding subspecies, brownish rather than blackish dorsally in winter and much lighter, more yellowish on the sides and ventrally; skull shorter (SL $\bar{x}$ 18.5), braincase flatter and rounder and bony bridge across the infraorbital canal narrower than in preceding subspecies. In addition, the length of the unicuspid row is shorter (2.5–2.8 mm, versus 2.8–3.2 mm) and the individual unicuspids broader and more crowded. Craniometrically this isolated form differs from *arcticus* to a similar degree, as the latter differs from *Sorex tundrensis*. The taxonomic status of *maritimensis* needs further study. Distribution: eastern New Brunswick and mainland Nova Scotia.

The single known specimen from the Yukon, known only from a skull, differs considerably from other *arcticus* specimens in size and possibly represents an undescribed subspecies [15].

Bee and Hall [1] considered S. *arcticus* and S. *tundrensis* to be conspecific as they found the differences in the cranial characters, cited by Jackson [8] as differentiating the two forms, to be insignificant. However the morphological distinctness of the two forms, and the apparent lack of intergradation in specimens from juxtaposed populations, as well as the difference in ecological adaptation to boreal forest and tundra respectively, leaves little doubt that we are dealing with two separate species. I have been unable to confirm the reported difference in the auditory ossicles of the two forms [15]. On the basis of the material examined by me, I can only conclude that the difference reported is based on an artifact or individual anomaly. The karyotype of S. *arcticus* has been reported from two specimens collected in the Whiteshell Provincial Park, Manitoba [10]. It consists of 26 autosomes (3 pairs of submetacentrics, 1 pair of subtelocentrics, 9 pairs of acrocentrics) giving a FNa of 34. The X chromosome is a large metacentric and the male has 2 Y chromosomes. The karyotype of S. *tundrensis* is unfortunately still unknown.

S. *arcticus* and S. *tundrensis* are New World representatives of a Holarctic group of shrews, the *Sorex-araneus-arcticus* group, which has several representatives in the Old World. All share a number of characters, including, in the species whose karyotypes have been determined, trivalent sex chromosomes in the male (XYY) [10]. The systematics of this morphologically uniform group are still confused, but recent karyological analyses have done much to clarify the situation. S. *arcticus* is known from Pleistocene deposits dating back to the Illinoian.

Biology

In the boreal forest and forest–grassland transition the black-backed shrew is found in grass-sedge marshes, meadows, willow-alder copses, and to a lesser extent, in forests, black spruce and larch bogs [3, 14]. In the prairies it is only found along aspen forest edges and in the larger muskeg and moist shrub communities. Near treeline it prefers the sedge-shrub borders of ponds and creeks [14]. In the Maritimes, its most favoured habitats include edges of freshwater swamps and marshes with grass and rushes, and damp grassy banks of ditches, dikes, and railway embankments. The level of the water table appears to affect the abundance of this species [3].

Habitat

The black-backed shrew feeds almost exclusively on insects. In spruce and tamarack bogs the cocoon stage of sawflies constitutes a major proportion of this shrew's diet during late summer and autumn. One study showed the stomach contents of this species to be composed of 60 to 70 per cent larch sawfly in September and October [2]. It is estimated that the daily requirement for an individual shrew is 123 sawfly eonymphs or 8.2 g. The black-backed shrew shares its habitat with *Microtus pennsylvanicus* and S. *cinereus*, and in the southeastern part of its range, with *Blarina* as well. There is no evidence of either positive or negative interactions between these species. It is probable that the ecological requirements of the three shrews are sufficiently different to minimize competition. Buckner's report [3] that the numbers of S. *arcticus* varied inversely with those of S. *cinereus* may indicate possible direct interaction

Food

Associated Mammals

between the two or changes in the environment favouring either one or the other species. For example a high water-table appears to favour *S. cinereus*, a low one *S. arcticus*. Low levels of infestations of ticks (*Dermacentor variabilis*) and fleas (*Corrodopsylla curvata*, *Monopsyllus wagneri*) have been reported from this species in Manitoba [3]. Mites, chigger mites, ticks and a flea have been reported from this shrew in Michigan and Minnesota [13].

Parasites

The population turnover is rapid. Juveniles appear in the population in late spring and early summer, and peak numbers are present in August and September. Juveniles, born in the spring to adults who were largely subadults the previous autumn, are themselves reproducing by August and many of them disappear from the population by autumn [3]. It appears, therefore, that there is a population turnover of about two generations in a year. There is severe mortality in the first month of life between birth and the time the young leave the nest. By the time the new generation reaches sexual maturity after three or four months, approximately 80 per cent have died [3]. From then on mortality levels off. Fifteen months after birth most of the generation has disappeared from the population. There is evidence that some survive beyond this age. Population density fluctuates annually between less than one and 10 animals per hectare. The home range of *S. arcticus*, determined by recaptures of marked individuals, occupies around 0.59 ha [3].

Population

S. arcticus is active throughout the 24-hour cycle [2, 5]. Fourteen activity peaks have been recorded, including a main activity peak during the night. In captive shrews, activity has been observed to occur in short periods, lasting on the average 3.3 minutes. During the frequent periods of inactivity, the animal rests by lying on its side or rolled up with its back up and its head tucked under the body. Grooming consists of rapid wiping of both forefeet along the snout. The black-backed shrew will dig into loose substrate using its forefeet and pushing motions of the head. The only vocalization reported for this species is a low rapid chatter when the shrew is running about. It drinks water by lapping. There is one interesting observation of *S. arcticus* hunting grasshoppers (*Melanoplus femurrubrum*) that were resting on vegetation, by climbing adjacent plants to a height of approximately 30 cm and then jumping violently on the prey, grasping it with jaws and feet [4]. Within a 15-minute interval, 37 strikes were observed, of which 33 were successful. The grasshoppers were sluggish because of cool temperature, which undoubtedly explains the high success rate. Vision was evidently used in this case. Little is known about the relative development of the senses in this species.

Behaviour

The time of the breeding season probably varies in different parts of the species' range. In the southern part of its range (Wisconsin) it is reported to last from late winter to mid-summer [5]. Males taken in this area from February through June all had active testes. In southern Manitoba, juveniles seldom appear before June and are rarely found later than September, which suggests a breeding period from early May to mid-August [3]. In Alberta the breeding season is said to be from late May to August [12]. Pregnant females have been reported from 27 April (Wisconsin) [9] and 3 May (Nova Scotia) [11] to 31 July (Alberta) [12]. The number of embryos range from 5 to 9

Reproduction and Ontogeny

with an average of about 6 [3, 5]. The duration of gestation and lactation are unknown, but in closely related European forms, it is 21 to 25 days and 21 to 24 days respectively [6, 7]. Three litters a year may be produced. There is no agreement on when sexual maturity is attained. One observer [3] claims that offspring born in spring breed in their fourth or fifth month and may breed in consecutive seasons. Another observer [5] states that young animals do not commonly breed in their first summer. It is quite probable that the age at which sexual maturity is attained varies between different localities, depending, among other things, on the quantity and quality of available food.

References

[1] Bee, J.W., and E.R. Hall, 1956
[2] Buckner, C.H., 1964, [3] 1966, [4] 1970
[5] Clough, G.C., 1963
[6] Crowcroft, W.P., 1957
[7] Godfrey, G.K., 1979
[8] Jackson, H.H.T., 1928 [9] 1961
[10] Meylan, A., and J. Hausser, 1973
[11] Smith, R.W., 1940
[12] Soper, J.D., 1964
[13] Whitaker, J.W., Jr., and D.D. Pascal, Jr., 1971
[14] Wrigley R.E., J.E. Dubois, and H.W.R. Copland, 1979
[15] Youngman, P.M., 1975

Sorex tundrensis Merriam
(Latinized, of the tundra)

Tundra Shrew   **Musaraigne de la toundra**

1900 *Sorex tundrensis* Merriam, Proc. Wash. Acad. Sci. 2:16
1956 *Sorex arcticus tundrensis*, Bee and Hall, Univ. Kans. Mus. Nat. Hist. Misc. Publ. 8:22
1975 *Sorex tundrensis* Youngman, Nat. Mus. Nat. Sci. (Ottawa) Publ. Zool. 10:45
Type locality: St. Michael, Norton Sound, Alaska

External Measurements and Weight

	TL	T	HF	W
N	72	72	72	23
X̄	94.9	28.6	13.3	6.1
SD	6.63	2.28	0.78	1.32
CV	6.98	7.97	5.85	21.60
OR	83–120	22–36	11–15	5–10

Cranial Measurements

	SL	CB	IOW	MW
N	80	80	79	69
X̄	17.6	8.9	3.4	4.9
SD	0.28	0.19	0.12	0.14
CV	1.59	2.16	3.54	2.88
OR	16.8–18.4	8.6–9.2	3.0–3.8	4.5–5.2

Description (Colour Plate II)

A medium-sized shrew; summer pelage tricoloured, back brown, sharply contrasting with much lighter, pale-brown or brownish-grey sides, underparts pale, greyish, dorsal band in juveniles and subadults lighter and demarcation between colour of back and sides less distinct; winter pelage bicolour, sides and underparts greyish, back brown; tail bicolour, brownish above, darkening towards tip, buff below; feet dull light-brown. Spring moult in April and May, some continuing into June; winter pelage begins to grow in late August to September, specimens collected between 24 August and 4 September in the central Yukon were all unprime and in various stages of growing winter pelage, 72 per cent of specimens collected in October (Mackenzie Delta) were in winter pelage, most individuals with incomplete moult appear to be young from late litters; all November specimens were in winter pelage. Skull similar to that of *S. arcticus*, but smaller and with shorter unicuspid row (2.4–2.6 mm).

Similar species: *S. arcticus* has longer tail (usually > 34 mm), darker, blackish back, longer skull (SL > 18.4 mm), longer unicuspid row (2.5–3.2 mm); juvenile *arcticus* resembles juvenile *tundrensis* but the former has a longer tail and brownish underparts, the latter a short tail and greyish underparts.

Distribution

The tundra shrew has a rather limited distribution in Canada from the northern Yukon east to the Anderson River near Liverpool Bay and south to extreme northwestern British Columbia. Peripheral localities: *British Columbia: (***1***)* Nadahini Creek. *Northwest Territories: (***2***)* Toker Point; (**3**) Anderson River near Liverpool Bay; (**4**) Parsons Lake. *Yukon: (***5***)* Firth River, 24 km south of Joe Creek; (**6**) 32 km south of Chapman Lake.

The species is also found in most of Alaska including Kodiak Island and across the Bering Strait in northeastern Siberia.

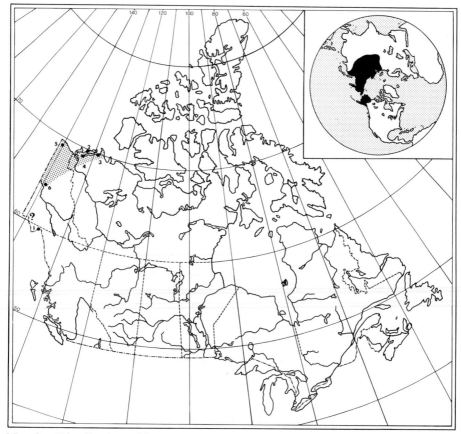

Map 3.   Distribution of *Sorex tundrensis*

Systematics

Aside from a possible clinal change in size from the arctic coast to the southern fringes of its distributional range, *Sorex tundrensis* displays little geographic variation over its North American range. One subspecies, *S. t. tundrensis*, is recognized in North America. The neighbouring Siberian form (*S. t. borealis* Kashchenko) is very similar to the North American tundra shrew. Unlike *S. arcticus*, *S. tundrensis* is a Beringian species. See comments under *S. arcticus*.

Biology

The tundra shrew is most commonly found on hillsides and other well-drained localities with dense vegetation of dwarf trees (*Betula, Alnus, Salix*), shrubs (*Ledum*), and grasses. It is less common on flat wet tundra, where *S. ugyunak* is more abundant [1]. It is also found in the northern fringes of the boreal forest. Small mammals associated with the tundra shrew are northern red-backed voles (*Clethrionomys rutilus*), singing voles (*Microtus miurus*), and variable lemmings (*Dicrostonyx*). It is less commonly found together with brown lemmings (*Lemmus*) and tundra voles (*Microtus oeconomus*), which prefer wetter conditions [3]. Little is known of the food habits of this species. Insects, earthworms, and floral parts of a small grass have been identified from the digestive tracts of specimens taken on the Seward Peninsula, Alaska [4].

During the summer, two age classes can be recognized on the basis of toothwear and pelage characteristics (see description). Nothing is known about the population dynamics of this species, but wide fluctuations in abundance occur. The tundra shrew is active at any time of a 24-hour period in the summer, but nothing is known about its activity in winter when it leads a largely sub-nivean existence. The behavior of this shrew has never been studied.

Information on reproduction in this species is meagre. Pregnant females have been taken in June, July and September. Embryo counts from seven pregnant females ranged from 8 to 12 and averaged 10 [3, 4]. This indicates a much higher reproductive potential in this species than in its southern relative, *S. arcticus*, which has a mean embryo count of about 6. The high reproductive capacity of *S. tundrensis* can be interpreted as an adaptation to ecological conditions in the Arctic. The presence of a pregnant lactating female shows the occurrence of postpartum heat in this species [4]. This would allow the production of several litters in quick succession during the short northern summer. Males in breeding condition with enlarged testes are common in summer, but their numbers decrease rapidly toward autumn. The known facts suggest a breeding season from spring (May) to late summer or early autumn (September) [1, 3, 4].

Habitat

Associated Mammals

Food

Population

Reproduction and Ontogeny

References

[1] Bee, J.W., and E.R. Hall, 1956
[2] Jackson, H.H.T., 1928
[3] Martell, A.M., and A.M. Pearson, 1978
[4] Quay, W.B., 1951

Sorex cinereus Kerr
(f. L cinis ashes, cinereus ash-coloured)

Common Shrew **Musaraigne cendrée**
(Masked Shrew, Cinereus Shrew)

1792 *Sorex arcticus cinereus* Kerr, Anim. Kingdom, p. 206.
1827 *Sorex personatus* I. Geoffroy Saint-Hilaire, Dict. Classique
   d'Hist. Nat. 11:319.
1925 *Sorex cinereus cinereus* Jackson, J. Mammal. 6:55–56.
Type locality: Severn Settlement, mouth of Severn River, Ontario.

External Measurements

	TL	T	HF	W
N	140	143	142	90
X̄	96.6	39.9	11.8	3.6
SD	8.26	4.27	0.83	0.85
CV	8.55	10.72	7.09	23.4
OR	75–125	28–50	8–13	2.2–5.4

Cranial Measurements

	SL	CB	IOW	MW
N	103	103	103	42
X̄	15.9	7.7	2.6	4.1
SD	0.36	0.27	0.11	0.10
CV	2.29	3.50	4.32	2.43
OR	15.2–16.9	7.1–8.5	2.4–2.85	3.8–4.3

Description (Colour Plate II)

A small shrew, back brown to dark brown, underparts greyish white,
tail brown above, lighter below with dark tip. Winter pelage tends
to be darker and greyer than summer pelage. Colour in species as a
whole rather variable, yellowish and reddish-brown individuals
occasionally occur, and in some areas there is a tendency to a tricolour pattern. Moults from April to the latter part of June, depending on sex and latitude. Tail generally of medium length, but varies
geographically, being longest along the east (*S. c. acadicus, S. c.
miscix*) and west coasts (*S. c. streatori*), and shorter in central
Canada.

Skull with long, narrow rostrum, anterior margin of orbit situated
approximately above the mesostyle of M2, the lacrimal foramen at
or just anterior to the interface of M1–M2 and the border of the infraorbital foramen anterior to the M1–M2 interface, and posterior to
the mesostyle of M1. Unicuspids forming a nearly evenly graded

series, with fourth unicuspid smaller than the third or subequal; unicuspids with ridge, usually pigmented, extending lingually to cingulum and ending in a cusplet. Unicuspids usually longer than wide.

Similar species: *Sorex haydeni*, ventral coloration of tail with pale terminal tuft (brownish rather than blackish), length of upper unicuspid row usually < 2.20 and unicuspids usually wider than long (for doubtful cases see van Zyll de Jong 1980). *S. ugyunak*, short tail, light fur extending high up the sides of body and head contrasting with darker colour of the back, colour of tail light, lacking dark terminal tuft. Length of unicuspids < 2.2, unicuspids usually wider than long. *S. vagrans* and *S. monticolus*, rostrum relatively shorter and broader, third unicuspid smaller than fourth. *Sorex hoyi* has shorter tail (< 40% of TL), shorter snout (Figure 8) and the third and fifth unicuspids reduced.

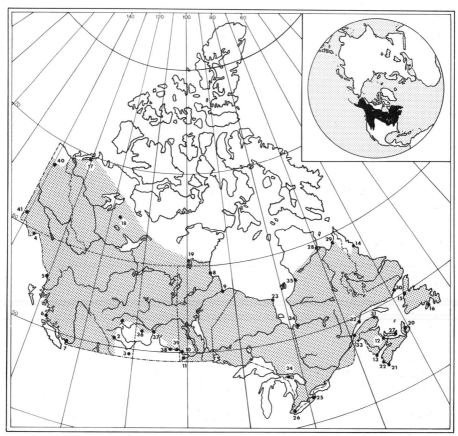

Map 4.   Distribution of *Sorex cinereus*

Distribution

The common shrew is the most widely distributed and abundant Canadian shrew. The species occurs in nearly all parts of the country, except on the tundra, the arctic islands, extreme northern Quebec, the Queen Charlotte Islands, Vancouver Island, Anticosti Island, the Madeleine Islands and smaller offshore islands. It was introduced to Newfoundland in 1958 and occurs now over the entire island in suitable habitats [15, 25]. Peripheral localities: *Alberta:* (**1**) Camrose; (**2**) Calgary; (**3**) Manyberries. *British Columbia:* (**4**) Stonehouse Creek; (**5**) Observatory Inlet; (**6**) Koeye River; (**7**) Mount Seymour. Also reported from the following offshore islands (not marked on map): Campbell; Hunter; King; Pitt; Princess Royal; Smyth; Spider; Townsend; Yeo. *Manitoba:* (**8**) 8 km north of mouth of the Seal River; (**9**) York Factory; (**10**) Kenton; (**11**) 2.4 km south, 12.8 km west of Hartney. *New Brunswick:* (**12**) Buctouche; (**13**) Deer Island. *Newfoundland (Labrador):* (**14**) Okak; (**15**) 1.6 km north of Woody Point; (**16**) 1.2 km east of Rocky Harbour. *Northwest Territories:* (**17**) Liverpool Bay; (**18**) Lac Ste. Croix; (**19**) Windy Bay, Nueltin Lake. *Nova Scotia:* (**20**) Kellys Mountain; (**21**) Seal Island; (**22**) Overton. *Ontario:* (**23**) Cape Henrietta Maria; (**24**) Gore Bay; (**25**) Point Abino; (**26**) Point Pelee National Park. *Prince Edward Island:* (**27**) Fortune Bridge. *Quebec:* (**28**) Irony Lake; (**29**) Kangiqsualujjuaq (formerly George-River); (**30**) La Tabatière; (**31**) Saint-Hélier; (**32**) Godbout; (**33**) Trois-Pistoles; (**34**) Rupert-House; (**35**) Papp's Cove, Lake Guillaume-Dèlisle (formerly Richmond Gulf). *Saskatchewan:* (**36**) Revenue; (**37**) Saskatoon; (**38**) Grenfell; (**39**) Spy Hill. *Yukon:* (**40**) Old Crow; (**41**) Tepee Lake.

Outside Canada the common shrew is found in Alaska and the northern United States, south to southern Washington, Idaho, central Utah, northern New Mexico, Colorado, Montana, Minnesota, Iowa, Illinois, northern Kentucky, Ohio, Pennsylvania, in the Appalachians south to North Carolina and Tennessee.

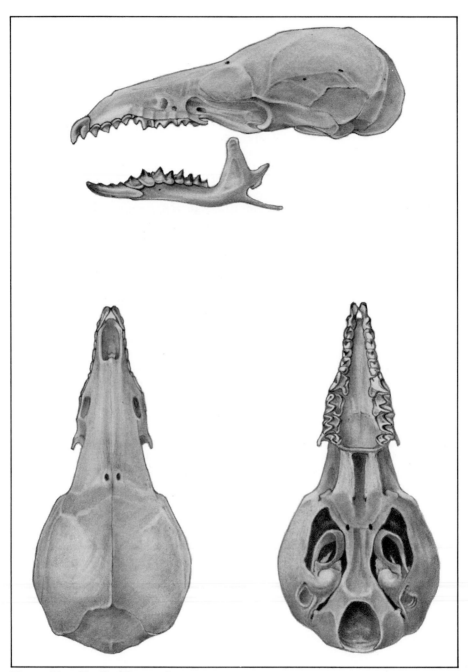

Figure 20.   Skull of *Sorex cinereus*

Systematics

The common, prairie, and barrenground shrews belong to a group of closely related species referred to as the *cinereus* group. The inter-relationships of all the forms in the group have not yet been analyzed in detail and the taxonomic arrangement in the *cinereus* group should, therefore, be regarded as provisional. The nominal species usually included in the *cinereus* group are: *S. cinereus, S. lyelli, S. preblei, S. pribilofensis, S. jacksoni,* and *S. milleri.* The forms *haydeni* Baird and *ugyunak* Anderson and Rand, until recently regarded as subspecies of *S. cinereus,* are here considered specifically distinct on the basis of morphological distinctness, sympatry, and the absence of intergradation [22, 23]. Specific status seems probable also for the form *fontinalis* Hollister from the eastern United States [13, 14].

The *cinereus* group can be subdivided into forms characterized by a relatively long skull with high braincase, long and narrow rostrum with relatively long upper unicuspid row (including *S. cinereus*) and those with a relatively short skull, with flatter braincase, short and broad rostrum with a relatively short upper unicuspid row (including the tundra forms *S. jacksoni, S. pribilofensis, S. ugyunak,* and the forms from northeastern Siberia [23] and the southern forms *S. haydeni, S. preblei, S. lyelli,* and *S. fontinalis*). Also see comments under *S. haydeni* and *S. ugyunak.*

S. cinereus is subdivided into eight subspecies, four of which occur in Canada.

S. c. acadicus Gilpin 1867, Proc. and Trans. N. S. Inst. Nat. Sci. 1 (pt. 2).
TL 95–113, x̄ 103.5 (N = 8); T 40–49, x̄ 45.4 (N = 15); skull SL x̄ 16.4, SD 0.23 (N = 28); CB x̄ 7.9, SD 0.26 (N = 17); IOW x̄ 2.9, SD 0.10 (N = 18); MW x̄ 4.2, SD 0.14 (N = 17). Colour like *S. c. cinereus,* in some areas (e.g. Cape Breton Island) tendency to tricolour pattern. Distribution: The Maritimes.

S. c. cinereus Kerr 1792, Anim. Kingdom, p. 206.
TL 82–109, x̄ 96.5 (N = 25); T 30–45, x̄ 39.8 (N = 25); skull SL x̄ 16.0, SD 0.21 (N = 26); CB x̄ 7.7, SD 0.24 (N = 27); IOW x̄ 2.8, SD 0.17 (N = 28); MW x̄ 4.2, SD 0.24 (N = 21). Colour brown in summer, greyish brown in winter. Distribution: most of Canada from the Yukon and British Columbia to Ontario and Quebec.

S. c. miscix Bangs 1899, Proc. New Engl. Zool. Club 1:15.
TL 88–117, x̄ 99.5 (N = 12); T 38–45, x̄ 41 (N = 12); skull SL x̄ 16.3, SD 0.26 (N = 23); CB x̄ 7.8, SD 0.22 (N = 22), IOW x̄ 2.7, SD 0.10 (N = 24); MW x̄ 4.1, SD 0.14, (N = 21). Colour like *S. c. cinereus.* Distribution: Labrador.

S. c. streatori Merriam 1895, N. Am. Fauna 10:62.
TL 102–111, x̄ 106 (N = 8), T 42–58, x̄ 46 (N = 8); skull, SL x̄ 16.4, SD 0.32 (N = 9); CB x̄ 7.6, SD 0.20 (N = 9); MW x̄ 4.2, SD 0.08, (N = 9). Colour dark. Distribution: Pacific coast.

Biology

The common shrew is found in a variety of habitats including forests, grasslands, and weed patches, from wet areas to those that are quite dry [26]. It occurs in deciduous and coniferous woods up to timberline; in alder and willow thickets; and along the margins of marshes, bogs, and streams.

The bulk of this species' food consists of insects and other inverte- brates such as earthworms, sow bugs, centipedes, spiders, and molluscs [11]. Vertebrates such as young mice and salamanders are also taken. Throughout the boreal forest, this shrew is an important predator of sawfly cocoons [3]. Predation of 14–88 per cent of sawfly-cocoon populations by the common shrew has been reported. Some vegetable matter (seeds) is also used; in winter seeds may even form the bulk of the diet [6]. Ants are apparently avoided and captive shrews of this species did not eat frogs, slugs, carrots, and apples [1]. The common shrew has a high basal metabolism and the amount of food eaten is considerable [17]. A daily consumption of $3.3 \times$ the animal's own body weight has been recorded [1], but given high-quality food (e.g. beef liver) consumption will be only one-half that much [18]. The shrews themselves are preyed upon by snakes, birds of prey, mammalian carnivores, and larger shrews.

Populations fluctuate considerably from year to year. A catch of 0.3 animals per 100 trap nights during a year of low abundance may be $50 \times$ that figure during a year of peak abundance [7]. Density esti-mates vary from approximately 2 to 30 shrews per hectare [4]. The turnover in the population is rapid. Individuals usually do not survive beyond 14 months, producing usually two and rarely three litters in a lifetime. Four age-classes are distinguishable on the basis of tooth wear [19].

The common shrew is most active at night, when approximately 85 per cent of activity occurs, with a peak between 01:00 to 02:00 hrs. Light is the most important factor affecting the 24-hour activity rhythm. Activity is greater on dark cloudy nights. Rainfall also increases nocturnal activity [3, 8, 24]. The behaviour of this species is not well known. Movements are rapid. When running, the animal carries the tail straight to the rear with the tip curved up. It can jump approximately 10–15 cm and is capable of climbing in low vegetation and shrubs [12]. Burrowing has not been observed, although it is able to dig in loose substrate. Some time is spent grooming each day. Inaccessible parts of the body are scratched with the hind foot. When tearing at large prey, one or both front feet are used to hold the food in place. The senses of sight [1] and smell appear to be well developed. This species has been observed hunting butterflies in the daytime [5]. The butterflies were detected by the shrew at a distance of approximately 6 m, presumably visually. Buried cocoons and other immobile prey are detected by smell and dug up. Hearing is probably acute for certain sounds, and there is evidence that echoloca-tion may be used. Three types of vocalizations have been described: staccato squeaks associated with aggressive behaviour; a faint twitter when the animal is searching for food; and gritting of teeth when resting [1]. Ultrasonic sounds have also been detected and are probably used in echolocation. Caravan behaviour, common in crocidurine shrews and also reported for some Old World species of *Sorex*, has recently been observed in this species as well [10]. So far, it is the only report of this behaviour in an American soricine. Caravan behaviour is displayed by young shrews when they are disturbed or forced to leave the nest. It consists of the animals moving in single-file formation, each maintaining contact with the rump of the animal in front by burying its nose in the fur near the tail. They were not observed to grip each other with their teeth, as has been reported for some crocidurine shrews.

The reproductive biology of the common shrew is poorly known. The species is probably polyoestrous. Breeding activity starts in spring (April) and continues into autumn. The dates at which breeding commences probably vary with latitude. In the far north, there may be only one main breeding season in summer. In the southern part of the range, pregnant or lactating shrews have been reported as late as October [16, 21]. Litter size varies from 4 to 10 and averages about 7. The newly born young, which are born in a spherical nest of dry vegetation, are hairless with eyelids fused and teeth not yet erupted. They are approximately 15 to 17 mm long including the 3 mm long tail and weigh a little over 0.25 g. Incisors erupt between 13 and 14 days, eyes open at 17 to 18 days and ears at 14 to 17 days. The young are weaned when approximately 20 days old [9].

Reproduction and Ontogeny

References

[1] Blossom, P.M., 1932
[2] Buckner, C.H., 1957, [3] 1964, [4] 1966, [5] 1970
[6] Criddle, S., 1973
[7] De Vos, A., 1957
[8] Doucet, G.J., and J.R. Bider, 1974
[9] Forsyth, D.J., 1976
[10] Goodwin, M.K., 1979
[11] Hamilton, W.J., Jr., 1930
[12] Horvath, O., 1965
[13] Junge, J.A., and R. Hoffmann, 1982
[14] Kirkland, G.L., Jr., 1977
[15] Macleod, C.F., 1960
[16] Moore, J.C., 1949
[17] Morrison, P.R., and O.P. Pearson, 1946
[18] Morrison, P.R., M. Pierce, and F.A. Ryder, 1957
[19] Pruitt, W.O. Jr., 1954a, [20] 1954b
[21] Short, H.L., 1961
[22] van Zyll de Jong, C.G., 1980, [23] 1982a
[24] Vickery, W.L., and J.R. Bider, 1978
[25] Warren, G.L., 1970
[26] Wrigley, R.E., J.E. Dubois, and W.H.R. Copland, 1979

Sorex haydeni Baird
(named after collector F.V. Hayden)

Prairie Shrew   **Musaraigne des steppes**

1858 *Sorex haydeni* Baird, Mammals, *in* Rep. Expl. Surv. 8, (1):29.
1896 *Sorex personatus haydeni* Allen, Bull. Am. Mus. Nat. Hist.
    8:257.
1925 *Sorex cinereus haydeni* Jackson, J. Mamm. 6:56.
Type locality: Fort Union, now Mondak, Montana, near present
town of Buford, North Dakota.

External Measurements and Weight

	TL	T	HF	W
N	100	133	128	50
X̄	87.0	31.6	10.7	3.0
SD	5.20	2.47	0.67	0.44
CV	5.98	7.81	6.30	14.67
OR	77–101	25.0–38.0	9–12	2.0–5.0

Cranial Measurements

	SL	CB	IOW	MW
N	137	132	142	93
X̄	14.9	7.4	2.6	4.2
SD	0.32	0.23	0.11	0.11
CV	2.13	3.08	4.22	2.67
OR	14.1–15.6	6.8–7.8	2.4–2.9	3.9–4.6

Description (not illustrated)

Similar to *S. cinereus* but smaller, with shorter tail; winter and
summer pelage paler than in *S. cinereus* with a tendency to tricolour
pattern especially in older adults, tail paler usually lacking the dark
terminal tuft. Skull smaller than that of *S. cinereus* with shorter,
broader rostrum, lacrimal foramen and border of infraorbital
foramen usually placed more anterior than in *S. cinereus*, above or
before the mesostyle of M1, or at least tangential to a line drawn
from the tip of the mesostyle perpendicular to the alveolar border.
Unicuspids as in *S. cinereus*, but wider than long, and the unicuspid
row more compressed and shorter; teeth in general more robust than
those of *cinereus*; pigmentation usually more intense and extensive
— a high proportion has two pigmented areas on the lower incisor,
the first and larger including the tip and the first two cusps, the
second including the third cusp.

Similar species: *S. cinereus*, tail longer, ventral coloration of tail
with terminal hairs dark, length of unicuspid row usually > 2.2 mm,
individual unicuspids usually longer than wide. *S. ugyunak* found
on tundra distinctly tricolour, lower incisor with pigmentation
usually occurring in three separate areas. *S. vagrans* and *S. monticolus*,
larger, third unicuspid smaller than fourth; *Sorex hoyi*, third and
fifth unicuspid reduced.

Distribution

The distribution of the prairie shrew in Canada is restricted to the prairie and parklands of Manitoba, Saskatchewan, and Alberta [2]. The possibility of its occurrence in the Peace River parklands of British Columbia cannot be ruled out as it is known from Beaverlodge, Alberta, not far from the border. Peripheral localities: *Alberta* (**1**) Beaverlodge; (**2**) Warspite; (**3**) Pigeon Lake; (**4**) Calgary; (**5**) Milk River. *Manitoba* (**6**) 0.3 km north, 4.6 km west of St. Lazare; (**7**) 7.4 km south, south, 6 km west of Pratt; (**8**) Oak Hammock Marsh; (**9**) 16 km east of Emerson. *Saskatchewan:* (**10**) Turtleford; (**11**) Hanley; (**12**) Dysart.

In the United States, this species is found in the northern great plains in Montana, North Dakota, South Dakota, Minnesota, Wyoming, Colorado, Nebraska, and Iowa.

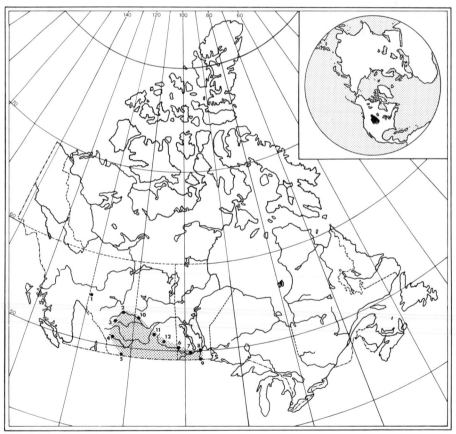

Map 5.   Distribution of *Sorex haydeni*

Systematics

Until recently the prairie shrew was considered to be a subspecies of
S. cinereus. For his revison of the American long-tailed shrews,
Jackson [1] examined a large series of shrews from Aweme, Manitoba,
which contained some typical *haydeni* and *cinereus* skulls, as well
as a few that he regarded as intermediate. He interpreted the latter as
integrades between the two. Re-examination of these and other
specimens from the prairie provinces showed that the two forms
should be regarded as species as they do not intergrade and are
morphologically distinct in areas of sympatry [2]. No evidence of
hybridization between the two was found. No subspecies are recognized in *S. haydeni*. The relationships between *S. haydeni* and
S. preblei and other similar southern forms of the *cinereus* group
need to be investigated. *S. haydeni* resembles *S. ugyunak* to a much
greater extent than it does the neighboring *S. cinereus*. Whether this
resemblance is owing to common ancestry or to convergence needs
further study.

Biology

The grasslands of the prairies and parklands of the north central
plains with their semi-arid to sub-humid climate are the preferred
habitat of the prairie shrew. Where *S. cinereus* and *S. haydeni* occur
together, in the prairie-forest transition, the two species exhibit
habitat segregation; *S. cinereus* preferring the cover of trees, shrubs,
or tall herbaceous vegetation and *S. haydeni* the low cover of the
prairie vegetation [2].

Next to nothing is known about the general biology of this species.
It is probably similar to that of *S. cinereus*. On 14 October 1924
Criddle found eight young of this species in a nest of brome grass
under a sheaf near Treesbank, Manitoba [1].

References

[1] Jackson, H.H.T., 1928
[2] van Zyll de Jong, C.G., 1980

Sorex ugyunak Anderson and Rand
(from *ug-yū-nak*, the Eskimo name for shrew)

Barrenground Shrew   **Musaraigne de Béringie**

1945 *Sorex cinereus ugyunak* Anderson and Rand, Can. Field-Nat.
    59(2):62.
Type locality: Tuktoyaktuk (= Tuktoyaktok), about 32 km southwest of Toker Point on the arctic coast.

External Measurements and Weights

	TL	T	HF	W
N	31	33	35	4
X̄	82.4	25.8	11.5	3.6
SD	6.09	2.45	0.84	1.08
CV	7.40	9.51	7.35	30.24
OR	74–103	22–31	10–13.5	2.9–5.2

Cranial Measurements

	SL	CB	IOW	MW
N	26	26	26	19
X̄	14.8	7.3	2.6	4.03
SD	0.29	0.20	0.08	0.13
CV	1.93	2.76	3.05	3.21
OR	14.2–15.4	6.7–7.8	2.4–2.8	3.8–4.4

Description (Colour Plate II)

A small, short-tailed shrew, colour distinctive, light colour of underparts extending far up the sides, with brown back forming a well-
defined dorsal stripe, tail light, pale brown above, whitish below,
terminal tuft in ventral view pale buff to light brownish. Summer
pelage short (2–3 mm on the back) back brown, sides and underside
buffy; in winter pelage longer (5–6 mm on the back) back brownish,
sides grey and underside light grey. Juveniles are somewhat darker
than adults and the demarcation between dark back and light sides
is less distinct. Winter pelage is acquired in mid-October (Tuktoyaktuk). Date of spring moult unknown but one specimen collected on
6 June was already in summer pelage.

   Skull like that of *S. cinereus*, but resembling that of *S. haydeni*
more in being smaller than that of the former, having a shorter
broader rostrum, less inflated cranium, posterior border of infraorbital foramen and lacrimal foramen placed more anterior, at or
before the mesostyle of M1. Unicuspid row relatively short, similar

to that of *haydeni*, and individual unicuspids usually wider than long, pigmentation of teeth as in *cinereus*, the unworn lower incisor usually shows three separate areas of pigmentation, the tip and first cusp, the second cusp, and the third cusp.

Similar species: *S. haydeni*, found in prairie region, light colour generally not extending far up the sides. *S. cinereus*, light colour of underside does not extend far up on the side and lacks abrupt demarcation between light- and dark-coloured pelage, tail dark on the ventral side, blackish terminal tuft usually contrasts with light colour of the rest of the tail, length of unicuspids > 2.2 mm. *S. monticolus*, larger, lacking distinct colour pattern of *ugyunak*; *S. tundrensis* much larger.

Distribution

In Canada, the barrenground shrew occurs on the vast mainland tundra west of Hudson Bay. Peripheral localities: *Northwest Territories:* (1) Tuktoyaktuk; (2) mouth of Kugaryuak River;

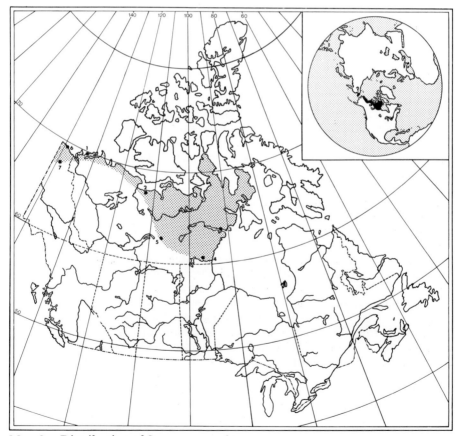

Map 6.   Distribution of *Sorex ugyunak*

(3) Chesterfield Inlet; (4) 72 km southwest of Padlei; (5) Ptarmigan Lake; *Yukon:* (6) Head Point; (7) Driftwood River 96.5 km northeast of Old Crow.

The world distribution of this species cannot be delineated with certainty because of the unresolved taxonomic status of the shrews of the *cinereus* group in Siberia. In Alaska, the species is found on the north slope of the Brooks Range, west to Point Barrow. Siberian forms of the *cinereus* group (see below) have been recorded from the Chukotka and Kamchatka peninsulas, the upper reaches of the Omolon River and from Paramushir, the northernmost island of the Kuril Islands chain [5, 8, 9].

Systematics

This shrew was originally described in 1945 as a subspecies of *S. cinereus*. Morphometric analysis has not produced any evidence of intergradation between neighboring populations of *cinereus* and *ugyunak* [6, 7]. As different from *cinereus* as *haydeni*, *ugyunak*, moreover, resembles the latter closely. Beside *ugyunak*, the tundra forms of the *cinereus* group are represented in North America by two other forms, *S. pribilofensis* on St. Paul Island and *S. jacksoni* on St. Lawrence Island in the Bering Sea. Across the Bering Strait, in the northeastern Palearctic Region, three forms, *portenkoi* from the Chukotka Peninsula, *camtschatica* from Kamchatka and the upper Omolon River, and *leucogaster* from Paramushir have been described [5, 8].

S. pribilofensis is the most differentiated of the tundra forms, probably owing to its long isolation, which may have lasted since 16 000 years B.P. It seems reasonable to assume, on morphological grounds, that *pribilofensis* has attained full specific status [2, 7]. *S. jacksoni* is more similar to *ugyunak*, from which it differs mainly in size and the darker coloration of its pelage [7]. St. Lawrence Island has been separated from the mainland more recently (approximately 7000 years B.P.).

Morphometric comparison of shrews of the *cinereus* group from both sides of the Bering Strait has shown that the American forms *ugyunak* and *jacksoni* resemble the Siberian forms *portenkoi* and *leucogaster* closely [7]. Indeed the tundra-dwelling mainland forms, *ugyunak* and *portenkoi*, are hardly distinguishable. It is probable that all four forms are conspecific. Should further research, such as comparison of the morphology of the penis and karyotypes, confirm this, the new combination would take the name *Sorex jacksoni* Hall and Gilmore 1932. The third Siberian form, *camtschatica*, differs considerably from the four just mentioned and may represent a separate species [7]. Superficially *camtschatica* resembles the Nearctic woodland form *S. cinereus* in size, length of tail and the colour of its pelage, which is not tricoloured as in the tundra forms; however, cranially, it is closer to the tundra forms [5, 7]. The relatively large hind foot with its well-developed fringe of stiff hairs sets it apart from both *S. cinereus* and the tundra forms. Ecological differences with respect to the tundra forms are suggested by its reported greatest relative abundance in moist woods along riverbanks [5].

The *cinereus* group probably evolved in North America in the early Pleistocene. Fossils assigned to this group are known from the Kansan Glacial Stage. The present distribution of the distinctive tundra and woodland forms of the *cinereus* group suggests two main evolutionary centres during the last glaciation, one in Beringia and the other south of the glaciated area [3, 7]. The Beringian population gave rise to the present tundra forms including *camtschatica*. The southern woodland form moved north with the expanding forest, while the tundra forms expanded eastwards to occupy the present range in the barrens west of Hudson Bay. If the similarity of *S. haydeni* to the tundra forms, especially to *S. ugyunak*, is the result of common ancestry, this could date back to an early southward migration of tundra forms along the ice-free corridor during the mid-Wisconsin or at the end of the Wisconsin glaciation [7].

Geographic variation in *S. ugyunak* has not yet been studied in detail, but comparison of some cranial measurements of specimens from the Canadian Arctic east of the MacKenzie River with those from Alaska indicates that the latter may be larger.

Biology

The barrenground shrew is found north of tree-line in the arctic tundra [4]. It appears to select low, wet, sedge-grass meadows and thickets of dwarf willow and birch [1]. It has also been found in old winter houses of the Eskimo. In winter it has been observed to enter food caches to feed. Little else is known about this species.

References

[1] Bee, J.W., and E.R. Hall, 1956
[2] Hoffmann, R.S., and R.S. Peterson, 1967
[3] Macpherson, A.H., 1965
[4] Martell, A.M., and A.M. Pearson, 1978
[5] Okhotina, M.V., 1977
[6] van Zyll de Jong, C.G., 1976*a*, [7] 1982*a*
[8] Yudin, B.S., 1969, [9] 1973

Sorex fumeus Miller
(f. L *fumus* smoke)

Smoky Shrew   **Musaraigne fuligineuse**

1885 *Sorex forsteri* True, Proc. U.S. Nat. Mus. 7:606
1895 *Sorex fumeus* Miller, N. Am. Fauna 10:50
Type locality: Peterboro, Madison County, New York

External Measurements and Weight

	TL	T	HF	W
N	50	50	50	4
X̄	113.5	46.7	13.5	6.7
SD	5.16	2.74	0.85	0.94
CV	4.54	5.86	6.29	14.02
OR	104–125	42–54	12–15	5.8–8

Cranial Measurements

	SL	CB	IOW	MW
N	50	45	50	26
X̄	18.1	8.6	3.6	5.1
SD	0.33	0.39	0.11	0.14
CV	1.82	4.53	3.06	2.74
OR	17.5–18.8	7.5–9.1	3.4–3.9	4.8–5.4

Description (Colour Plate III)

A medium-sized shrew, summer pelage brown, underparts brownish, only slightly lighter than the sides and back. In winter the pelage is dark grey to blackish. Moults from spring to mid-July and in autumn to late October and early November. Tail usually bicolour, yellowish below, brown above. Skull with broad and relatively flat braincase; infraorbital foramen situated just anterior to the M1–M2 interface and the lacrimal foramen at the M1–M2 interface, the anterior margin of the orbit is situated just posterior to the mesostyle of M2, unicuspids wider than long with unpigmented lingual ridge to cingulum and the third unicuspid larger than the fourth.

Similar species: *S. cinereus* is smaller and more lightly built, feet smaller and narrower (approximately 2 mm wide); underparts usually much lighter (greyish) than sides and back. Skull smaller (SL < 17 mm). *S. dispar* and *S. gaspensis* resemble *S. fumeus* in winter pelage, but can be distinguished from it by their relatively longer tails, which are not bicolour and by their lighter skulls and narrow unicuspids (longer than wide) as well as the position of the infraorbital foramen behind the M1–M2 interface.

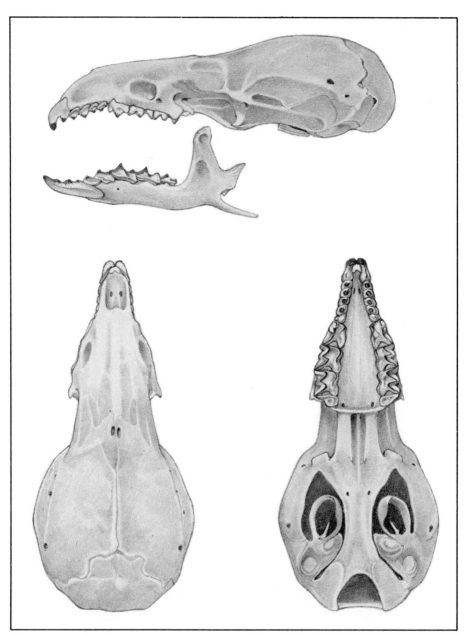

Figure 21.   Skull of *Sorex fumeus*

Distribution

The smoky shrew is restricted to eastern Canada where it occurs south of a line connecting the north shore of Lake Superior and the mouth of the Saguenay River, in all of Quebec east of the St. Lawrence and in New Brunswick and Nova Scotia. Cameron [1] reported this species from Prince Edward Island and Cape Breton Island, but the two single specimens on which these reports were based were re-examined and found to be *S. cinereus*. Therefore the occurrence of the species on these islands remains in doubt. Extensive collecting on Cape Breton Island has so far failed to produce any evidence of *S. fumeus* there. In Ontario the species has not been reported from Lambton, Elgin, Norfolk, Haldiman, Kent, and Essex counties. The species may be rare or absent in these areas possibly because of lack of suitable habitat. Peripheral localities: *New Brunswick:* (**1**) Burnt Church; (**2**) Browns Flat. *Nova Scotia:* (**3**) East Roman Valley; (**4**) Wolfville; (**5**) Barrington Passage. *Ontario:* (**6**) Fraserdale; (**7**) Port Carling; (**8**) Niagara Glen; (**9**) London; (**10**) Johnson

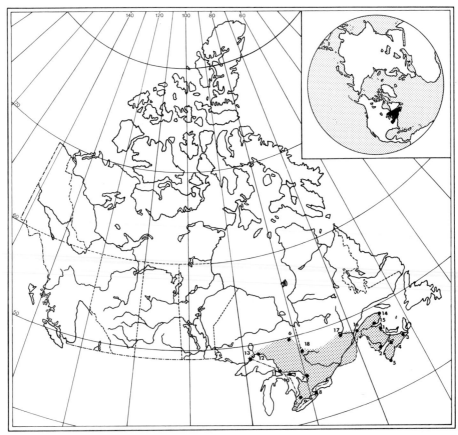

Map 7.   Distribution of *Sorex fumeus*

Harbour; (11) Garden River; (12) Schreiber; (13) Thunder Bay. *Quebec:* (14) Cap des Rosiers; (15) Cascapédia; (16) Saint-Simon; (17) Chambord; (formerly Val Jalbert); (18) 16 km west of Arntfield.

Outside Canada the species occurs in the eastern United States from New England south to North Carolina and Tennessee.

Systematics

S. fumeus is a rather uniform species showing little marked geographic variation. The two indistinct subspecies recognized are said to be somewhat different in size and colour. A comparison of the samples in the collection of the National Museum of Natural Sciences indicates joint nonoverlap in external measurements of less than 75%, a value well below the conventional level of subspecific difference of 90% joint nonoverlap.

S. f. fumeus Miller, N. Am. Fauna 10:50, 1895.
TL 92–124, $\bar{x}$ 111.7 (N = 20); T 39–50, $\bar{x}$ 45.6 (N = 20); HF 12–14.5, $\bar{x}$ 13.38 (N = 20); SL $\bar{x}$ 18.0, SD 0.33 (N = 19). Slightly smaller and more reddish brown in summer pelage than *S. f. umbrosus*. Distribution: Ontario and Quebec.

S. f. umbrosus Jackson, Proc. Biol. Soc. Wash. 30:149, 1917.
TL 100–126, $\bar{x}$ 116.5 (N = 30); T 41–54, $\bar{x}$ 48.5 (N = 30); HF 13–15, $\bar{x}$ 13.8 (N = 30); SL $\bar{x}$ 18.2, SD 0.34 (N = 31). Slightly larger than *S. f. fumeus*, upper parts greyish brown in summer pelage. Distribution: Gaspé Peninsula, New Brunswick, and Nova Scotia.

Biology

The smoky shrew is most abundant in deciduous or mixed woods of the Great Lakes–St. Lawrence and Acadian Forest regions. It prefers damp sites with abundant leaf litter, rotten logs, and stumps. Here, this species uses runways and tunnels in the leaf mould made by other small mammals. The smoky shrew's spherical nests, made of shredded leaves, are located at various places in these subterranean labyrinths, generally beneath stumps or fallen and rotted tree trunks [2]. *Habitat*

The diet of the smoky shrew, as that of most other shrews, is made up predominantly of animal matter. The results of one analysis indicated that insects are most important (80% frequency of occurrence), followed by centipedes (13.1%), earthworms (10.1%), snails, (10.1%), spiders (5.9%), sow bugs (5.2%), mammals (3%), salamanders (1.8%), and birds (0.6%). Vegetable matter was found in 14.9% of the sample. In winter, when most prey species are dormant or not available, the smoky shrew feeds mostly on pupae and dormant insects. In captivity this species has been observed to consume half or more of its weight in a day. In its natural environment, this shrew probably obtains most of its water requirements from its food. Captive individuals drink by dipping their snouts in the water and then tilting their heads back [2]. *Food*

The smoky shrew shares the forest floor with a number of species of small mammals including *Blarina brevicauda, Peromyscus* *Associated Mammals leucopus, P. maniculatus, Clethrionomys gapperi, Synaptomys cooperi, Napaeozapus insignis,* and *Parascalops breweri.* There may be interspecific intolerance between *S. cinereus* and *S. fumeus* where they occur together. *Blarina* preys on small mammals including *S. fumeus,* and may affect its abundance. Other predators are weasels, bobcats, hawks, and owls. Parasites recorded from *S. fumeus* include fleas, mites, nematodes and cestodes [2].

Predators

Parasites

Populations of the smoky shrew fluctuate considerably from year to year. In peak years and in optimum habitat, the species may reach densities of 62 to 124 animals per hectare. The life span of the smoky shrew like that of other shrews, is short and usually does not exceed 14 to 17 months. Mortality is heavy in winter. Adults disappear rapidly from the population in summer and are virtually absent after August [2].

Population

Not much is known of this species' behaviour but it is believed to be similar to that of other long-tailed shrews. Alarmed shrews utter a high-pitched grating sound. When greatly disturbed, the animal will throw itself on its back and, with spread and threshing legs, utter squeaking staccato notes. These shrews produce an almost inaudible continuous twittering as, with twitching noses and extended vibrissae, they search for food. Scats are deposited in piles near the nest. The eyes are small, and the role of vision in the animal's life unknown. The sense of smell appears to be not particularly well developed, although no careful tests have been carried out to confirm this. Olfaction almost certainly plays an important role in social behavior, especially during the breeding season. Hearing and touch are well developed. Evidence from trapping indicates that the smoky shrew is active throughout the day and night [2].

Behaviour

The breeding season begins in early spring (early March in New York) and lasts into late summer (late August in New Brunswick). This species does not appear to breed in the year of birth. At the onset of the breeding season, reproductive organs increase in size very rapidly. The males become sexually mature before the females. Gestation is estimated at somewhat less than three weeks and litter size averages 5.5 young (5-6). Embryo counts vary from 2 to 7 (mode 6). Number of litters produced is unknown, but as mating occurs directly following parturition, judging from the presence of actively nursing females with well-developed embryos, it seems probable that each female may produce two or three litters [2].

Reproduction and Ontogeny

References

[1] Cameron, A.W., 1958
[2] Hamilton, W.J., Jr., 1940*b*
[3] Jackson, H.H.T., 1928

Sorex gaspensis Anthony and Goodwin

Gaspé Shrew	Musaraigne de Gaspé

1924 *Sorex gaspensis* Anthony and Goodwin, Am. Mus. Novit.,
  109:1–2
Type locality: Mount Albert, Gaspé Peninsula, Quebec, 600 m
elevation

External Measurements and Weight

	TL	T	HF	W
N	21	23	23	9
X̄	103.4	49.5	12.1	3.0
SD	6.54	2.33	0.36	0.60
CV	6.32	4.71	2.98	20.00
OR	95–120	45–55	11–12.5	2.3–4.3

Cranial Measurements

	SL	CB	IOW	MW
N	18	17	17	7
X̄	15.9	7.5	3.0	3.8
SD	0.34	0.30	0.21	0.11
CV	2.14	4.00	7.00	2.89
OR	15.4–16.4	7.2–8.2	2.8–3.5	3.6–3.8

Description (Colour Plate II)

A small dark-grey, long-tailed shrew, with underparts only slightly
paler than dorsum; tail dark grey to black, slightly lighter below,
feet pale. Winter pelage unknown, but a tuft of winter hair on the
rump of a moulting male specimen (29 June) and newly grown
winter hair on the posterior part of the back of a female (September)
suggest that the winter pelage is like the summer pelage in colour,
but longer. Vibrissae are long. Skull long and narrow and brain case
flattened dorsoventrally, rostrum relatively long and narrow,
posterior border of the infraorbital foramen and the lacrimal foramen
are located posterior to the M1–M2 interface, anterior margin of
the orbit approximately at the metastyle of M2. Mandible slender, its
depth less than the height of the unworn molars, mental foramen
anterior to the protoconid of m1, and base of i1 (cingulum) situated
below p3. Unicuspids narrower than long and third unicuspid
greater or subequal to the fourth unicuspid.
Similar species: *S. dispar*, larger, HF > 12, SL > 16.4. *S. fumeus*,
relatively shorter bicoloured tail, SL > 17 mm. *S. cinereus*, brownish,
posterior border of infraorbital foramen anterior to M1–M2 interface.

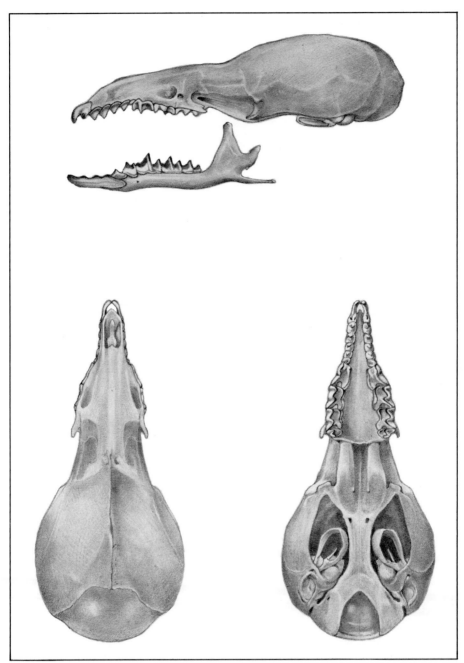

Figure 22. Skull of *Sorex gaspensis*

Distribution

This species has the most restricted range of any native shrew.
Specimens have been collected in the Gaspé, New Brunswick (Mount
Carleton) and Nova Scotia (Cape Breton Island). Microgeographic
distribution within this area appears to be patchy, possibly because
of specific habitat requirements.
Peripheral localities: *New Brunswick:* (**1**) Mount Carleton;
(**1**) Sagamook Mountain; (**2**) Moose Mountain. *Nova Scotia:* (**3**) Cape
Breton Highlands National Park; (**3**) valley of the Northeast
Margaree River; (**4**) Kellys Mountain. *Quebec:* (**5**) Mount Albert;
(**6**) Berry Mountain.

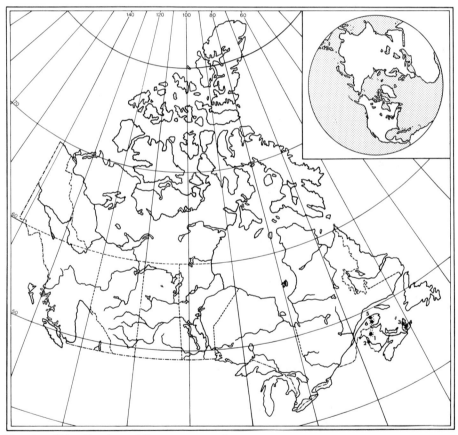

Map 8. Distribution of *Sorex gaspensis*

Systematics

S. gaspensis is closely related to the larger *S. dispar* to the south. The two forms may prove to be conspecific. Available information shows that *dispar* exhibits clinal variation in size, decreasing at a steady rate from North Carolina and Tennessee in the south to New England in the north. Samples of *gaspensis* from the Gaspé and Cape Breton Island indicate that the size of this form is smaller than would be expected if we assume the rate of decrease in size per unit distance to remain unchanged. Kirkland and Van Deusen [8] concluded from this that *gaspensis* is specifically distinct. The possibility exists, however, that the cline linking the two forms becomes much steeper between New England and the northern extremities of the group's range. Until now insufficient material was available from the intervening area to decide the question. A study, now underway, of a recent collection from two localities in New Brunswick may clarify the situation [2]. Other than size, there do not appear to be any differences between *gaspensis* and *dispar* [7, 8].

Biology

S. gaspensis is without a doubt our least-known and rarest shrew. The type specimen was collected in 1923 by G.G. Goodwin of the American Museum of Natural History. Since that time the total number of specimens in collections has grown slowly and probably did not exceed 30 until recently, when a sample of 68 was collected in New Brunswick [2]. Next to nothing is known of its biology, but capture data suggest that it is restricted to rocky, mountainous or hilly terrain, where it has been collected along small, bouldered streams in coniferous and mixed forest and in hardwoods with a substrate of boulders and broken rock [1, 2, 9, 10]. The only information on food habits thus far comes from the stomach contents of two animals [5]. They contained, respectively, beetle and spider remains in addition to plant matter. Three adult females caught during the latter half of June and July had 5(1) and 6(2) embryos [2].

References

[1] Anthony, H.E., and G.G. Goodwin, 1924
[2] Dalton, M., and B.A. Sabo, 1980
[3] Goodwin, G.G., 1924, [4] 1929
[5] Hamilton, W.J., Jr., and W.J. Hamilton III, 1954
[6] Jackson, H.H.T., 1928
[7] Kirkland, G.L., Jr., 1981
[8] Kirkland, G.L., Jr., and H.M. Van Deusen, 1979
[9] Peterson, R.S., and A. Symansky, 1963
[10] Roscoe, B., and C. Majka, 1976

Sorex dispar Batchelder
(f. L *dispar* unlike, different)

Long-tailed Shrew	**Musaraigne longicaude**
(Rock Shrew)	

1896 *Sorex macrurus* Batchelder, Proc. Biol. Soc. Wash. 10:133
1911 *Sorex dispar* Batchelder, Proc. Biol. Soc. Wash. 24:97
Type locality: Beedes, Essex County, New York

External Measurements and Weight

	TL	**T**	**HF**	**W** [8]	
N	6	6	6	17 ♂ ♂	9 ♀ ♀
X̄	125.5	57.8	14.5	5.5	4.7
SD	4.13	2.71	0.49	—	—
CV	3.29	4.69	3.37	—	—
OR	121–131	55–62	14–15	3.9–8.3	3.5–5.5

Cranial Measurements

	SL	**CB**	**IOW**	**MW**
N	6	5	5	5
X̄	17.8	8.0	3.3	4.3
SD	0.32	0.08	0.08	0.13
CV	1.83	1.03	2.42	3.04
OR	17.3–18.2	7.9–8.1	3.3–3.5	4.2–4.5

Description (not illustrated)

External appearance and skull characters similar to those of *S. gaspensis*, but larger, and pelage somewhat darker and less greyish. Winter pelage as well as summer pelage, slate coloured. Vibrissae longer than in *S. cinereus* and *S. fumeus*. For similar species, see under *S. gaspensis*.

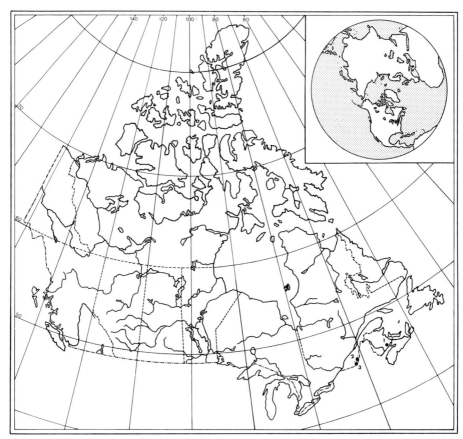

Map 9.   Distribution of *Sorex dispar*

Distribution

This species is found in the mountains from Maine to southern West
Virginia and eastern Tennessee. In Canada, it is known from only
six specimens, four of which were collected in 1955 near the interna-
tional border in Quebec, near Lac du Portage, 16 km southeast of
Armstrong, and south of Cartierville [7], and two were collected in
Albert County, New Brunswick, in 1978 and 1979 [3, 4].

Systematics

See discussion under *S. gaspensis*. There are two subspecies: *S. d.
blitchi* and *S. d. dispar*. The Canadian specimens belong to the latter
subspecies.

Biology

This shrew appears to prefer loose talus in wooded country [2, 8]. The distribution of this species is not limited by altitude, but its restriction to hilly and mountainous areas is related to the availability of talus there. The species spends most of its time in crevices and spaces among rocks and boulders covered by leaf mould and roots. — Habitat

Limited information on the food habits of this species suggests that it feeds predominantly on centipedes [8]. Remains of insects and spiders were also found. Small mammals associated with *S. dispar* in its limited habitat are red-backed voles (*Clethrionomys gapperi*), and three species of shrews, *S. fumeus*, *B. brevicauda*, and *S. cinereus*, of which the last-mentioned is most numerous. Competition is avoided, presumably by different specialization and exploitation of different food resources. *S. cinereus*, from localities inhabited by *S. dispar*, feeds mainly on spiders and to a lesser extent on beetles, other insects, and pupae. — Food / Associated Mammals

There is no information on the population structure and dynamics of this species. This shrew is probably more common, at least locally, than its relative rarity in collections would indicate. Because of the type of habitat in which it is found, and because of its largely subterranean habits, *S. dispar* is rarely caught in conventional traplines. — Population

Nothing is known of its behaviour or activity patterns. It is probably active in the day as well as at night. — Behaviour

The reproductive season apparently starts in the latter half of April (in Pennsylvania) judging from the presence of enlarged uteri at that time. Two females collected on 3 and 6 May were pregnant and contained five small (< 0.5 mm) embryos each [8]. Five females collected in February, March, and July showed no evidence of reproductive activity. The meagre evidence suggests that *S. dispar* breeds later than other shrews. — Reproduction and Ontogeny

References

[1] Jackson, H.H.T., 1928
[2] Kirkland, G.L., Jr., 1981
[3] Kirkland, G.L., Jr., D.F. Schmidt, and C.J. Kirkland, 1979
[4] Kirkland, G.L., Jr., and D.F. Schmidt, 1982
[5] Kirkland, G.L., Jr., and H.M. Van Deusen, 1979
[6] Martin, R.L., 1966
[7] Peterson, R.L., 1966
[8] Richmond, N.D., and W.C. Grimm, 1950

Sorex monticolus Merriam
(f. L *mons* mountain; *colere* to inhabit)

Dusky Shrew   **Musaraigne sombre**

1890 *Sorex monticolus* Merriam, N. Am. Fauna 3:43
1891 *Sorex dobsoni* Merriam, N. Am. Fauna 5:33
1891 *Sorex vagrans similis* Merriam, N. Am. Fauna 5:34
1895 *Sorex obscurus* Merriam, N. Am. Fauna 10:72
1955 *Sorex vagrans obscurus* Findley, Univ. Kans. Publ., Mus. Nat. Hist. 9:54
1977 *Sorex monticolus* Hennings and Hoffmann, Occas. Pap. Mus. Nat. Hist. Univ. Kans. 68:12

Type locality: San Francisco Mountain, 3500 m, Coconino County, Arizona

External Measurements and Weight

	TL	T	HF	W
N	196	201	201	32
X̄	118.9	50.9	30.8	6.9
SD	9.99	5.76	1.00	1.62
CV	8.40	11.31	7.25	23.50
OR	95–139	30–62	11–16	4.4–10.2

Cranial Measurements

	SL	CB	IOW	MW
N	105	103	105	83
X̄	17.4	8.5	3.4	5.1
SD	0.57	0.32	0.17	0.22
CV	3.26	3.75	5.01	4.32
OR	15.8–18.8	7.8–9.2	3.0–3.7	4.6–5.5

Description (Colour Plate II)

Size small to medium; summer pelage brownish, sides the same colour as back or slightly paler, underparts brownish to silver grey, tail brown, dark above, paler below without a black tip; feet pale brownish; winter pelage darker, from nearly black in coastal forms to greyish brown inland. Females moult in spring from late March to early April and males from late May to August; winter pelage develops in autumn (September, October). Skull with relatively short, broad rostrum, anterior margin of the orbit at the level of the mesostyle of M2, border of infraorbital foramen posterior to mesostyle of M1. Unicuspids with well-developed, usually heavily pigmented lingual ridge from apex to cingulum, ending in a distinct

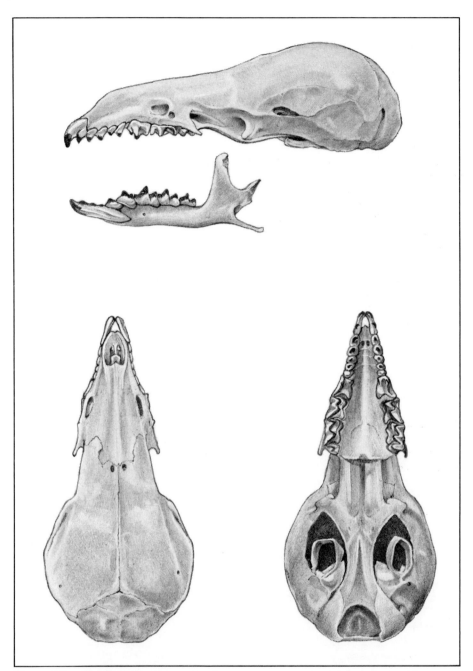

Figure 23.   Skull of *Sorex monticolus*

cuspule; third unicuspid smaller than fourth. The small median cusp on the upper incisor is below the margin of pigmentation.

Similar species: *S. vagrans*, smaller on the average, with shorter tail; skull and teeth smaller; medial accessory cuspule of I1 small, above or at the margin of pigmentation [8]; smaller hind feet and shorter toes with fewer paired digital callosities (no more than four on digits II to IV of the hind foot) [13]. In areas of sympatry in British Columbia the large, long-tailed subspecies of *S. monticolus* can usually be distinguished from the sympatric subspecies of *S. vagrans* by size and tail length. On Vancouver Island and the southern mainland west of the Cascades, *S. m. isolatus* and *S. v. vancouverensis*, and *S. m. setosus* and *S. v. vagrans*, respectively, can be separated using size and tail length with a probability of misidentification in the range of 0.08 to 0.11, or approximately one wrong identification out of 9 to 13. East of the Cascades, where *S. v. vagrans* converges with the sympatric *S. m. obscurus*, which is smaller and has a shorter tail than the coastal forms of *S. monticolus*, the probability of misidentifying a specimen is much higher ($P \approx 0.30$). One out of three can be expected to be identified incorrectly using total length and tail length. In all areas, positive identification can be achieved using the form and pigmentation of I1 and the characters of the feet.

S. cinereus, smaller, tail usually with dark tip, rostrum relatively longer and slenderer, 4th unicuspid smaller than, or subequal to, 3rd unicuspid.

S. trowbridgii has a distinctly bicoloured tail, light feet, laterally compressed unicuspids, and a postmandibular canal.

Distribution

S. monticolus occurs in western Canada from British Columbia and the Yukon east to western and northern Manitoba. It is also found on the Queen Charlotte Islands, Vancouver Island, and smaller offshore islands. Peripheral localities: *Alberta:* (1) Wood Buffalo National Park; (2) Pigeon Lake; (3) Sylvan Lake; (4) Hand Hills. *British Columbia:* (5) Bennett; (6) Port Simpson; (7) Pitt Island; (8) Princess Royal Island; (9) King Island; (10) Spider Island; (11) Calvert Island; (12) Texada Island; (13) Port Moody; (14) Victoria; (15) Nootka; (16) Cape Scott; (17) Kunghit Island (formerly Prevost Island); (18) Skidegate; (19) Lucy Island. Also reported from the following islands (not marked on map): Banks; Campania; Chatfield; Dufferin; Goose; Hecate; Horsfall; Hunter; McCauley; Reginald; Ruth; Smyth; Stuart; Swindle; Townsend. *Manitoba:* (20) Thompson; (21) The Pas; (22) Porcupine Mountain; (23) Singush Lake; (24) Lake Audy. *Northwest Territories:* (25) Aklavik; (26) Punk Mountain; (27) Nahanni Mountains; (28) Fort Simpson; (29) Fort Resolution. *Saskatchewan:* (30) Stony Rapids; (31) Windrum Lake; (32) Trappers Lake; (33) Flotten Lake; (34) Cypress Hills near Maple Creek; (35) Middle Creek. *Yukon:* (36) Old Crow. Outside Canada, the species is found in Alaska and the western United States to Mexico.

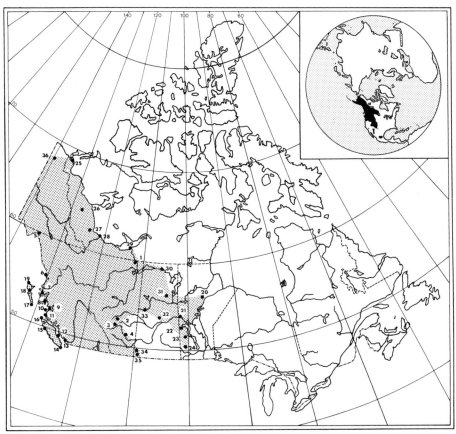

Map 10.   Distribution of *Sorex monticolus*

Systematics

S. monticolus is very similar to *S. vagrans* and in certain areas of
overlap the two forms were found to be difficult or impossible to
separate. Findley [4] interpreted this convergence in size and
colour in areas of sympatry as evidence of introgression between the
two forms and concluded that they belonged to the same species-
complex. He, therefore, combined them in one species, *S. vagrans*,
in which he also included *S. pacificus* and *S. yaquinae* (see
Jackson [10]). However, recent studies by Hennings and Hoffmann [8, 9], and by Hawes [6, 7], on the morphology and ecology of
S. monticolus and *S. vagrans* support their specific independence.
The recent taxonomic revision of the two species also revealed that
S. monticolus Merriam 1890 takes priority over the familiar name
S. obscurus Merriam 1895 [8]. *S. monticolus* had previously been
regarded as a subspecies of *S. vagrans*.
   Karyotypes of different forms of the *S. monticolus-vagrans* group
were reported by Brown [1], but his results and conclusions need

to be re-evaluated in the light of the newly described diagnostic characters.

The earliest fossil evidence of the *S. monticolus-vagrans* group possibly dates back to the Illinoian (Conard Fissure, Arkansas) [4]. Related Recent species occur in the western (*S. ornatus*, *S. pacificus*) and southeastern United States (*S. longirostris*), and in Mexico (*S. verapaecis*) [4].

S. monticolus varies considerably in size, tail length and colour in different parts of its range [3, 4, 5, 8]. In southwestern British Columbia, the species is relatively small and dark brown. Farther north along the coast, the species becomes larger and has a longer tail. East of the Cascade and Coast mountains, in the interior of British Columbia and the remainder of the species' range in Canada, this shrew is smaller, has a shorter tail and is lighter in colour, greyish rather than brownish or reddish. The extent of geographic variation is evident from the large number of subspecies that have been described, of which in Canada alone there are ten.

S. m. calvertensis Cowan, 1941, Proc. Biol. Soc. Wash. 54:103.
TL 118–129, $\bar{x}$ 123.2 (N = 5); T 48–57, $\bar{x}$ 52.4 (N = 5); HF 13–15, $\bar{x}$ 14.3 (N = 5). Summer pelage pale brown above, underparts paler brown, tail brown above, somewhat paler below, winter pelage blackish or greyish. Distribution: Calvert and Banks Island, British Columbia.

S. m. elassodon Osgood, 1901, N. Am. Fauna 21:35.
TL 120–125, $\bar{x}$ 122 (N = 4); T 50–58, $\bar{x}$ 54.5 (N = 4); HF 14–15, $\bar{x}$ 14.5 (N = 5). Summer pelage brown, underparts paler brown, tail brown; winter pelage darker brown. Distribution: Queen Charlotte Islands, British Columbia, and nearby islands in southeastern Alaska.

S. m. insularis Cowan, 1941, Proc. Biol. Soc. Wash. 54:103.
TL 111–134, $\bar{x}$ 122.3; T 46–58, $\bar{x}$ 52.6; HF 13–15, $\bar{x}$ 14.6 (after Cowan and Guiguet 1965). Similar to *S. m. longicauda*, but smaller and winter pelage brown not blackish or greyish. Distribution: Smyth, Townsend, and Reginald islands, British Columbia.

S. m. isolatus Jackson 1922, J. Wash. Acad. Sci. 12:263.
TL 107–125, $\bar{x}$ 117.3 (N = 20); T 46–57, $\bar{x}$ 51.8 (N = 20); HF 13–14, $\bar{x}$ 13.5 (N = 20). Colour dark brown, underparts brownish, sometimes with silvery cast, winter pelage blackish. Distribution: Vancouver Island.

S. m. longicauda Merriam, 1895, N. Am. Fauna 10:74.
TL 107–139, $\bar{x}$ 126.5 (N = 87); T 42–63, $\bar{x}$ 55.1 (N = 91); HF 12–16, $\bar{x}$ 14.5 (N = 91). Summer pelage like *isolatus*, brown, with underparts brownish, tail brown; winter pelage blackish. Distribution: British Columbia, west slopes of Coast Mountains from Burke Channel northwards.

S. m. mixtus Hall, 1938, Am. Nat. 72:462.
TL 108–117, $\bar{x}$ 111 (N = 5); T 44–49, $\bar{x}$ 48 (N = 5); HF 12–13, $\bar{x}$ 12 (N = 5).

Similar to *isolatus* and *setosus*, but with shorter tail and smaller hind foot. Distribution: Texada Island, British Columbia.

S. m. obscurus, Merriam, 1895, N. Am. Fauna 10:72.
TL 100–118, x̄ 109.8 (N = 20); T 38–50, x̄ 45 (N = 20); HF 12–14, x̄ 12.8 (N = 20). Colour greyish brown, underparts greyish; winter pelage more greyish. Distribution: interior of British Columbia, the Yukon, western Northwest Territories, northern and western Alberta.

S. m. prevostensis Osgood, 1901, N. Am. Fauna, 21:35.
TL 120–126, x̄ 123 (N = 7); T 52–58, x̄ 54.7 (N = 7); HF 13.5–15, x̄ 14.5 (N = 7). Summer pelage dark brown, underparts brownish; winter pelage blackish. Distribution: Kunghit Island, British Columbia.

S. m. setosus Elliott, 1899, Field Columb. Mus. Publ. 32, zool. ser. 1:274.
TL 106–125, x̄ 116.4 (N = 20); T 44–56, x̄ 51.6 (N = 20); HF 12–14; x̄ 13.4 (N = 20). Summer pelage brown, underparts brownish; winter pelage blackish. Distribution: coastal British Columbia from Burke Channel southwards, east to the Coast Mountains divide.

S. m. soperi Anderson and Rand, 1945, Can. Field-Nat. 59:47.
TL 99–119, x̄ 109.1 (N = 6); T 37–50, x̄ 44.7 (N = 6); HF 11.5–13.5, x̄ 12.4 (N = 6). Resembles *obscurus* closely, but said to be darker. Distribution: Saskatchewan and Manitoba.

Biology

The dusky shrew is found in many different habitats subject to a wide range of climatic conditions; from the temperate deciduous and coniferous forests to the subarctic tundra–taiga transition, and from the humid Coast Forest to the relatively arid prairies. In the subarctic, it is found along streams and around springs, where relatively tall arborescent shrubs, such as willows and alders, provide overhead cover. In the short-grass range of southern Alberta and Saskatchewan, the species appears to be similarly restricted to thickets along streams and in coulees. The food of this shrew is essentially similar to that of other long-tailed shrews, consisting predominantly of insects, earthworms, and other invertebrates.

Habitat

Food

The dusky shrew coexists with the smaller *S. vagrans* and *S. cinereus* where their ranges overlap. In southern British Columbia, where *S. monticolus* occurs together with *S. vagrans*, interspecific competition is reduced by differences in habitat preference [7, 12]. *S. monticolus* appears to have the competitive advantage on acidic soils, whereas *S. vagrans* does better on relatively richer soils. Unlike *S. vagrans*, *S. monticolus* appears to be rare or absent in open grassy areas and is usually associated with the forest floor litter [12]. The scent produced by the side glands of the two species during the breeding season is noticeably different and serves as a possible isolating mechanism [6]. The size difference between *S. monticolus* and *S. cinereus* probably reduces competition between these species. In

Associated Mammals

the western part of its range, the dusky shrew appears to be the more common of the two, but its abundance relative to that of the common shrew appears to decline toward the east.

Like most other shrews, the dusky shrew is not a long-lived species. The oldest individuals are probably not more than 18 months old. The mean area for the home range of an individual shrew has been estimated to cover 1227 m^2 for non-breeding animals and 4020 m^2 for breeding animals. Non-breeding (first-year) animals are territorial toward members of their own species as well as towards other sympatric *Sorex* [7]. During the breeding season, the animals roam more widely and appear to be non-territorial. The breeding season is from April to August. The average litter size is about 5, ranging up to 7. Information on reproduction from widely separated parts of the species' extensive range is still lacking.

Population

Reproduction and Ontogeny

References

[1] Brown, R.J., 1974
[2] Clothier, R., 1951
[3] Cowan, I. McT., and C.J. Guiguet, 1965
[4] Findley, J.S., 1955
[5] Foster, J.B., 1965
[6] Hawes, M.L., 1976, [7] 1977
[8] Hennings, D., and R.S. Hoffmann, 1977
[9] Hoffmann, R.S., 1971
[10] Jackson, H.H.T., 1928
[11] Slipp, J.W., 1942
[12] Terry, C.J., 1981
[13] van Zyll de Jong, C.G., 1982*b*

Sorex vagrans Baird
(f. L *vago* to wander, pr. part. *vagrans*)

Wandering Shrew   **Musaraigne errante**
(Vagrant Shrew)

1858 *Sorex vagrans* Baird, Mammals *in* Rep. Expl. Surv. 8 (1):15.
Type locality: Shoalwater Bay, Pacific County, Washington.

External Measurements and Weight

	TL	T	HF	W
N	275	277	278	12
X̄	103.9	42.9	12.4	5.7
SD	5.63	2.86	0.64	1.16
CV	5.42	6.66	5.16	20.20
OR	86–119	35–50	10–14	4–7.8

Cranial Measurements

	SL	CB	IOW	MW
N	90	65	47	18
X̄	16.4	8.1	3.0	4.5
SD	0.32	0.21	0.13	0.14
CV	1.95	2.55	4.12	3.22
OR	15.7–17.2	7.5–8.5	2.9–3.4	4.3–4.9

Description (not illustrated)

Very similar to *S. monticolus*, but somewhat smaller, with shorter
tail and lighter skull and dentition. Spring moult occurs in March
in females and in April to mid-May in males. Another moult occurs
in late summer (August and September). This species can be separated
from *S. monticolus* by the small median cusp of I1 being situated
at or above the level of pigmentation, and by a smaller number of
paired digital callosities (not more than 4 on each side of digits II to
IV of the hind foot).

   Other similar species: *S. cinereus*, tail with dark tip, viewed
ventrally; nose relatively longer, more slender; greater number of
paired digital callosities and third unicuspid larger than or subequal
to fourth unicuspid.

Distribution

The range of this shrew in Canada is restricted to southern British
Columbia, including the southern half of Vancouver Island and
some of the islands in the Strait of Georgia. Peripheral localities:
British Columbia: (**1**) Lac la Hache; (**2**) Hemp Creek; (**3**) Glacier
National Park; (**4**) Morrissey; (**5**) Newgate; (**6**) Silver Lake;
(**7**) Lihumption Park; (**8**) Colwood; (**9**) Bowen Island; (**10**) Alberni;
(**11**) Sayward. Also reported from the following islands (not marked
on map): Saltspring; South Pender; and Saturna islands.

In the United States, this species is found from the international
boundary south to California, Nevada, and Utah and eastwards to
western Montana and Colorado.

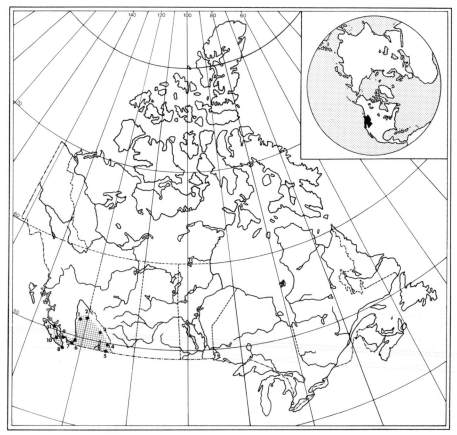

Map 11.   Distribution of *Sorex vagrans*

Systematics

See the discussion under *S. monticolus*. Only two subspecies of
S. vagrans are found in Canada [5].

S. v. vagrans Baird, 1858, Mammals, *in* Rep. Expl. Surv. 8 (1):15.
TL 98–112, x̄ 104.6 (N = 20); T 35–48, x̄ 44 (N = 20); HF 12–14, x̄ 12.8
(N = 20). Colour brown above, underparts grey mixed with brown.
Distribution: southern British Columbia.

S. v. vancouverensis Merriam, 1895, N. Am. Fauna 10:70.
TL 96–119, x̄ 106 (N = 20); T 40–50, x̄ 43.8 (N = 20); HF 12–13, x̄ 12.4
(N = 20). Colour similar to *vagrans*, but darker and more reddish;
underparts brownish, winter pelage darker, more brownish than
that of *vagrans*. Distribution: southern half of Vancouver Island
from Sayward south and on islands in the Gulf of Georgia (Saltspring,
South Pender, and Saturna islands).

Biology

S. vagrans inhabits wooded and open grassy habitats on well-drained   Habitat
to moist sites. It is most common in grassy moist habitats with rich
soils of low acidity [2, 4, 6, 8]. It preys on insects, earthworms, and   Food
other small invertebrates. Small vertebrates such as salamanders may
occasionally be taken. In feeding experiments, this shrew accepted a
wide range of foods including seeds of various trees, shrubs, and
herbs, as well as invertebrates, carrion, and some mushrooms [7].

The ecological interrelationship of *S. vagrans* and *S. monticolus*   Associated
is discussed under the species account of the latter. Where the geo-   Mammals
graphical range of *S. vagrans* overlaps that of *S. cinereus*, the two
species coexist in the same area, although apparently in unequal
abundance. In its preferred habitats, *S. vagrans* apparently always
outnumbers *S. cinereus*, presumably being competitively superior
there.

The mean home range of *S. vagrans* in southern British Columbia   Population
has been estimated to cover 1039 m² for non-breeding and 3258 m²
for breeding animals [4]. In an old field-community of western
Washington, an annual crude density of 36.6 animals per hectare
was estimated, varying from a high of 58.2 individuals per hectare
in summer to a low of 25.8 in late autumn–early winter [6]. Populations of this shrew exhibit an annual turnover, which appears to be
characteristic for most if not all species of shrews. The average life–
expectancy was estimated as 6.6 months in one study, with the
highest mortality occurring in juveniles and one-year-old animals.
Only a few shrews (3 per cent) attained ages of between 24 and 25
months. The sex ratio is nearly equal over the year, but shows seasonal
changes, with females outnumbering males in summer and *vice
versa* in autumn [6].

The wandering shrew is predominantly active at night throughout   Behaviour
the year, with an increase in diurnal activity in spring [6]. The use of
echolocation by this species has been demonstrated [1]. It is used
most often when the animal finds itself in unfamiliar surroundings
and the shrew uses it to locate suitable cover—for example when it

must cross an exposed stretch of ground. The ability to echolocate may be widespread in species of the subfamily Soricinae.

The breeding season extends from March to September, but most breeding takes place in spring (March to May), with only a small proportion of animals breeding in late summer [6]. The average number of young born is 5.2, with an observed range of 2 to 9. The gestation period is estimated at approximately 20 days. Populations of *S. vagrans* in lowland grassland habitats, where food is abundant, have a shorter generation time, mature earlier and have a longer breeding season than woodland populations.

Reproduction and Ontogeny

References

[1] Buchler, E.R., 1976
[2] Clothier, R.R., 1955
[3] Hawes, M.L., 1976, [4] 1977
[5] Hennings, D., and R.S. Hoffmann, 1977
[6] Newman, J.R., 1976
[7] Terry, C.J., 1978, [8] 1981

Sorex trowbridgii **Baird**
(Named after W.P. Trowbridge)

Trowbridge Shrew   **Musaraigne de Trowbridge**

1858 *Sorex trowbridgii* Baird, Mammals, *in* Rep. Expl. Surv. 8(1):13
Type locality: Astoria, mouth of the Columbia River, Clatsop
County, Oregon.

External Measurements and Weight

	TL	T	HF	W
N	41	41	41	—
x̄	113.0	54.3	13.1	5.02*
				3.85**
SD	4.85	2.39	0.56	—
CV	4.30	4.40	4.28	—
OR	104–124	50–59	12.1–14.5	—

*Mean weight for breeding animals
**Mean weight for non-breeding animals

Cranial Measurements

	SL	CB	IOW	MW
N	20	20	19	10
x̄	17.2	8.6	3.8	4.9
SD	0.15	0.13	0.07	0.07
CV	0.89	1.60	1.84	1.56
OR	16.8–17.5	8.3–8.9	3.7–3.9	4.9–5.1

Description (Colour Plate II)

A medium-sized shrew with a relatively long, distinctly bicoloured
tail, which is dark dorsally and white below. Pelage dark grey,
slightly more brownish in summer than in winter; underparts similar
to back, but slightly lighter, feet whitish. Juveniles are more brownish
until their first moult. Spring moult in late May and June; autumn
moult from late August to the first or second week of November.
Skull with orbit placed relatively far back at the level of the metastyle
of M2, lacrimal foramen at the interface of M1 and M2 and the border
of the infraorbital foramen on a line between the mesostyle and metastyle of M1, third unicuspid smaller than the fourth; unicuspids
laterally compressed and lingual ridge from apex not ending in a
cusplet. A postmandibular foramen is present.

  Similar species: *S. trowbridgii* is not easily confused with other
native shrews, because of its distinct colour pattern. The skull and
mandible of *S. trowbridgii* can be distinguished from that of *S.*

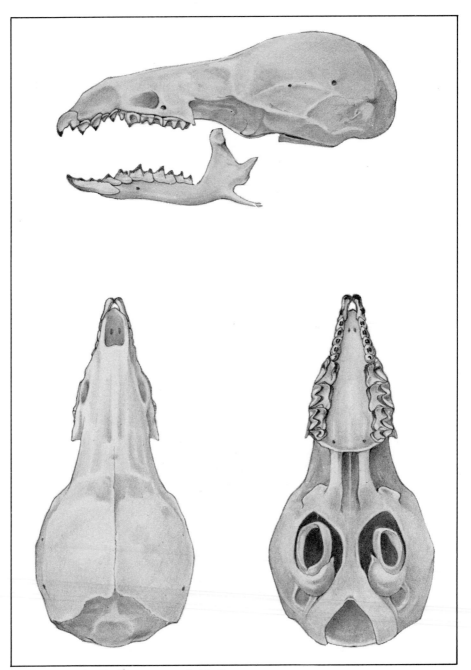

Figure 24. Skull of *Sorex trowbridgii*

obscurus by the laterally compressed unicuspids and the presence of a postmandibular foramen, and from that of *S. vagrans* by the same characters and its larger size.

Distribution

In Canada, Trowbridge shrew is restricted to extreme southwestern British Columbia, north to the Fraser River Delta and Hope. Peripheral localities: *British Columbia:* (**1**) Hope; (**2**) 2nd summit, Skagit River; (**3**) Cultus Lake and Chilliwack River Valley; (**4**) Fraser River Delta.

In the United States, it occurs in western Washington, western Oregon, and northern California.

Systematics

Five subspecies are recognized, but only one *S. t. trowbridgii*, occurs in Canada. *S. trowbridgii* has been included by Findley and others in the subgenus *Sorex* on the basis of the presence of a postmandib-

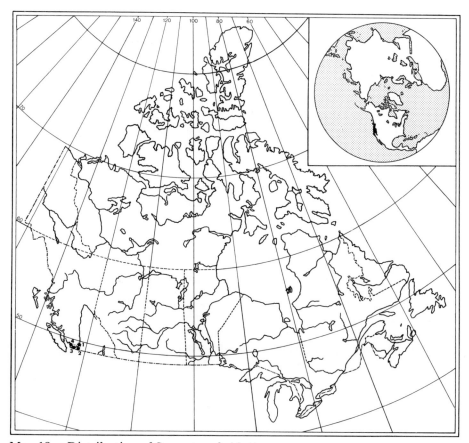

Map 12.   Distribution of *Sorex trowbridgii*

ular foramen. However, this character occurs at lower frequencies also in species of the subgenus *Otisorex*, and can therefore not be used as conclusive evidence by itself for placing *S. trowbridgii* in the subgenus *Sorex*. Other characters, particularly the structure of the unicuspids and the reduced size of the third unicuspids, as well as the presence of 13 pairs of ribs, link it to the subgenus *Otisorex*, in particular to the western species of that group, in which the third unicuspid is smaller than the fourth. *S. trowbridgii* has a diploid number of 34 chromosomes with 2 metacentric, 4 sub-metacentric and 26 acrocentric autosomes (FN = 38) [1].

Biology

S. trowbridgii is a forest-dwelling shrew, preferring the low vegetation and ground litter of well-drained coniferous forests [2, 3, 4]. It
occurs less frequently in brushlands and cut-over areas and it is rare
in wet meadows. This species preys chiefly on small arthropods
(insects, spiders, centipedes) and to a lesser extent on other invertebrates [6, 7, 9]. Conifer seeds (*Pseudotsuga*) are consumed mainly in
winter, when other food, presumably, is less available. In captivity,
this shrew will eat seeds of a variety of plants and some mushrooms.
S. trowbridgii probably competes with *S. vagrans*, and is usually
excluded from moister sites favoured by this species. In its absence, it
will occupy such sites. Interspecific competition does not seem to be
a major factor in the local distribution and abundance of *S. trowbridgii*
and *S. monticolus* who often share the same habitat. *S. trowbridgii*
burrows in the organic surface layer of the soil, while *S. monticolus*
is active in the debris on the forest floor [10].

Habitat

Food

Associated Mammals

This shrew is intermittently active throughout the 24-hour period
in short-term cycles of approximately one hour [8]. Activity takes up
about 39 per cent of the total period. Breeding adults are more than
twice as active as immatures and non-breeding adults.

Behaviour

In this species, as in other *Sorex* species, population turnover is
rapid. The maximum life-span of this shrew is estimated to be
approximately 18 months. Two age classes can be easily recognized;
adults are grey and have worn teeth, whereas young shrews are
brownish and show relatively little wear on their teeth. Adults
disappear rapidly from the population during May, June, and July
of their second year [6].

Population

Nothing is known about the reproductive biology of this species
in Canada. In California, both sexes become sexually mature in
February, judging from the rapid increase in weight and size of the
reproductive organs [6]. The testes increase in size from the non-
breeding condition, when they are 1 to 3 mm long, to a length of 4.7
to 6.0 mm. Females appear to attain reproductive readiness about
two weeks after the males. At this time, the uterine horns are 2 mm
or more in width. Breeding activity wanes in the latter half of May;
most adults taken after that time are in post-breeding condition. The
earliest date on which embryos were observed in California was
25 February. All other pregnant animals were found in April and
May. The breeding season appears to be over in June, when reproductive organs have regressed to non-breeding size. However there is
some evidence of late breeding (8 August). In western Oregon both

Reproduction and Ontogeny

sexes were found to be capable of breeding between February and October, but most breeding occurred early and the majority of females had bred by the end of June [5]. Postpartum pregnancies were found in 12 per cent of fecund females, with the highest percentage being found in the early part of the breeding season. In Washington, a pregnant female and males with enlarged testes were taken in April [4]. It seems probable that breeding in the Canadian part of the range takes place in spring and early summer. A mean number of 5 embryos with a range of 3 to 6 was reported, based on 8 females from California [6]. A larger sample from Oregon gave an average of 3.89 embryos per female [5].

References

[1] Brown, R.J., 1974
[2] Cowan, I. McT., and C.J. Guiguet, 1965
[3] Dalquest, W.W., 1941, [4] 1948
[5] Gashwiler, J.S., 1976
[6] Jameson, E.W., Jr., 1955
[7] Moore, A.W., 1942
[8] Rust, A.K., 1978
[9] Terry, C.J., 1978, [10] 1981

Sorex palustris Richardson
(f. L *palus*, marsh, adj. *paluster* fem., *palustris*
neut., dwelling in marshes)

Water Shrew   **Musaraigne palustre**
(American Water Shrew, Navigator Shrew)

1828 *Sorex palustris* Richardson, Zool. J. 3:517
Type locality: central Canada

External Measurements and Weight

	TL	T	HF	W
N	50	50	50	12
X̄	149.9	71.2	19.5	12.9
SD	8.69	4.55	1.20	2.91
CV	5.80	6.39	6.15	22.56
OR	130–163	61–89	18–24	8.5–17.9

Cranial Measurements

	SL	CB	IOW	MW
N	77	73	78	63
X̄	20.0	9.8	3.8	6.0
SD	0.50	0.34	0.17	0.29
CV	2.50	3.47	4.47	4.83
OR	19.1–21	9–10.6	3.4–4.3	5.4–6.5

Description (Colour Plate III)

A large shrew, dark grey to black above, colour rather variable,
some with a sprinkling of silvery hairs, underparts usually white or
grey, or in some forms brownish, chin generally pale whitish or
grey, lighter than other parts; tail bicolour, dark above, white below,
or concolour. The winter pelage tends to be more contrasting, somewhat darker above and lighter below. Hind feet large, bearing a
fringe of stiff hairs along outer and inner margins of feet and toes,
with a greatest length of approximately 1.25 mm along the outer
margin of the foot. Similar hairs are also present on the front feet.
Moults in spring (May, June) and autumn (mid-August, September).
Skull large, bony bridge over infraorbital canal relatively narrow,
anterior margin of orbit extending anteriorly to the mesostyle of
M2, border of infraorbital foramen anterior to the M1–M2 interface,
approximately at the mesostyle of M1, lacrymal foramen anterior to
the M1–M2 interface. Teeth, unicuspids with lingual ridge to
cingulum, third unicuspid smaller than fourth.

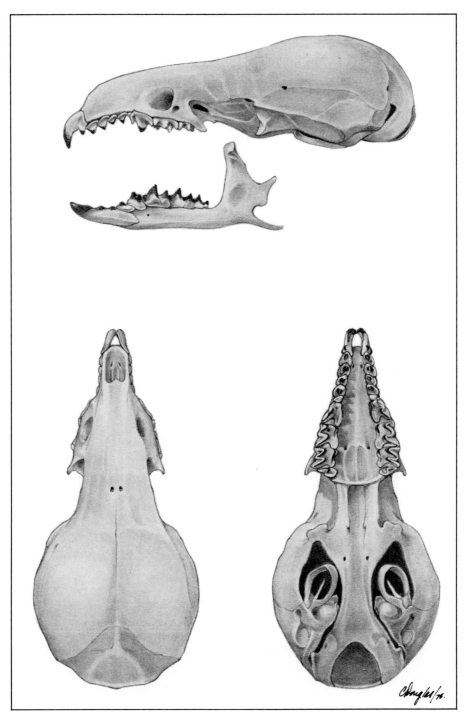

Figure 25.   Skull of *Sorex palustris*

Similar species: *S. bendirii* is dark above and below, with abdomen only slightly paler than back, feet brown, unicuspid row relatively longer (> 70 per cent of premolar–molar length), rostrum curved.

Distribution

The water shrew occurs in most of the forested parts of Canada, where suitable habitat is available, north to the southern Yukon, southwestern Northwest Territories, northern Saskatchewan, Manitoba, Ontario, and Quebec. Along the Labrador coast, it is known as far north as Hamilton Inlet. The species also occurs on Cape Breton Island, Prince Edward Island, and Vancouver Island, but is unknown on Anticosti Island, and the Queen Charlotte archipelago. Peripheral localities: *Alberta:* (**1**) Wainwright; (**2**) Bashaw; (**3**) Banff; (**4**) Bertha Brook. *British Columbia:* (**5**) Hagensborg; (**6**) Quatsino; (**7**) Millstream near Victoria. *Manitoba:* (**8**) Churchill; (**9**) 16 km north, 14.5 km east of Middlebro; (**10**) Winnipeg; (**11**) Aweme. *New Brunswick:* (**12**) 24 km southeast of Bathurst;

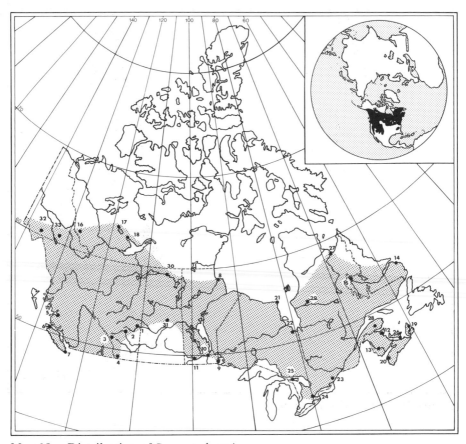

Map 13.   Distribution of *Sorex palustris*

(13) Scotch Lake; *Newfoundland (Labrador):* (14) Cartwright;
(15) Astray Lake. *Northwest Territories:* (16) Glacier Lake;
(17) Grandin River; (18) Old Fort Rae. *Nova Scotia:* (19) Ingonish
Centre; (20) Digby. *Ontario:* (21) Cape Henrietta Maria; (22) Moosonee;
(23) North Kemptville Creek; (24) Freelton; (25) Silver Water. *Prince
Edward Island:* (26) Bridgetown; (26) 1 km west of Sturgeon; *Quebec*
(27) Kuujjuaq (formerly Fort-Chimo); (28) Kelly's Camp, Cascapedia
River; (29) Kanaaupscow. *Saskatchewan:* (30) Stony Rapids;
(31) Prince Albert National Park. *Yukon:* (32) Dezadeash Lake;
(33) Nisutlin River, Canol Road mile 40.

Outside Canada, the species is found in southern Alaska and the
northern United States, extending farther south on the major mountain ranges to California, Arizona and New Mexico in the west and
Tennessee in the east.

Systematics

S. palustris and *S. bendirii* are closely related species. Both are
adapted to a semi-aquatic way of life. Aside from adaptations for
swimming and diving, these species do not differ fundamentally
from other *Sorex* species. In the Old World, the equivalent niche is
occupied by the genus *Neomys*, a more highly specialized soricid of
the tribe Neomyini.

Ten subspecies of *S. palustris* have been described, some on the
basis of one or two specimens, others on the basis of what appear to
be highly variable characters, such as colour. Variation in size is slight
for such a widespread species. The largest and the smallest subspecies
overlap greatly in cranial as well as external measurements. A study
of geographical variation in this species and a revision of the subspecies is needed. The subspecies found in Canada are the following.

S. p. palustris Richardson, 1818, Zool. J. 3:517.
TL 135–160, x̄ 145 (N = 24); T 57–74, x̄ 66 (N = 24); SL, x̄ 20.4,
SD 0.35 (N = 6). Underparts brownish to grey in summer, pale grey
in winter, back blackish grey in summer, somewhat darker in winter,
demarcation between dorsal and ventral colour distinct; tail bicolour.
Distribution: central Mackenzie District, northeastern British
Columbia, east-central Alberta, Saskatchewan, Manitoba, northern
Ontario, and western Quebec.

S. p. albibarbis (Cope), 1862, Proc. Acad. Nat. Sci. Phila., 14:188.
TL 131–157, x̄ 149 (N = 13); T 63–75, x̄ 70 (N = 13); SL x̄ 20, SD 0.47
(N = 10). Underparts scarcely paler than dorsum, dark in summer,
grey or brown, sometimes blackish in winter; back blackish grey in
summer, darker in winter; tail not bicolour or indistinctly bicolour;
demarcation between dorsal and ventral coloration indistinct.
Distribution: eastern and central Ontario, southern Quebec, western
New Brunswick.

S. p. brooksi Anderson, 1934, Can. Field-Nat. 48(8):134.
Type specimen, TL 150, T 70.5; SL 20.3. Underparts grey or brown,
back black, tail whitish below. Distribution: Vancouver Island.

S. p. gloveralleni Jackson, 1926, J. Mamm. 7(2):57.
TL 130–159, x̄ 145 (N = 14); T 61–75, x̄ 70.2 (N = 14); SL x̄ 20,
SD 0.25 (N = 9). Underparts much paler than back, usually pale grey,
back blackish grey or black; tail bicolour. Distribution: Nova Scotia,
including Cape Breton Island.

S. p. hydrobadistes Jackson, 1926, J. Mamm. 7(3):57.
TL 139–163, x̄ 153 (N = 18); T 66–80, x̄ 72 (N = 18); SL x̄ 20.4,
SD 0.39 (N = 19). Underparts dark in summer, pale in winter, back
brownish, or blackish grey in summer, dark blackish-grey in winter,
tail bicolour; demarcation between ventral and dorsal pelage colour
indistinct in summer, more distinct in winter. Distribution: east
shore of Lake Superior.

S. p. navigator (Baird), 1858, Mammals *in* Rep. Expl. Surv. 8(1):11.
TL 134–170, x̄ 154 (N = 82); T 62–89, x̄ 75 (N = 82); SL x̄ 19.6,
SD 0.39 (N = 34). Underparts grey in summer, paler grey in winter,
back grizzled blackish grey, brownish in winter, tail bicolour;
demarcation between ventral and dorsal pelage coloration distinct.
Distribution: southern Yukon, British Columbia, and western
Alberta.

S. p. labradorensis Burt, 1938, Occas. Pap. Mus. Zool. Univ. Mich.
383:1–2.
TL 155, 146; T 75, 71; SL 19.7, 20.4. Underparts grey, back blackish
(winter pelage): tail bicolour. Distribution: described from Red Bay,
Labrador.

S. p. turneri Johnson, 1951, Proc. Biol. Soc. Wash. 64:110.
TL 153, 149; T 73, 69; SL 19.6, 19.1. Underparts grey, back blackish;
tail bicolour. Distribution: northern Quebec, near Kuujjuaq
(formerly Fort-Chimo).

Biology

The water shrew, as its name indicates, occurs near water. Lakes, · Habitat
ponds, swift and sluggish small streams, all provide suitable habitat
if adequate cover is available in the form of overhanging banks,
boulders, tree roots, logs, etc. In the mountains, the species occurs
along cold fast mountain streams. On the other extreme, it is also
found in stagnant water of marshes or bogs, and a few have been
caught in places with very little water. The water shrew appears to
have some flexibility in adapting to habitats with little water or even
to habitats where water is present only seasonally. However, the
species appears to be most abundant along small cold streams with
abundant cover.

Food taken by this shrew is composed largely of insects, particularly · Food
the larvae and nymphs of aquatic insects, such as mayfly, caddisfly,
and stonefly [2]. Other invertebrates (e.g. planaria) are also caught.
Small fish (*Notropis, Cottus*) and larval amphibians are taken [1, 6, 7],
but constitute an insignificant portion of the overall diet. One
10 g specimen ate an average of 10.3 g in a day [3]. Based on

O_2 consumption ($\bar{x}$ 7.8 cc/g/hr compared to 15.8 and 5.3 cc/g/hr in *S. cinereus* and *Blarina* respectively) and food utilization, the food requirement has been estimated at 0.95 g/g/day [8].

Food is grasped with the teeth and pieces severed by vigorous upward jerks of the head, while the forefeet are used to hold down the prey. Smaller prey may be lifted up while being eaten. When more food is available than can be consumed, it is hoarded. The water shrew drinks, usually after eating and sleeping, with a scooping motion, after which the muzzle is raised [8].

A number of parasites have been reported for this species. Ecto-parasites include fleas (*Nearctopsylla hyrtaci*, *Corrodopsylla curvata*) and mites (*Hirstionyssus* spp., *Euphaemogamasus liponyssoides*, *E. nidi*). Endoparasites found include nematodes (larval *Porrocaecum* spp. under the skin, *Capillaria rauschi* in the stomach, and an undescribed *Capillaria* from the bladder) and cestodes (*Hymenolepis* in the duodenum and plerocerci of *Tetrathyridium* in the coelomic cavity) [3].

Parasites

Like other species of *Sorex*, *S. palustris* is short-lived with a maximum age not exceeding 18 months. Nothing is known about the size of the home range or population densities in different habitats.

Population

The water shrew is active day and night [8]. An average of 30 minutes of activity are followed by 60 minutes of inactivity. There are two major activity peaks. One occurs from sunset to about four hours after sunset, and the other occurs one hour before sunrise. In winter this species remains active and swims under the ice.

Behaviour

Water shrews are adept swimmers and divers. They are very buoyant in the water, floating on top of the water rather than in it. They move rapidly with jerky motions, and have been observed actually running on the surface of the water [5]. Below the surface, they swim rapidly and skillfully using all four legs as in running [9]. The main thrust is provided by the large hind feet with their fringe of stiff hairs. When the animals hunt under water the fur is at first surrounded by a layer of air, giving it a silvery appearance and reducing heat loss to one-half of what it would be if the animal were wet. In water of 10–12°C, the rectal temperature drops 1.03°C in 30 seconds [1]. The fur begins to get wet after approximately a minute in the water and this would result in a serious increase of heat loss. Dives are, therefore, of short duration. Surfacing after a dive, the shrew pops up like a cork and appears dry. The shrew leaves the water shortly after and begins to groom itself with its hind feet. It dries rapidly and rewarms itself at a rate of approximately 1°C/min. During grooming and drying the shrew will eat the prey it captured. Running shrews utter high-pitched squeaks continuously [8].

Acuteness of the different senses needs further investigation [8]. Vision and smell seem to be used over short distances [9]. Detection of submerged minnows by water shrews, presumably by vision from above the surface at distances of approximately 12 and 15 cm, has been reported [1]. Hearing may be the most acute sense, but it is probably of little use underwater. The possibility of echolocation has been suggested for this species, but it has not yet been demonstrated [8]. In all probability the animal depends on several of its senses in getting around and in capturing prey.

Water shrews build nests by quickly turning around in gathered nesting material until they form a small depression [8]. Then, using their muzzles with a stitching motion, they form the walls of the nest. The nest is entered and left by burrowing through its wall. Damaged nests are repaired or reconstructed by the shrew using its muzzle. New nests are constantly built. Water shrews will burrow short tunnels, 10 to 12 cm long, by digging with their forefeet, while the hind feet kick the loosened soil back out of the tunnel [8]. They are solitary animals and intraspecific behavior is predominantly agonistic [8]. Fighting behavior is more or less stereotyped. A fight is generally preceded by squeaking. If no retreat occurs, one of the shrews will rise on its hind legs, exposing the usually light-coloured ventral side, and squeak. The other shrew remaining on all fours will generally flee at this point. If both animals rise and squeak they will move their heads to one side with their mouths wide open and make rapid slashing movements at each other's head. If contact occurs, both animals will fall to the ground fighting, tightly curled into a ball. The fight ends when one of the shrews breaks away and flees. There is no evidence of territoriality.

Spermatogenesis begins in the winter following birth (December and January in Montana) [3]. During this time there is an increase in body weight. Sexually active males weigh approximately 15 g (13–18 g) and are significantly heavier than the females, which average 10 g (8–12 g). The testes of sexually mature water shrews weigh 100–200 mg. Between January and August all males born in the previous year show active spermatogenesis. Mature sperm begins to appear in February. Ovaries and uterus also develop in January, and pregnant or lactating females are present between February and August. Ovulation is possibly induced by copulation. A postpartum heat occurs, which is followed by pregnancy in at least some lactating females. The majority of breeding females are adult animals, born during the preceding year, but there is evidence that some females may breed during their first summer. Embryo counts range from 5 to 7 with a mean of 5.8 and a mode of 6. Numbers of young in litters reported in the literature vary from 4 to 7. Gestation and duration of lactation are unknown. In all probability two or three litters are produced.

Reproduction and Ontogeny

References

[1] Buckner, C.H., 1970
[2] Calder, W.A., 1969
[3] Conaway, C.H., 1952, [4] 1960
[5] Jackson, H.H.T., 1961
[6] Lampman, B.H., 1947
[7] Nussbaum, R.A., and C. Maser, 1969
[8] Sorensen, M.W., 1962
[9] Svihla, A., 1934

Sorex bendirii (Merriam)
(Named after C.E. Bendire)

Pacific Water Shrew   **Musaraigne de Bendire**
(Marsh Shrew, Bendire Shrew)

1884 *Atophyrax bendirii* Merriam, Trans. Linn. Soc. N.Y. 2:217
1912 *Neosorex bendirii bendirii* Miller, N. Am. Land Mamm., p. 12
1926 *Sorex bendirii* Jackson, J. Mamm. 7(1):57–58
Type locality: Near Williamson River, 29 km southeast of Fort
Klamath, Klamath County, Oregon

External Measurements and Weight

	TL	T	HF	W
N	20	19	18	16
X̄	150.8	67.1	18.9	13.3
SD	8.28	7.52	1.27	3.07
CV	5.49	11.22	6.71	23.07
OR	137–167	62–81	17–21	7.5–18

Cranial Measurements

	SL	CB	IOW	MW
N	8	9	9	9
X̄	20.8	10.1	4.2	6.2
SD	0.49	0.33	0.08	0.18
CV	2.36	3.27	1.90	2.90
OR	19.7–21.1	9.5–10.4	4–4.3	5.8–6.3

Description (Colour Plate III)

The largest of our long-tailed shrews, pelage velvet-like blackish
brown to black in colour, underparts dark, only slightly paler than
back, summer pelage more brownish than winter pelage, tail dark
above and below, feet brownish and fringed with stiff hairs, their
greatest length approximately 1 mm.

Skull large, rostrum long and curved ventrally, position of orbit,
lacrymal foramen, and infraorbital foramen similar to that in
S. palustris, upper unicuspid series relatively longer than that of
S. palustris, the third unicuspid usually smaller than the fourth or
subequal. Similar species: *Sorex palustris:* hair fringe on hind feet
longer (approx. 1.25 mm), underparts lighter, tail usually bicolour,
feet lighter (only *S. b. albiventer* from the Olympic Peninsula in
Washington has light underparts in winter), skull with shorter
straight rostrum, length of the upper unicuspid row is less than
70 per cent of the upper premolar–molar length.

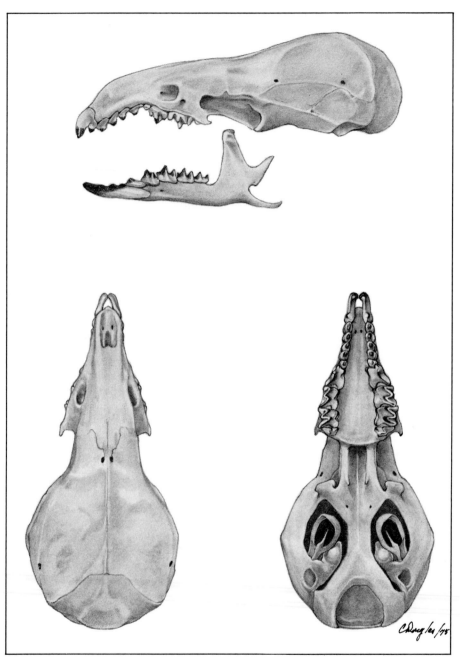

Figure 26.   Skull of *Sorex bendirii*

Distribution

The Pacific water shrew is restricted to a relatively narrow humid
zone along the Pacific coast from California to southern British
Columbia. In Canada, it is only found in the Fraser River delta area.
Peripheral localities: *British Columbia:* (**1**) Point Grey; (**2**) Hunting-
don; (**3**) Cultus Lake and Chilliwack River Valley, 29 km east of
Vedder Crossing.

Systematics

S. bendirii and *S. palustris* have similar adaptations and are probably
derived from a common ancestral population. Three subspecies are
recognized, of which only *S. b. bendirii*, the smallest form, occurs in
Canada. The largest of the subspecies, *S. b. palmeri*, is found in
Oregon. The third, *S. b. albiventer*, is intermediate in size and is
restricted to the Olympic Peninsula. The karyotype of one female of
S. b. bendirii has been reported. It contained a diploid number of

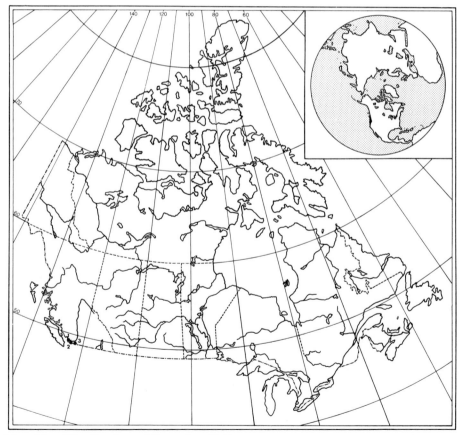

Map 14.   Distribution of *Sorex bendirii*

54 chromosomes with 6 metacentrics, 12 submetacentrics, and 38 acrocentrics [1].

Biology

Little is known about this species. It is found in marshy areas, along sluggish streams, in beach debris, and in wet lands in heavily wooded areas [2, 5]. In winter, during rain, it may be found well away from water, sometimes up to 1 km distant. Its food includes soft-bodied arthropods (sow bugs, spiders, centipedes) and other invertebrates, terrestrial as well as aquatic.

Habitat

Food

The Pacific water shrew enters water readily and swims and dives well [4]. It runs on top of the surface with its belly above or barely touching the water. In the water, it is constantly in motion. Usually it swims hither and thither using all four legs, and then it suddenly dives to explore the bottom, using its snout and vibrissae. Underwater, the hind limbs, kicked alternately, provide the main propulsion. Front feet are used occasionally but less than on the surface of the water. This species generally swims for short periods of less than 2 minutes. The longest swimming-time record was 3.5 minutes. After a shrew emerges, it will groom itself with hind feet and mouth. It drinks after feeding, in a manner quite different from that reported for *S. palustris*, with the lower jaw submerged and by lapping up the water. When alarmed, this shrew has been heard to produce a shrill twittering call frequently. It also twitters in agonistic encounters over food. There is little information on the relative acuity of the senses. Eyesight appeared to be poor to one observer [4].

Behaviour

Virtually nothing is known of the reproductive biology of this species. The breeding season begins early in the year (January or February) [4].

Reproduction and Ontogeny

References

[1] Brown, R.J., 1974
[2] Cowan, I. McT., and C.J. Guiguet, 1965
[3] Jackson, H.H.T., 1928
[4] Pattie, D.L., 1969, [5] 1973

Sorex hoyi (Baird)
(Named after P.R. Hoy)

Pygmy Shrew   **Musaraigne pygmée**

1858 *Sorex hoyi* Baird, Mammals, *in* Rep. Expl. Surv. 8(1):32
1895 *Sorex (Microsorex) hoyi* Merriam, N. Am. Fauna 10:89
1901 *Microsorex hoyi* Elliot, Field Columb. Mus. Publ. 45 (Zool.
       series 2), p. 377
1980 *Sorex hoyi* Diersing, J. Mamm. 61(1):83
Type locality: Racine, Racine County, Wisconsin

External Measurements and Weight

	TL	T	HF	W
N	53	53	55	9
X̄	85.5	30.5	10.0	3.6
SD	7.23	2.68	0.82	0.90
CV	8.46	8.78	8.29	25.36
OR	71–104	24–35	8–11.5	2.4–5.35

Cranial Measurements

	SL	CB	IOW	MW
N	33	31	32	29
X̄	14.5	6.8	2.9	4.1
SD	0.44	0.31	0.13	0.20
CV	2.99	4.60	4.49	4.76
OR	13.6–15.2	6.3–7.4	2.7–3.1	3.8–4.5

Description (Colour Plate II)

A small reddish to greyish-brown shrew with lighter, greyish or
brownish underparts and a relatively short indistinctly bicolour tail.
Winter pelage greyer and longer than summer pelage with belly
sometimes whitish. Moulting specimens have been reported from
late April and July and early October. Mature males show lateral
glands from April to September. This species differs from other
Sorex in the extreme reduction of the third and fifth unicuspids; the
third unicuspid is anteroposteriorly flattened, the fifth unicuspid is
a minute peg-like structure. Only three unicuspids are usually visible
in side view; first and second unicuspid with pigmented lingual
ridge ending in well-developed pigmented secondary cusp near
cingulum, fourth more peg-like with pigmented ridge. Skull
flattened and narrow with short rostrum; anterior border of orbit
at or just anterior to the metastyle of M2, lacrymal foramen anterior
to M1–M2 interface, between metastyle and mesostyle of M1, border

of infraorbital foramen approximately at the mesostyle of M1. Mandible short and heavy, cingulum of i1 and mental foramen placed well back, beneath or behind the paraconid of p4 and beneath or behind the hypoconid of m1 respectively.

Similar species: *S. cinereus*, externally similar, but can be distinguished by its longer tail, which is > 50% head-body length. The snout of *S. cinereus* is longer (3 × width of rhinarium), and four unicuspids are easily visible in lateral view. *S. ugyunak* can be distinguished by its colour pattern, and *S. haydeni* has four unicuspids easily visible.

Distribution

The pygmy shrew is found across Canada, except on the tundra, the prairies and along the west coast. It is known also from Prince Edward Island and Cape Breton Island, but has not been reported from the other large islands off the coast. Peripheral localities: *Alberta:* (1) Lindbrook; (2) Blindman River at Red Deer River;

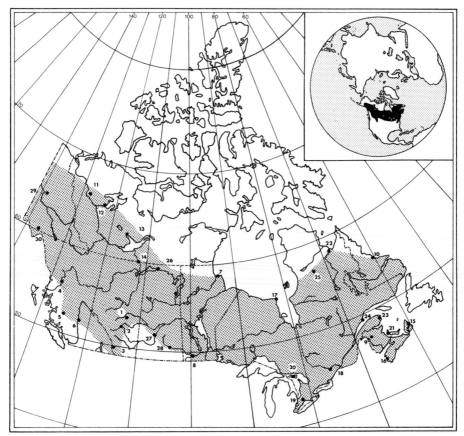

Map 15.   Distribution of *Sorex hoyi*

(3) Racehorse Creek at Oldman River. *British Columbia:* (4) Hazelton; (5) Anahim Lake; (6) Williams Lake. *Manitoba:* (7) Churchill; (8) Aweme. *New Brunswick:* (9) Trousers Lake. *Newfoundland (Labrador):* (10) Hopedale. *Northwest Territories:* (11) Chick Lake; (12) Fort Franklin; (13) Old Fort Rae; (14) Fort Smith. *Nova Scotia:* (15) Ingonish Centre; (16) Maxwellton. *Ontario:* (17) Cape Henrietta Maria; (18) Leitrim; (19) Coldstream; (20) Gore Bay; *Prince Edward Island:* (21) Alberton. *Quebec:* (22) Kuujjuaq (formerly Fort-Chimo); (23) Gaspé; (24) Godbout; (25) Petit lac des Loups Marins (formerly Upper Seal Lake). *Saskatchewan:* (26) Fond-du-Lac; (27) Swanson; (28) Indian Head. *Yukon:* (29) 22 km east of Dawson City; (30) Haines Road.

Outside Canada the species is found in Alaska, the northeast corner of Washington, northern Idaho, extreme northeastern Montana from the Dakotas east to the New England states and in the Appalachians south to North Carolina. A relict population, *S. h. montanus*, is found in the mountains of Wyoming and Colorado.

Systematics

Long [6] concluded, on the basis of cranial differences and slight colour differences, that *Microsorex* contained two species, *hoyi* and *thompsoni*. The latter is said to differ in having a smaller, flatter skull, a ratio of cranial breadth to depth of about 1.7 in old adults, and small teeth. A subsequent analysis of these differences indicated that they can be explained as a consequence of the difference in overall size [11]. A recent revision by Diersing [4] also concluded that there is only one species in the subgenus. Geographic variation in this widely distributed species is mainly that of size and, to a lesser extent, colour. Available data suggest that size displays clinal variation from south (small forms) to north (large forms) with several zones of rapid change. Five subspecies are recognized, of which two are found in Canada [4].

S. h. hoyi Baird, 1858, Rep. Pacific RR Surv. 8, part 1, p. 32. A large subspecies; TL 77–104, T 24–35, mean M2M2 breadth 3.9–4.2. Distribution: Across Canada from the Atlantic coast and the St. Lawrence west to the Rocky Mountains and British Columbia north to the Yukon and the District of Mackenzie.

S. h. thompsoni Baird 1858, Mammals, *in* Rep. Expl. Surv. 8(1):34. A smaller subspecies with relatively long tail; TL 71–91, T 29–33, mean M2M2 breadth 3.6–3.9. Distribution: Maritime Provinces including Prince Edward Island and Cape Breton Island; extreme southern Quebec and counties east of the St. Lawrence River, southern Ontario. *S. (Microsorex)* has been reported from Middle and Late Pleistocene deposits [8].

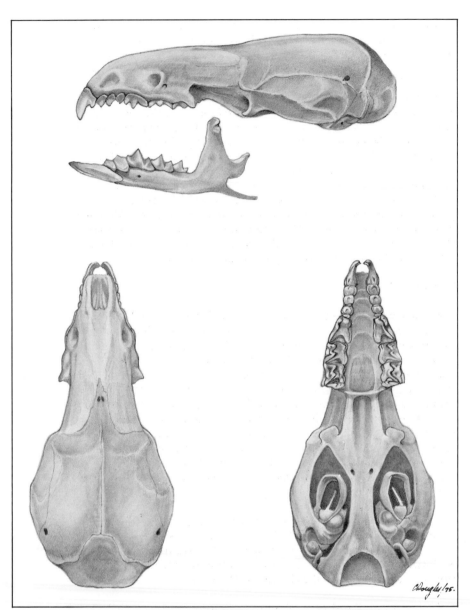

Figure 27.   Skull of *Sorex hoyi*

Biology

The pygmy shrew is found in a wide variety of habitats, in deciduous and coniferous forests, bogs, swamps, marshes, and occasionally in meadows, dry clearings, sand dunes, and savanna parkland [7, 12]. Though tolerant of many widely varying conditions, the species displays a preference for mesic forest habitats. There is very little information on the pygmy shrew's food habits. Adults and larvae of Lepidoptera, Coleoptera, and Diptera have been reported [8], as well as unidentified insects and jack pine seeds in winter [3]. The minimum number of larch sawfly eonymphs needed to meet the daily metabolic requirements of a single individual was found to be 98 by one investigator [1]. The actual number of eonymphs that would be destroyed because of wasteful feeding and digestive inefficiency is probably much higher, and was estimated at approximately 711 a day. Food preferences of captive *S. hoyi* were similar to those of *S. cinereus* and *S. arcticus*. The pygmy shrew preferred hepialid larvae (*Sthenopsis argentiomaculatus*), grasshoppers, larch sawfly eonymphs, elaterid larvae and adults, large lepidopterous larvae, larch sawfly adults, and dipterous larvae. Ants were avoided [1].

The pygmy shrew itself is probably preyed upon by a number of predators, although there are only two reported observations—one involved predation by a garter snake, the other by a hawk (*Buteo platypterus*) [8].

The pygmy shrew is apparently a relatively rare species. Two estimates of population density reported for this species are 0.52 per hectare [8] and 0.7 to 1.2 per hectare [1], which indicates that the pygmy shrew is considerably less abundant ($< 1/10 \times$) than the common shrew in most habitats. The underlying causes of the relative rarity of this species are not understood.

The activity pattern of the pygmy shrew resembles that of *S. cinereus* [1]. Total daily activity of one animal was 239 minutes, occurring in short periods throughout the 24-hour period, lasting on the average 2.9 minutes. Peak activity occurred at nights. What little is known of the pygmy shrew's behaviour is based on the observation of a captive individual and indicates that their behaviour is similar to that of other *Sorex* species [9].

Information on reproduction is meagre [7, 8, 10]. Litter size is unknown. Reported embryo counts from different, mainly southern, parts of the range vary from 3 to 8 embryos with an average of 5.75 embryos. There is some indication that the embryo counts in northern populations may be higher than in the south. Pregnant individuals are known from July and the first half of August; lactating females from the end of July to the end of August. The number of litters produced is unknown. The lateral glands in the males are visible from April through August. Since these glands are believed to be related to sexual activity in the male, this may provide a clue to the onset and duration of reproductive activity in the male.

Habitat

Food

Predators

Population

Behaviour

Reproduction and Ontogeny

References

[1] Buckner, C.H., 1964, [2] 1966
[3] Criddle, S., 1973
[4] Diersing, V.E., 1980
[5] Jackson, H.H.T., 1928
[6] Long, C.A., 1972*a*, [7] 1972*b*, [8] 1974
[9] Prince, L.A., 1940
[10] Scott, T.G., 1939
[11] van Zyll de Jong, C.G., 1976*b*
[12] Wrigley, R.E., J.E. Dubois, and H.W.R. Copland, 1979

Genus *Blarina* Gray, 1838
(Name invented by Gray)

This genus is characterized externally by dark-grey colour, large size, short tail ($<$ ¼ TL), thick fleshy feet and a conical head with no apparent external ears, and minute eyes. Mammae 6, side glands and also pectoral scent gland present. Penis sigmoid with slender tapering glans.

Skull massive for a shrew, with prominent mastoid processes. Number of teeth as in *Sorex*, first and second unicuspids are large, third and fourth much smaller, and fifth minute; tips of teeth darkly pigmented. Mandible stout, cingulum of i1 placed far back, approximately below protoconid of m1, mental foramen posterior to protoconid of m1; coronoid process has conspicuous spicule and external temporal fossa.

Blarina is a Nearctic genus with four Recent species. Fossil evidence of the genus goes back to the late Pliocene.

Blarina brevicauda (Say)
(f. L *brevis* short; *cauda* tail)

Short-tailed Shrew   **Musaraigne à queue courte**
(Mole Shrew, Big short-tailed Shrew)

1823 *Sorex brevicaudus* Say *in* Long, Account of an exped. . . .to the
      Rocky Mts. 1:164.
1858 *Blarina brevicauda* Baird, Mammals, *in* Rep. Expl. Surv.
      8(1):42
Type locality: West bank of Missouri River, near Blair, Washington
County, Nebraska

External Measurements and Weight

	TL	T	HF	W
N	75	75	75	50
X̄	122.4	26.6	15.6	19.8
SD	8.96	3.61	1.02	3.12
CV	7.31	13.55	6.53	15.74
OR	90–145	17–35	13.5–18	16–28.6

Cranial Measurements

	SL	CB*	IOW	MW
N	119	113	120	111
X̄	22.8	12.3	5.8	7.8
SD	0.71	0.47	0.21	0.29
CV	3.11	3.79	3.64	3.67
OR	20.2–24.6	10.2–13.5	5.1–6.3	6.7–8.5

*CB in this species is mastoid width

Description (Colour Plate III)

This large, short-tailed shrew with its greyish-black fur is not easily
confused with any other Canadian shrew (for details see description
under the genus). Spring moult, beginning in February, starts on
the nose and progresses posteriorly except in second-year males,
which have a completely irregular moulting pattern. Autumn moult
(October, November) starts on the rump and progresses anteriorly.
The moult from juvenile to adult pelage begins in the head region
and proceeds caudad on dorsal and ventral surfaces [14, 21].

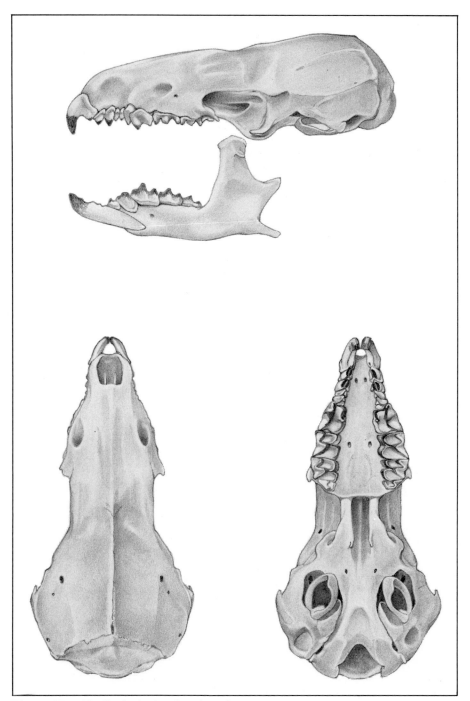

Figure 28.　Skull of *Blarina brevicauda*

Distribution

This species is found from the Maritimes across the southern part of
Quebec, Ontario, and Manitoba to eastern Saskatchewan. Peripheral
localities: *Manitoba* (**1**) The Pas; (**2**) Island Lake. *New Brunswick:*
(**3**) Buctouche; (**4**) Nackawic. *Nova Scotia:* (**5**) Cape North; (**6**) St.
Peters; (**7**) Barrington Passage. *Ontario:* (**8**) Moosonee; (**9**) Gore
Bay; (**10**) Wabinosh Bay. *Prince Edward Island:* (**11**) Mount Herbert.
Quebec: (**12**) Saint-Hélier; (**13**) Saint-Omer; (**14**) Godbout; (**15**) Saint-
Méthode, (**16**) 1 km west of Matagami airport. *Saskatchewan:*
(**17**) Keatley; (**18**) 5 km west of Bittern Lake; (**19**) Regina.

South of the border it is distributed in the northern half of the
central and eastern United States.

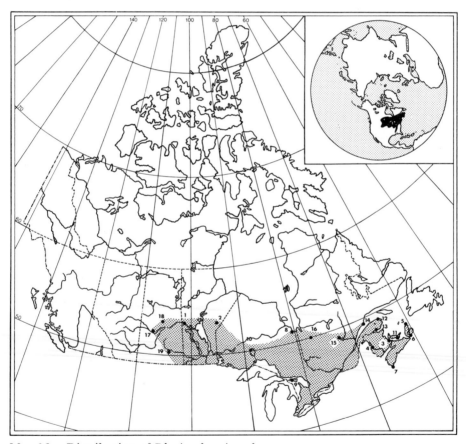

Map 16.   Distribution of *Blarina brevicauda*

Systematics

The geographic variation of *B. brevicauda* throughout its range is in need of study. Variation in colour and size appears to be slight. None of the six subspecies listed as occurring in Canada can be regarded as distinct and their taxonomic status is in need of re-evaluation. The subspecies reported from Canada are the following:

B. b. angusta Anderson, 1942, Annu. Rep. Provancher Soc. Nat. Hist. Que., p. 52.
TL 108–140, x̄ 121.9 (N = 19); T 21–28, x̄ 24.0 (N = 20); SL x̄ 22.8, SD 0.64 (N = 29); CB x̄ 12.4, SD 0.35 (N = 26). Said to be darker than *pallida* and to have a long, narrow skull. Distribution: Gaspé, northern New Brunswick.

B. b. brevicauda (Say), 1823, *in* Long, Account of an exped. . . .to the Rocky Mts. 1:64.
TL 118–126, x̄122.0 (N = 4); T 24– 29, x̄ 26.0 (N = 4); SL x̄ 23.0, SD 0.38 (N = 4); CB x̄ 12.6, SD 0.08 (N = 3). Distribution: western Ontario.

B. b. hooperi Bole and Moulthrop, 1942, Sci. Publ. Cleveland Mus. Nat. Hist. 5(6):110–112.
TL 107–128, x̄ 118.8 (N = 12); T 25–34, x̄ 27.7 (N = 13); SL x̄ 22.4, SD 0.39 (N = 10); CB x̄ 12.2; SD 0.27 (N = 10). Said to be characterized by large head and feet and long tail. Distribution: Eastern Townships, Quebec, near Vermont border.

B. b. manitobensis Anderson, 1946, Catalogue of Canadian Recent Mammals. Nat. Mus. Can. Bull. 102.
TL 109–128, x̄ 117.3 (N = 11); T 17–29, x̄ 24 (N = 11); SL x̄ 23.7, SD 0.58 (N = 9); CB x̄ 13.0, SD 0.36 (N = 8). Said to be larger than *B. b. brevicauda*. Distribution: Manitoba and Saskatchewan.

B. b. pallida Smith, 1940, Am. Midl. Nat. 24(1):223–24.
TL 115–144, x̄ 127.4 (N = 20); T 23–33.5, x̄ 29.83 (N = 20); SL x̄ 22.8, SD 0.59 (N = 12); CB x̄ 12.3, SD 0.44 (N = 12). Said to be larger than *B. b. talpoides* and paler. Distribution: New Brunswick, Nova Scotia, Prince Edward Island.

B. b. talpoides (Gapper), 1830, Zool. J. 5:202.
TL 90–135, x̄ 120.8 (N = 20); T 23–32, x̄ 27.6 (N = 20); SL x̄ 23, SD 0.71 (N = 37); CB x̄ 12.3, SD 0.40 (N = 35). Distribution: Ontario, Quebec.

B. brevicauda has a diploid number of 50 chromosomes (FN = 52) consisting of 48 acrocentric autosomes and 2 metacentric sex chromosomes, a large X and a very small Y [30]. A few animals have one large submetacentric autosome, formed by the centric fusion of 2 acrocentrics (2N = 49).

Three forms occurring in the southern United States, and until recently regarded as subspecies of *brevicauda*, have been unmasked as independent species. They differ from *B. brevicauda* in their smaller size, coloration and karyotype [16*b*, 26].

Biology

The short-tailed shrew is found in a wide variety of habitats including deciduous and coniferous forests, seral woodlands, bogs and grass-lands resulting from cultivation [39, 45]. The species is, however, most abundant in hardwoods with deep leaf-litter and humus in eastern North America. It is less common in coniferous and seral woodlands and occurs at much lower densities in bogs and grassland. In Manitoba it is reported to be most common in grass-sedge marsh, willow-alder shrubs and deciduous beach ridge forest. This shrew is active on the surface and below it to a depth of around 50 cm under leaf litter and in tunnel systems in the humus and soil layers. The short-tailed shrew is more fossorial than other native shrews, although it is not highly specialized in this direction. It uses already existing tunnels of other small mammals and also digs its own in the rela-tively loose humus layer. The ridges sometimes pushed up by this species in soft woodland soil resemble those of moles, but are much smaller. The protective woodland canopy promotes the stability of soil temperature and moisture that are important to the survival of this shrew in summer. Snow cover, insulating the soil underneath, is equally important in limiting the penetration of frost and tempera-ture extremes in the soil during the winter.

Habitat

Nests are constructed from locally available plant material, such as dry leaves, grass, sedges, and sometimes hair, which is worked into a hollow sphere [11, 19]. Nests are usually located in protected places under logs or stumps. Breeding nests are bulkier than resting nests.

The short-tailed shrew preys on a large number of invertebrates and also on small vertebrates [5, 20, 22]. A certain amount of vegetable matter is also consumed. Of the invertebrates, insects (particularly the larvae of Lepidoptera, Diptera and Coleoptera), annelids, molluscs (snails and slugs) and sow bugs are important foods. Centipedes, millipedes, and spiders are eaten less frequently. Vertebrates are less important than invertebrates, but during the winter when inverte-brates are less available small mammals (*Microtus, Sorex*) may be important as a source of food [12, 13]. Evidence of food hoarding has been found [22]. A few reports indicate that this shrew occasionally attacks animals much larger than itself (e.g. a young snowshoe hare, a garter snake and a ribbon snake) [10, 32, 41]. The average daily consumption in terms of larch sawfly eonymphs is about 10 g, which corresponds to a metabolic requirement of 9.7 cal./animal/ day [4].

Food

Blarina is unique among Canadian mammals in having a poisonous bite [25, 33, 37]. The poison is produced by coarsely granular cells in the secretory tubules of the submaxillary salivary gland. The toxin, highly toxic and water soluble, is present in the saliva. It is transferred to the victim through a groove between the long lower incisors when the shrew bites. Only 5.7 mg of fresh sub-maxillary tissue, injected into a mouse weighing 20 g, killed the animal in a few minutes. The extract from 10 mg of the gland killed a rabbit weighing 1.36 kg in less than five minutes. The effects of the poison are similar to those of the neurotoxic, elapine type, snake venom, and consist of a local reaction, a lowering of the blood pressure, a slowing of the heartbeat and inhibition of respiration. The poison is believed to enable this shrew to kill prey larger than itself [25, 43]. Another probably more frequent function of the venom is to immobilize prey animals such as snails, earthworms, and beetles, which have been found alive but paralyzed in this shrew's storage chambers [28].

The main predators of the short-tailed shrew are probably raptorial birds. Adult shrews appear to be unpalatable to mammalian predators because of their lateral gland odour.

Predators

During summer and autumn, two distinct age classes can be distinguished on the basis of tooth wear [9]. These represent adults born during the previous breeding season and young of the current breeding seasons. The sex ratio is about even, although slightly more males than females are caught in traps [3, 19, 34]. This is probably related to the fact that males have, on the average, larger home ranges and are therefore more prone to get caught. The turnover of the population is rapid, as in other shrews. Young enter the population in spring and summer. Adults disappear from the population at a steady rate until, by late October and early November, animals born during the preceding breeding season have virtually been eliminated [5, 9]. Only a few animals appear to survive two winters. One study estimated that only 6 per cent of the population was over a year old at the start of winter. Extreme ages reported for captive short-tailed shrews are 30 months for a female and 33 months for a male [35]. Always one of the common shrews in its range, the short-tailed shrew may be exceedingly abundant some years. In one such year the species constituted 65 per cent of all small mammals trapped in an area of Algonquin Provincial Park [15]. One estimate of over 200 short-tailed shrews per hectare has been reported, but average densities lie well below that figure. Population density in the preferred habitat (deciduous wood) was estimated at approximately 20 shrews per hectare. In less favoured habitats (swamps, bogs, grassland) densities vary from approximately 2 to 10 shrews per hectare. Estimates of individual home ranges vary from approximately 40 m² to 9000 m² [3, 5], those of males averaging somewhat larger than those of females. Individual home ranges usually overlap with one or more neighboring home ranges of conspecifics of either sex.

Population

The short-tailed shrew is active for short periods throughout a 24-hour period, with the greatest activity occurring during the hours of darkness. Captive shrews are, on the average, active from 6 to 16 per cent of the time [27, 29]. The majority of time is, therefore, spent at low resting metabolism, nearly 15 hours a day in a state of sleep. This way of conserving energy is probably an important factor in this species' survival in cold temperate climates [40]. In nature, where the search for food is undoubtedly more time-consuming, the amount of activity may be considerably greater.

Behaviour

Blarina is semi-cursorial, with greater fossorial tendencies than any of the long-tailed shrews. Socially more tolerant than most other native shrews, they can be kept together more easily. As many as five captive short-tailed shrews have been reported to have lived amicably in the same cage and even slept together [42]. Most of the behaviour patterns described are, however, agonistic [31]. Four of these are action patterns termed approach, retreat, attack, and combat; five consist of threat postures. In male–female encounters during the breeding season, the male appears to play a rather passive role initially. He tolerates her bites, while giving off odour, rubbing his glandular secretions on the substrate, and uttering a continuous series of clicking noises. Females in heat, or those who are pregnant or lactating, have glands that are completely inactive, which apparently serves to subdue the normal aggressiveness of the male. The female's receptivity gradually increases and copulation follows. The male mounts the female from behind, holding her with his mouth by the fur of the neck or shoulders and clasping her between his front legs [35]. The pelvic region then vibrates rapidly when the male seeks to penetrate the female. This is followed by a deep thrust once the male has introduced his penis. The male dismounts immediately afterwards, but remains locked to the female because of a lock-and-key mechanism produced by the S-shaped flexure of the erect penis and the matching shape of the vagina. Pointed epidermal structures on the glans may help to prevent withdrawal of the penis. The male is dragged about by the female while the pair is coupled. They may remain coupled for as long as 25 minutes, although the average duration is much shorter, between 4 and 5 minutes. After separation the male returns the penis to its sheath with his mouth. Retraction apparently cannot be achieved unaided. Mating may be repeated twenty or more times in a day.

The clicking sounds referred to above are also produced by young short-tailed shrews when they are displaced from the nest, and by adults during solitary exploration of strange situations [17]. The use of a click in mother–infant relations, and in courtship, indicates that clicks function as contact calls. The short-tailed shrew has a number of other vocalizations. They can be divided into low–intensity sounds, which are difficult to detect by ear, and medium- and high-intensity sounds. The first category includes "put", "twitter", and "clicks". Both sexes produce the "put" sound, under similar circumstances as the click, when exploring strange situations. The sound has a frequency of 300–1000 cps, a duration of 0.16–0.9 seconds and is repeated at the rate of 10–14 "puts" per second. During encounters, the "put" appears to result from a more intense smelling. The "twitter" is produced in a similar context as the "put", but is associated with forward or upward body extensions. The "put" and the "twitter" probably function in spacing the animals, the latter working at greater distances than the former.

The medium–intensity sounds include receptive calls of females and ultrasonic sounds. The former consist of single and repetitive clicks and serve to signal the female's receptivity to the male. The ultrasonic sounds are emitted during intensive investigations and function in echolocation. Echolocation is probably used for exploring tunnels, finding cover on the surface and avoiding obstacles when the animal is moving fast in unfamiliar surroundings [18].

The high–intensity sounds comprise the "chirp" and the "buzz". The "chirp" is produced when the animal is picked up or suddenly frightened, and during aggressive encounters in the upright position. It seems likely that this sound functions to repel conspecifics or predators. The "buzz" is emitted under similar circumstances, primarily during close contact. Both "chirp" or "buzz" are also emitted when the animal threatens with its mouth open, the end of its snout turned up, and stamping its feet. Vision does not appear to play a discernable role in the behaviour of this species.

Short-tailed shrew males become sexually active in February but mating probably does not take place until March. Young are born from mid-April into September. Heat in the female lasts two to four days, but may last up to a month in the absence of mating. Ovulation is induced by copulation. Gestation is from 17 and 22 days, after which 3 to 7 (average 4.5) young are born. Embryo counts average somewhat higher (5.2–5.7), with the greatest reported number being 10 embryos. The female will not come into heat again until after her young are weaned, but if the young die she can become receptive shortly after parturition. A female may have three or more litters in a season [7, 9, 19, 34].

Reproduction and Ontogeny

The newborn young are naked and blind, and have closed external ears. At 13 days of age they are well-furred and the external ears are open. By 22 days the teeth are well developed but the eyes are still closed. The young are probably weaned shortly after this time. Both males and females may breed in their first year. Mating in captive males first occurred at 83 days. Females may mate between one and two months after birth.

References

[1] Allison, T., S.D. Gerber, S.M. Breedlove, G.L. Dryden, 1977
[2] Barbehenn, K.R., 1958
[3] Blair, W.F., 1940
[4] Buckner, C.H., 1964, [5] 1966
[6] Christian, J.J., 1950, [7] 1969
[8] Dapson, R.W., 1968a, [9] 1968b
[10] De Byle, N.V., 1965
[11] Dusi, J.L., 1951
[12] Eadie, W.R., 1949, [13] 1952
[14] Findley, J.S., and J.K. Jones, Jr., 1956
[15] Fowle, C.D., and R.Y. Edwards, 1955
[16a] Genoways, H.H., and J.R. Choate, 1972
[16b] George, S.B., H.H. Genoways, J.R. Choate, and R.J. Baker, 1982
[17] Gould, E., 1969
[18] Gould, E., N.C. Negus, and A. Novick, 1964
[19] Hamilton, W.J., Jr., 1929, [20] 1930, [21] 1940a
[22] Ingram, W.M. 1942
[23] Jameson, E.W., Jr., 1950
[24] Klugh, A.B., 1921

[25] Lawrence, B., 1946
[26] Lund, D., 1975
[27] Mann, P.M. and R.H. Stinson, 1957
[28] Martin, I.G., 1981
[29] Martinsen, D.L., 1969
[30] Meylan, A., 1967
[31] Olsen, R.W., 1969
[32] O'Reilly, R.A., Jr., 1949
[33] Pearson, O.P., 1942, [34] 1944, [35] 1945, [36] 1946, [37] 1956
[38] Platt, W.J., 1976
[39] Pruitt, W.O., Jr., 1953
[40] Richardson, J.H., 1973
[41] Rongstad, O.J., 1965
[42] Rood, J.P., 1958
[43] Tomasi, T.E., 1978, [44] 1979
[45] Wrigley, R.E., J.E. Dubois, H.W.R. Copland, 1979

Genus *Cryptotis* Pomel, 1848
(f. Gk *kruptos* secret, hidden + Gk *ous* genit. *otis* ear)

Small, short-tailed shrews, with inconspicuous ears and small eyes, resembling *Blarina* but smaller. The skull is short and broad and is characterized by only four upper unicuspids. The teeth are less pigmented than in *Blarina*. Mandible stout, with mental foramen beneath the hypoconid of m1. The talonid of m3 greatly reduced to a small heel with small conical cusp.

The genus has 12 nominal species; most are found in Central America. *Cryptotis* is the only representative of the Insectivora in South America.

It is known from the mid-Pliocene to Recent of North America. The late-Pliocene *C. adamsi* had five unicuspids. It is thought that *Cryptotis* shares a common origin with *Blarina*.

Cryptotis parva (Say)
(f. L *parvus* small)

Least Shrew   **Petite Musaraigne**
(Little Short-tailed Shrew)

1823 *Sorex parvus* Say, *in* Long, Account of an exped. . . .to the
      Rocky Mts. 1:163
1912 *Cryptotis parva* Miller, Bull. U.S. Nat. Mus. 79:24
Type locality: West bank of the Missouri River, near Blain,
Washington County, Nebraska

External Measurements and Weight

	TL	T	HF	W
x̄	81.9	17.5	11.2	—
OR	75–92	15–22	10–12.5	4.4–5.7

Cranial Measurements (2 specimens)

	SL	CB	IOW	MW
	15.3; 14.6	—; 7.2	3.5; 3.3	5.1; 5.0

Description (Colour Plate II)

A small, short-tailed shrew, with inconspicuous ears, brown above
and lighter below. The eyes are small and black, but relatively larger
than those of *Blarina*. (For further details see description under
genus). The winter pelage is darker than the summer pelage. Nothing
is known about the moult in the Canadian population, but it
probably occurs in late spring and late autumn. The glans penis is
short, bulbous, and heavily grooved [11]. This shrew's small size and
short tail distinguish it from all other Canadian shrews.

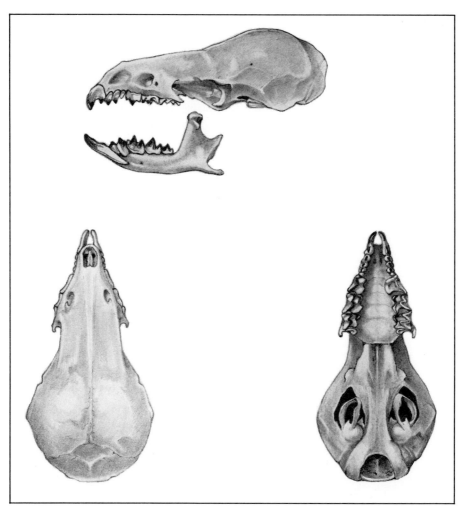

Figure 29.   Skull of *Cryptotis parva*

Distribution

This is a predominantly southern shrew found in the eastern, central, and southern United States and in Mexico. In Canada, this species is only known from Long Point, Ontario. The first specimens were collected there in 1927 [15]. Because of its apparent absence from other areas in southern Ontario, it has been suggested that the least shrew was rafted across Lake Erie. The limited range in Ontario may be related to the lack of suitable habitat, or it may reflect inadequate collecting in habitats where it is likely to exist.

Systematics

Nine subspecies have been described. The Canadian population belongs to *C. p. parva*. *C. parva* has been reported from Pleistocene deposits in the United States.

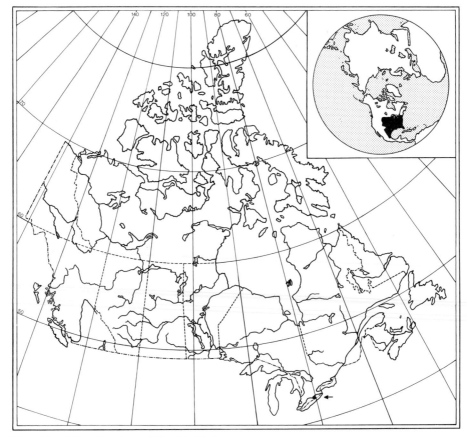

Map 17.   Distribution of *Cryptotis parva*

Biology

The least shrew prefers predominantly open country supporting
grassy, weedy, or brushy vegetation [8]. It is not found in woods. On
Long Point, the habitat consists of vegetated dunes and grassy areas
near marshes. Specimens collected there were found under driftwood
on the beach and under dry marsh-debris. This shrew digs its own
burrows or uses those of other animals [5]. The burrow made by this
species is approximately 13 mm high by 18 mm wide. Nests are
made of leaves and dry grasses [3].

Least shrews prey on insects, earthworms, centipedes, and
molluscs [7, 8, 9, 17]. They are also said to prey on frogs [9]. Insects
(especially larvae of Lepidoptera and Coleoptera, crickets, and grasshoppers) and earthworms appear to form the bulk of the food eaten.
Small amounts of plant material have also been reported (*Endogone*,
Setaria seeds). A captive least shrew weighing 3.6 g consumed on the
average 3.83 g of food in a day [2]. The least shrew itself is preyed
upon by owls, hawks, red foxes, cats, and snakes. Three young collected by Logier and Stovell were regurgitated by a captured milk
snake (*Lampropeltis doliata triangulum*) [15].

Very little is known about population structure and dynamics of
this species. The size of the home range has been estimated at 2800 m^2
and 1700 m^2 for one female and one male respectively. There is no
information on the longevity of the species in the field, but one
captive individual died at the age of 21 months [14].

The least shrew is active throughout the day but more so at
night [5, 8]. When well fed, captive individuals of this shrew will
sleep for considerable periods, averaging nine hours a day, curled up
with head, feet, and tail under the belly. The least shrew is the most
social of the native shrews. As many as 31 individuals have been
found in one nest [12] and no aggressive behaviour toward conspecifics has been observed in established captive individuals [4].
In a captive colony, all adults exhibited considerable care-giving
behaviour. This was evident from the retrieving of intentionally
scattered young and the co-operation in rebuilding the nest. The
least shrew digs with its forefeet, while the hind feet aid occasionally
in clearing the loosened earth. In loose soil, it burrows in the manner
of a mole, pushing up small ridges as it goes. Least shrews swim
voluntarily, floating high in the water. Little is known about the
relative importance of the senses. The eyes are relatively larger than
in the related *Blarina*. However, based on the lack of response
to moving objects, sight is thought to play a minor role in the life
of this shrew. Both sounds and scents are produced by the least shrew,
indicating that hearing and sense of smell play a part in social interaction. Little is known of the function and significance of scent
communication. The significance of vocal communication is much
better known [6]. The least shrew produces a number of sounds
similar to those of *Blarina*. Like those of the latter, the vocalizations
can be divided into low intensity ("put", "twitter", and "click"),
medium–intensity (receptive female calls, ultrasonic sounds), and
high–intensity (buzzes) sounds. Interestingly, the "chirp", a sound
produced in aggressive situations by *Blarina*, appears not to be
produced by the highly social least shrew. On the other hand, "clicks,"

Habitat

Food

Predators

Population

Behaviour

a contact sound, are uttered most frequently by this species. The functions of the other sounds are similar to those described for *Blarina*. Least shrews are clean animals. Grooming consists of washing and combing of the fur with the forefeet. Faeces are deposited away from the nest.

Courtship behavior consists of a protracted series of advances by the male, to which the female's initial response is agonistic, but which gradually becomes more and more receptive and culminates in copulation a day or two after the beginning of courtship [10]. Copulation is repeated with the same male and some times with other males of lower social status over a period of approximately three days.

During the initial precopulatory phase, males sniff the anal region, the lateral gland, and finally the aural gland. The aural gland, oval in shape and 1 to 2 mm long, is situated directly in front of the ventral part of the ear cartilage of the female. Investigation of the aural gland by the male occurs intermittently after the initial phase and is usually followed by an attempt to mount. During copulation the male sits on the female's back, clasping her with his front legs. Copulatory locking is frequent and may last a few seconds to several minutes. It is not uncommon for the male to be dragged backward behind the female during this phase. The penis is retracted with the aid of the mouth. After the copulatory period, when the female is presumably pregnant, males lose interest. It is believed that the scent of the aural gland of pregnant females contains a component that communicates her reproductive state to the male. This mechanism may be important in this species, exposed to frequent social contact, in order to ensure that pregnant and lactating females are not disturbed by courting males.

In the northern part of its range, the least shrew probably breeds from early March to November [8]. Heat lasts for one to two days. The gestation period is not more than 15 days according to one source [16]; 21 to 22 days according to others [4, 13]. Females generally breed again one to four days after they have given birth [4]. The litter size varies from 3 to 6, with a mode of 5. The newborn young are hairless, except for the vibrissae, and pink in colour. The external ears are closed, as are the eyes and there are no teeth [8]. One newborn young weighs less than 1 g and is about 22 mm long. Hair appears on the sixth day and the ears open after 10 to 12 days [4]. The young are fully furred and the eyes are open by 14 days after birth. The young are weaned when they are approximately 21 days old, and weigh more than 3 g. The young stick close to the mother until they are 20 to 23 days old, after which they assume an independent existence. Sexual maturity in both sexes is attained before the age of 40 days.

Reproduction and Ontogeny

References

[1] Allison, T., S.D., Gerber, S.M. Breedlove, and G.L. Dryden, 1977
[2] Barrett, G.W., 1969
[3] Broadbrooks, H.E., 1952
[4] Conaway, C.H., 1958
[5] Davis, W.B., and L. Joeris, 1945

[6] Gould, E., 1969

[7] Hamilton, W.J., Jr., 1934, [8] 1944

[9] Hatt, R.T., 1938

[10] Kivett, V.K. and O.B. Mock, 1980

[11] Martin, R.A., 1967

[12] McCarley, W.H., 1959

[13] Mock, O.B., 1970

[14] Pfeiffer, C.J., and G.H. Gass, 1963

[15] Snyder, L.L., 1929

[16] Walker, E.P., 1975

[17] Whitaker, J.O., Jr., and R.E. Mumford, 1972

Family TALPIDAE Gray, 1825

Moles   Taupes

Small insectivores with cylindrical bodies, short to long tails, conical mobile tactile snouts in some forms trunklike or provided with finger-like appendages (*Condylura*); eyes minute, sometimes subcutaneous; external ear greatly reduced or absent; limbs pentadactyl, little modified in the most primitive forms (*Uropsilus*), or showing varying degrees of adaptation to fossorial or aquatic existence; fur thick and soft in many forms, often with a pronounced sheen.

The skull is long, narrow and flattened in most forms, with thin zygomatic arches, no postorbital processes, tympanic bones attached to the braincase, the auditory bullae incomplete or well developed. Teeth are variable in number and size, upper canines always present but may be reduced, lower canine reduced or absent, the molars with dilambdadont (**W** or **M**) cusp pattern.

In the fossorial forms, clavicle and humerus are short and heavy, the humerus articulates with the clavicle to provide greater strength; manus broadened with falciform bone adjacent to the first finger, phalanges short, claw-bearing phalange with bifurcated tip. Hind limbs not modified, tibia and fibula fused distally.

Stomach long and narrow, intestine long and of uniform width, caecum absent, external genitalia of males and females similar, clitoris large, vagina closed by skin in anoestrous female, uterus bicornate, placenta discoidal of epitheliochorial or endotheliochorial type. Brain dorsoventrally flattened with smooth cerebral hemispheres. Sense of touch well developed, centred in the nose and in some forms, the edge of front feet; hearing appears to be well developed, development of olfaction is not well known; vision is poorly developed, eyes minute but complete, in some forms subcutaneous, presumably nonfunctional, although the presence of rods in the retina may indicate ability to perceive light.

The majority of talpids are adapted for a fossorial existence. *Uropsilus*, the most primitive living mole, is shrew-like in appearance and has no special adaptations for digging; two genera (*Galemys* and *Desmana*) are aquatic. Food consists predominantly of invertebrates and small vertebrates, although small amounts of vegetable matter are consumed by some species.

The moles are restricted to Eurasia and North America and comprise some 13 genera and 20 species in the world today. Of these five genera and seven species are restricted to North America. All North American species except one (*Scapanus latimanus*) form part of the Canadian fauna. The family has a long taxonomic history, reflecting the changes in our understanding of the relationships within the group. The most recent classification [1] subdivides the living Talpidae into three subfamilies — the Uropsilinae, including the most primitive living form *Uropsilus*; the Desmaninae, comprising the Eurasian aquatic moles; and the Talpinae, including all other living moles. The Talpinae are further subdivided in five distinct tribes, of which three are found in North America. These are the Urotrichini with *Neurotrichus*; the Condylurini with *Condylura*;

and the Scalopini with the genera *Parascalops*, *Scalopus* and *Scapanus*. The first and last tribes also have living representatives in eastern Asia.

More recent morphological, electrophoretic and karyological analysis of North American moles [3, 4] indicate the existence of three species groups: 1) *Scapanus* and *Parascalops*, 2) *Scalopus* and *Neurotrichus*, and 3) *Condylura*. The genetic distinctness between all North American species was found to be similar, excepting *Condylura*, which is more remote. The first four genera could be placed in the subfamily Scalopinae and *Condylura* in the Condylurinae. *Condylura* may have diverged from the other genera as much as 49 million years ago, whereas the lineages leading to *Neurotrichus*, *Scalopus* and *Scapanus-Parascalops* may have diverged from one another during the Miocene at about the same time.

The earliest known talpids are from the Upper Eocene of Europe. They were first represented in North America in the Oligocene by a now-extinct subfamily, the Proscalopinae. The Recent subfamilies first appeared in North America in the Miocene.

References

[1] Hutchison, J.H., 1968
[2] Jackson, H.H.T., 1915
[3] Yates, T.L., 1978
[4] Yates, T.L., and I.F. Greenbaum, 1982

Genus *Neurotrichus* Günther, 1880
(f Gk *nē* negative prefix not + Gk *oura* tail + Gk *thrix*
genit. *thrichos* hair. Referring to Günther's
conclusion that it did not belong in the genus
Urotrichus)

A small shrew-like mole with a relatively long, scaly, thinly haired tail (half of head–body length). Snout elongate, rhinarium naked, moist and deep pink; nostrils lateral and slightly crescentic with the concavity upwards. Eyes small and auditory orifice about 4 mm $\times$ 2 mm. Feet large, scaly, less modified for digging than those of other North American talpids, palms of forefeet longer than broad, claws long, but not broad and depressed; hind feet long and narrow with six plantar tubercles. Fur with distinct guard hairs and underfur, similar to that of *Condylura*, but finer, colour nearly black, vibrissae on anterior upper lip and two pair on each side of the head, about 5 mm in front of the ear opening. Mammae 8 (4 pectoral, 2 abdominal, 2 inguinal). Skull with incomplete auditory bullae and pterygoid only slightly inflated. Dental formula i 3/3, c 1/1, p 2/2, m 3/3, total 36; I1 enlarged and relatively broad and flattened antero-posteriorly, I2 and I3 small, C1 larger than I3, flattened laterally and similar to P1, P2 large, triangular, upper molars with W-shaped cusp pattern and bicuspidate lingual edge: i1 small and spatulate, i2, i3 and c1 similar but smaller, p1 and p2 triangular, lower molars with W cusp pattern. *Neurotrichus* possesses a pair of prominent ampullary glands (accessory genital glands) not found in other North American moles, but present in Soricids [1]. The karyotype of the only living species based on one female, consists of a diploid number of 38 biarmed chromosomes (FN = 72). This genus is now confined to western North America although it has been reported from the Pliocene of Poland [2]: a related genus, *Urotrichus* Temminck, 1841, with two species, is found in Japan.

References

[1] Eadie, W.R., 1951
[2] Skoczen, S., 1980

Neurotrichus gibbsii (Baird)
(named after collector George Gibbs)

Shrew-mole   **Taupe naine**
(American Shrew-mole)

1858 *Urotrichus gibbsii* Baird, Mammals, *in* Rep. Expl. Surv. 8(1):76
1885 *Neurotrichus gibbsii* True, Proc. U.S. Nat. Mus. 7:607
Type locality: Naches Pass, 1370 m, Pierce County, Washington

External Measurements and Weight

	TL	T	HF	W
N	50	50	50	—
X̄	105.4	34.5	15.1	10
SD	4.21	2.14	0.60	—
CV	3.99	6.21	3.97	—
OR	98–116	30–40	14–17	9.5–10.5

Cranial Measurements

	SL	CB	IOW
N	23	19	23
X̄	22.3	10.2	5.1
SD	0.39	0.23	0.16
CV	1.75	2.23	3.13
OR	21.6–23.1	9.6–10.6	4.8–5.4

Description (Colour Plate IV)

See description of genus.

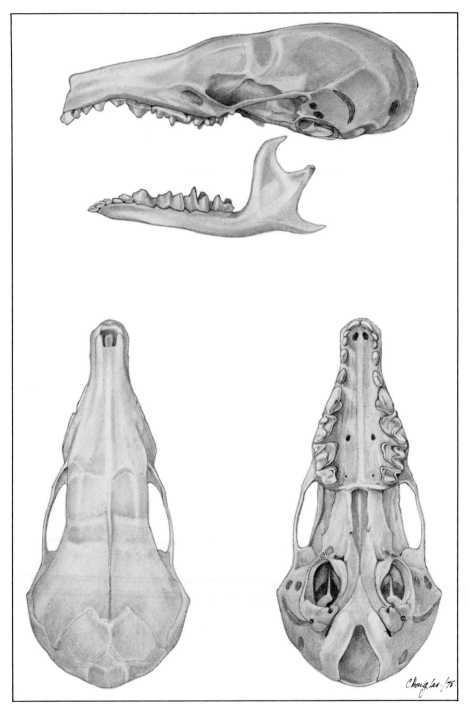

Figure 30.   Skull of *Neurotrichus gibbsii*

Distribution

This species is restricted to the lower Fraser Valley in Canada.
Peripheral localities: *British Columbia:* (**1**) Gibsons Landing;
(**2**) Langley; (**3**) Hope; (**4**) Allison Pass.

In the United States, its range extends along the Pacific slope
south to central California.

Systematics

Five subspecies are recognized, of which one occurs in Canada.
N. g. gibbsii (Baird), 1858, Mammals, *in* Rep. Expl. Surv. 8(1):76.

Biology

The shrew-mole lives on forested hillsides and valley bottoms with   Habitat
moist loose soils having a high humus content and an abundant leaf
litter, decaying vegetation, and rotting logs and stumps [1, 2, 6, 9]. It
is most common under deciduous vegetation along streams and in

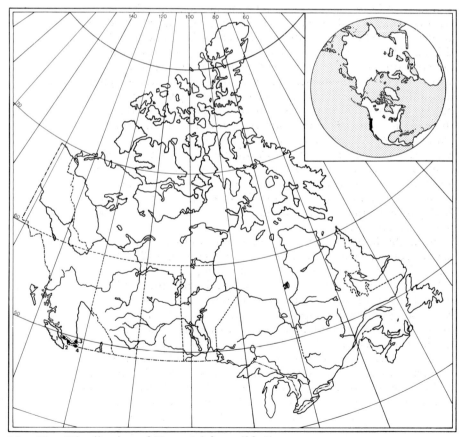

Map 18.   Distribution of *Neurotrichus gibbsii*

ravines. It is less frequently found in swampy places. The species is generally absent in dry hard soils and grassy meadows. The shrew-mole constructs runways between the surface litter and the soil, at depths of 1–13 cm below the surface [6], where it spends most of its time. Deep burrows are less common and rarely penetrate to a depth of more than 30 cm [2]. The tunnels are approximately 2.5 cm in diameter and have open entrances to the outside. The shallow burrows have ventilation ducts in their roofs, and enlarged empty chambers with a diameter and height of approximately 13 and 8 cm respectively are often present. Their function is unknown. Nests are made of dry leaves. In the loose forest soil they prefer, shrew-moles do not usually push up mole hills and their burrow systems are less extensive than those of other moles.

Shrew-moles hunt for food in their runways under the litter, as well as on the surface. Earthworms and isopods (sow bugs) appear to be the most-important prey species, accounting for 42 and 36 per cent by volume in one study [2], followed by insect larvae and pupae. Captive animals, according to this study, refused beetles, ants, myriapods, termites, and slugs [2]. Another study reports captive *Neurotrichus* accepting dead mice, a bird, large slugs, centipedes, and large beetles [8]. In addition, they ate a variety of plant seeds and mushrooms. The greatest quantity of food consumed by a captive animal in 12 hours amounted to 1.4 × the animal's weight. The food passes through the alimentary canal in about 35 minutes. The faeces are deposited wherever the animal happens to be. They are soft, shiny and black and approximately 4 mm long and 1 mm wide. Observations of captives indicate that they seem to drink rarely, apparently deriving sufficient water from their prey. Known predators of the shrew-moles include snakes (*Thamnophis ordinoides*), hawks (*Buteo jamaicensis*), raccoons and owls (*Otus asio*) [2]. The shrew-mole shares the forest floor with a number of other small mammals, of which *Peromyscus maniculatus*, *Sorex vagrans*, *S. trowbridgii*, and *Aplodontia rufa* are the most common [2, 9]. It rarely occurs together with other western moles, *Scapanus orarius* and *S. townsendii*, which prefer different habitats. The commonest parasites are small mites. Fleas and ticks have also been recorded. Endoparasites appear to be infrequent but nematodes and cestodes have been reported [2].

In suitable habitat, the population density of this species has been estimated at 12 to 15 shrew-moles per hectare [2]. There is no information on the size of the home range.

Like other moles, shrew-moles are active day and night [2]. Several individuals of this species have been trapped in the same runway, which suggests that the shrew-mole may be more gregarious than most moles. Among our native moles, this species is the least specialized for a fossorial existence. It spends more time on the surface and has been reported capable of climbing low bushes [2]. Compared to its more-fossorial relatives, the shrew-mole moves with agility on top of the soil, in a walk or fast scuttle. When the animal walks, the claws of the front feet are folded inwards, so that the animal walks on the back of its claws. Unlike our other moles, the shrew-mole is able to place the palms of its forefeet, which are

Food

Predators

Associated Mammals

Parasites

Population

Behaviour

usually turned outwards, flat on the ground. It can also raise itself on its hind feet, with the anterior part of its body not supported by the front legs [2, 7]. It can do so because of its well-developed hind feet and its long tail. The method of burrowing is similar to that of other moles that have been studied, but the shrew-mole is less powerful. It can push up only 20 × its own weight, less than the highly specialized fossorial species. The shrew-mole swims voluntarily and well, using the feet on each side alternately. This mole sleeps rolled up, with its head tucked down between its forelegs. Prey is grabbed with the teeth. Earthworms may be bitten along the entire length of the body, or the mole may start to eat the first portion encountered. Usually a worm is eaten from one end. Shrew-moles sometimes hold and strip earthworms through their forefeet.

Touch appears to be the best developed of the senses [2]. The nose is the animal's most sensitive tactile organ. While the animal hunts, the nose is constantly moved up, down, and sideways. When the animal moves forward, it raps its nose lightly and rapidly on the surface, first in front and then, turning its head about 40°, on the right and the left sides. The shrew-mole responds to sounds between 8000 to 30,000 vibrations per second and is best adapted to hear high-pitched sounds. It is not known what role hearing plays in food-finding or social behavior. Audible vocalizations have been heard only rarely [7]. Observations of captive animals suggest that the sense of smell is poorly developed and probably plays only a subordinate role in food-finding. However, the musky scent produced by breeding males suggests that the sense of smell is important in the species' reproductive behaviour. Vision is poorly developed. The lack of response to visual stimuli strongly suggests that the shrew-mole is effectively blind.

The shrew-mole appears to have an extended breeding season [2]. Reproduction and Ontogeny Males in breeding condition have been taken as early as 23 February, and nursing females have been recorded as late as 26 September (in Washington). However, most of the breeding records are between 10 March and 14 May, with few births recorded after that date. Embryo counts varied from 1 to 4. The period of gestation is unknown. The average litter size is probably about 3. The newborn young are hairless and pink; the eyes are covered by skin, but show up as black dots and there is no external ear-opening [5]. The forefeet are clawless, but shaped like those of the adult and the teeth have not erupted. The young weigh about 0.5 g (0.49–0.67 g). The period of lactation is unknown. The young probably become sexually mature during the breeding season following their birth.

References

[1] Cowan, I. McT., and C.J. Guiguet, 1965
[2] Dalquest, W.W., and D.R. Orcutt, 1942
[3] Eadie, W.R., 1951
[4] Kritzman, E.B., 1971, [5] 1972
[6] Racey, K., 1929
[7] Reed, C.A., 1944
[8] Terry, C.J., 1978, [9] 1981

Genus *Scalopus* Geoffroy Saint-Hilaire, 1803
(f. Gk *skallō* to dig + Gk *pous* foot)

A stocky mole; body depressed; tail, short, round, nearly naked. Nose distinct, long, thin, and pointed, tip naked, nostrils dorsal crescent-shaped with convex sides to outside; eyes minute and hidden in fur, auditory opening small, palms of forefeet broader than long with broad, flat, heavy claws, hind feet without plantar tubercles, toes of front and hind feet webbed. Fur dense and velvet-like, mammae 6 (2 pectoral, 2 abdominal, 2 inguinal). Skull with swollen frontal sinuses, relatively short rostrum; heavy zygomatic arches; auditory bullae complete, external pterygoid, basioccipital, and basisphenoid cancellous. Mandible heavy, angular process short and broad. Dental formula i 3/2(3), c 1/0(1), p 3/3, m 3/3, a total of 36 or 38 teeth. I1 large, broad and flattened, rodent-like, anterior surface convex. I 2, 3 very small and conical; C1 and upper premolars small; molars hypsodont; i1 small and situated anterior and below the much larger i2; i3 and c1 rudimentary, usually absent.

The karyotype is the same as that found in *Scapanus* (2N = 34; FN = 64) [2].

The genus comprises one Recent species, *S. aquaticus*. The formerly recognized species from Mexico, *S. inflatus* and *S. montanus*, apparently represent relict populations of *S. aquaticus*, dating back to a time when that species had a more extensive southern distribution [3]. The genus, which is known from the Pliocene to Recent, evolved in North America from more-primitive forms that invaded North America from Asia in the early Miocene. According to biochemical analyses the nearest living relative is *Neurotrichus* [1]. Both genera were probably derived from a common ancestor sometime during the Miocene.

References

[1] Yates, T.L., and I.F. Greenbaum, 1982
[2] Yates, T.L., and D.L. Schmidly, 1975, [3] 1977

Scalopus aquaticus (Linnaeus)
(f. L *aqua* water, because of the webbed toes and the mistaken
assumption that the animal was aquatic)

Eastern Mole	Taupe à queue glabre

1758 *Sorex aquaticus* Linnaeus, Syst. nat., 10th ed., vol. 1, p. 53

1803 *Scalopus virginianus* E. Geoffroy Saint-Hilaire, Catalogue des mammifères du Muséum National d'Histoire Naturelle, Paris, p. 78

1905 *Scalopus aquaticus* Oberholser, Mammals and summer birds of western North Carolina, Biltmore Forest School, Biltmore, North Carolina, p. 3

Type locality: Eastern United States

External Measurements and Weight

	TL	T	HF	WT
N	8	8	8	—
X̄	180.4	30.2	21.5	—
SD	6.88	1.58	0.75	—
CV	3.81	5.22	3.48	—
OR	173–191	28–33	20–22	75–120

Cranial Measurements

	SL	CB	IOW
N	10	10	10
X̄	37.1	19.5	8.2
SD	0.86	0.32	0.17
CV	2.31	1.64	2.11
OR	36.2–38.6	19.0–20.1	8.0–8.4

Description (Colour Plate IV)

See description under genus. The eastern mole can be distinguished externally from the somewhat similar hairy-tailed mole by its scantily haired tail, larger size, dorsal position of the nostrils, and its webbed toes.

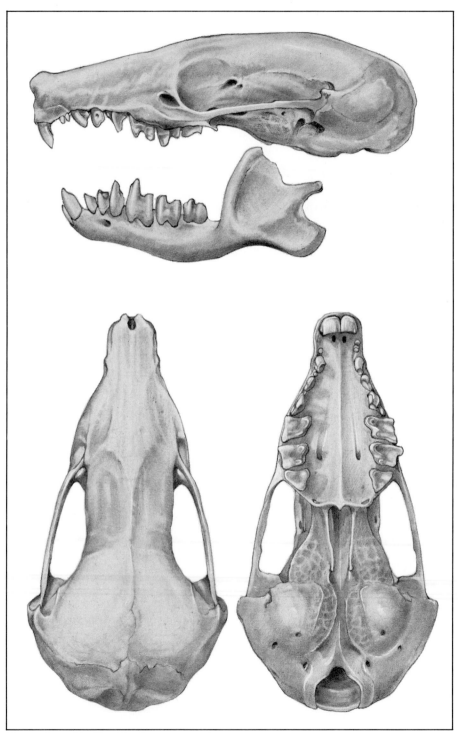

Figure 31.   Skull of *Scalopus aquaticus*

Distribution

The eastern mole is widely distributed in eastern North America from southern South Dakota, southern Minnesota, southern Wisconsin, Michigan, extreme southern Ontario, southern New York State, and Rhode Island in the north to the Gulf of Mexico in the south and from the Atlantic Coast in the east, to extreme eastern Wyoming and Colorado and the eastern half of Texas in the west. The distribution in Canada appears to be confined to (1) Essex County, where it is common in (2) Point Pelee National Park. There is one doubtful record for Strathroy, Ontario.

Systematics

Throughout its extensive range, the eastern mole exhibits considerable geographical variation, with 14 subspecies being recognized. The Canadian population belongs to the subspecies, *S. a. machrinus* (Rafinesque).

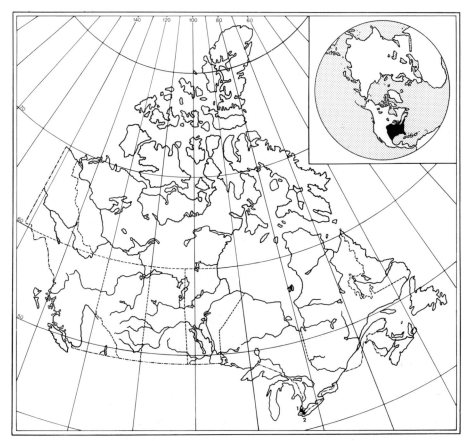

Map 19. Distribution of *Scalopus aquaticus*

Biology

Habitat

The eastern mole prefers soft moist soils with humus in forests or
fields. It avoids gravel or stony soil, although it is adapted to harder
and drier soils than *Parascalops*. Its tunnel system is from 2.5 cm to
60 cm below the surface and may cover an area from 1500 to
18 000 m² [5]. Males have larger home ranges (average size 10 000 m²)
than females (average size 3000 m²). The nest is situated from 8 to
46 cm below the surface [2]. It consists of a hollow area, about 20 cm
in diameter and 12 cm high. The cavity may be lined with dry leaves
or grass, or it may be bare. *Scalopus* rarely pushes up conspicuous
mounds like *Scapanus* [9].

Food

The eastern mole's food consists primarily of soil invertebrates [2, 6]. In order of their importance, these are earthworms,
insect larvae, adult insects and, in addition, a small amount of
vegetable matter. Earthworms, white grubs, and other insect larvae
are preferred to adult insects or vegetable matter. Captive moles will
eat mice, which they strip of the skin with their front paws [3]. It is
unlikely that the eastern mole is capable of capturing full-grown
mice under normal circumstances. Captives also eat corn, wheat,
oats, muskmelon seeds, squash seeds, ripe tomatoes, apples and
potatoes. One captive mole consumed the equivalent of about 32 per
cent of its body weight per day [6].

Predators

Parasites

Mammalian carnivores, hawks, and owls occasionally take this
mole when the opportunity presents itself [2], but the extent of their
predation is not known. A number of ectoparasites have been
reported from this mole, including a beetle *Leptinus testaceus*, a
louse *Euhaematopinus abnormis*, and a flea *Ctenophthalmus
pseudagyrtes* [8, 10]. Nothing appears to be known about the population structure and dynamics of the eastern mole.

Population

Behaviour

The eastern mole is active at any time of the day or night, with
two major inactivity periods from 04:00 to 07:00 hrs and one from
18:00 to 21:00 hrs [5]. Periods of sleep lasting 1 to 3 hours alternate
with active periods [1]. About 41 per cent of the time is spent sleeping, the rest awake. During winter, this mole appears to use a single
nest insulated with dry vegetation, whereas during the summer it
does not use a specific location for resting.

As in other moles, the sense of touch appears to be most important.
The tactile receptors are concentrated primarily in the nose and are
also present on the ventral surface of the tongue [2]. The eyes are
small, with the eyelids fused or forming a miniscule opening. The
sense of smell comes into play at short distances of a few centimetres
only. Hearing appears to be well developed in this species. Digging
is done exclusively with the front feet and consists of anteroposterior
strokes and lateral thrusts [2, 7]. In surface runways, the earth is
simply pushed up by means of the animal rotating its body 45° to
one side and extending the foot near the surface. The nose is held
between the feet during digging and is only extended intermittently
to make rapid examinations. In the construction of deep tunnels, the
earth is first loosened by the scraping action of the front paw. The
mole uses one paw at a time, while it uses the other to brace itself.
The loose earth is thrown beneath the belly and kicked back with the
hind feet from time to time. After a certain amount of earth has

accumulated, the animal turns around and uses one paw to push it to the surface. The mole has no difficulty turning around in its narrow tunnels. It does this by placing its head under its abdomen and creeping under itself, or by turning sideways, doubling itself, without rotating its body [3]. When sleeping, the mole keeps its head curled between its forefeet and under its body, with the top of the head on the ground and the nose pointing back. When the animal is searching for food, the nose is constantly in motion. Earthworms are grabbed with the mouth. The mole usually starts eating the worm at one end, either the anterior or posterior end, although occasionally it may begin eating the middle section. The forefeet are held close to the mouth, with the worm held between the dorsal surfaces of the feet and claws. The mole then pulls the worm through its feet, partially clearing it of soil within and without, bites off a piece and ingests it. The process is repeated until all of the worm has been consumed. The earthworm is sometimes stripped between the claws [2, 6]. Large insects are slammed against the wall of the burrow and held there while the mole examines its prey. If necessary, the prey is bitten and mauled further, after which it is consumed piece by piece. A large active prey is also attacked by piling loose earth on it. To defend itself, the mole uses its powerful front feet to strike out or push away the offender. The teeth are used infrequently in such situations.

The eastern mole breeds in spring [4]. The breeding season extends over three to four months, with a peak in the northern part of the species' range in late March and early April. After a gestation period of four weeks or less, 3 to 5 young are born. Most births occur in the latter half of April. The most frequent number in a litter is 4 and the average number is 3.91. The young are born hairless and without teeth. The deciduous dentition is shed before birth. A female produces only one litter per year. Breeding first occurs at one year of age. The vagina is closed by skin, except during the reproductive season. At oestrous the vaginal orifice is white and avascular, but after ovulation the lips of the vagina become reddish. Ovulation is probably induced by coitus. The testes of the male increase rapidly in size prior to the breeding season and then gradually decline, reaching their minimum size in summer.

Reproduction and Ontogeny

References

[1] Allison, T., and H. Van Twyver, 1970
[2] Arlton, A.V., 1936
[3] Christian, J.J., 1950
[4] Conaway, C.H., 1959
[5] Harvey, M.J., 1976
[6] Hisaw, F.L., 1923a, [7] 1923b
[8] Olive, J.R., 1950
[9] Scheffer, T.H., 1949
[10] Whitaker, J.O., Jr., and J.L. Schmeltz, 1973
[11] Yates, T.L., and D.L. Schmidly, 1978

Genus *Parascalops* True, 1894
(f. Gk *para* beside, near + Gk. *skalops* genit.
skalopos mole, rel. to *skallo* to dig.)

A mole with a cylindrical, slightly depressed body, tail short, round, thick and fleshy, slightly constricted at its base, annulated and covered with long coarse hair. Snout conical and mobile, with naked pink, moist rhinarium; nostrils lateral, crescent-shaped with the concavity pointing upwards. Auditory opening relatively large. Feet scantily hairy above, naked below; palms of forefeet as long as broad, and turned upwards; sole of hind feet with two plantar tubercles and heel pad. Fur dense and velvet-like, blackish with metallic sheen. In young aimals, hairs on feet and tail always dark, with age these become grizzled; in older animals snout, tail, and feet almost pure white. White spots on breast and abdomen often present. Moults twice a year in spring (end of March to end of May) and autumn (early September to mid-October). New hair appears first on breast and then on dorsal lumbar area anterior to tail; moult progresses caudad and laterad from the former and in opposite direction from the latter. A pair of large perineal glands opens at the anterior lip of rectal papilla; diffuse scent glands present on ventral body surface, consisting of sudoriferous glands and associated sebaceous glands. During breeding season, and for sometime after, secretions stain the fur brownish yellow or golden; in males from the ventral surface of lower jaw to inguinal area, in females stain is usually limited to underside of the jaw. Mammae 8 (4 pectoral, 2 abdominal and 2 inguinal). Skull with incomplete auditory bullae, region of pterygoid not inflated. Dentition, 44 teeth, i 3/3, c 1/1, p 4/4, m 3/3; first upper incisor large, broad and flat with a small external accessory cusp; remaining incisors, canine, and premolars in the upper jaw simple conical structures, canine slightly larger than the others; P4 is much larger and has an anterior cusp; upper molars have W-cusp pattern and three-lobed inner edge; i1 small, i2 larger and somewhat canine-like, i3, c1, and premolars small simple structures; lower molars with M-shaped cusp pattern. The living species has a karyotype of 2N = 34 (30 biarmed and 2 acrocentric chromosomes) and FN = 62.

The genus *Parascalops* has one known species (Pleistocene–Recent) confined to eastern North America. On the basis of biochemical evidence, the most closely related North American Recent form is *Scapanus* [1], while comparative morphological comparisons suggest that *Parascalops* is also close to the Chinese genus *Scapanulus*.

Reference

[1] Yates, T.L., and I.F. Greenbaum, 1982

Parascalops breweri (Bachman)
(Named after T.M. Brewer)

Hairy-tailed Mole   **Taupe à queue velue**

1842 *Scalops breweri* Bachman, Boston J. Nat. Hist. 4:32
1885 *Scapanus breweri* True, Proc. U.S. Nat. Mus. 7:606
1895 *Parascalops breweri* True, Science (Wash. D.C.), n.s., vol. 1,
     p. 101
Type locality: eastern North America

External Measurements and Weight

	TL	T	HF	W
N	14	14	14	—
X̄	153.4	28.9	18.4	—
SD	8.21	2.49	1.28	—
CV	5.35	8.61	6.96	—
OR	138–170	25–33	15–20	40–65

Cranial Measurements

	SL	CB	IOW
N	7	7	8
X̄	31.7	14.5	7.0
SD	0.82	0.39	0.16
CV	2.58	2.69	2.24
OR	30.8–32.8	14–15.2	6.8–7.3

Description (Colour Plate IV)

See the description under the genus. This mole can be distinguished
from similar species by its short hairy tail and lateral nostrils.

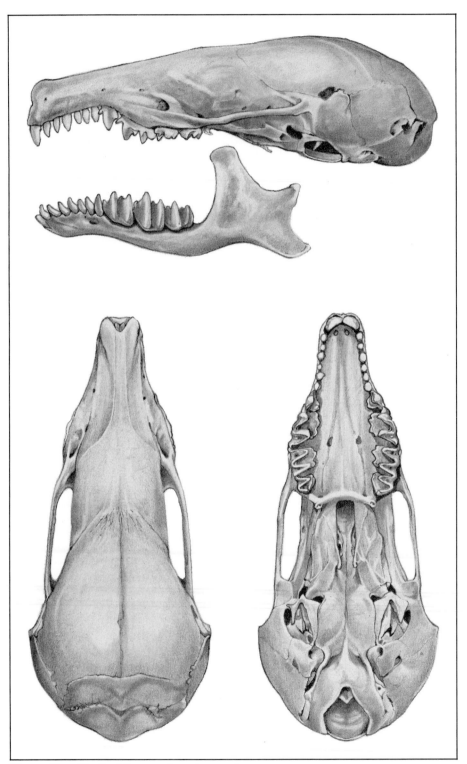

Figure 32.   Skull of *Parascalops breweri*

Distribution

The hair-tailed mole is found in eastern North America from Quebec in the north to the mountains of Virginia and Tennessee in the south. In the Canadian part of its range, the distribution of this mole is not founded on a great deal of information. However, from the available data and personal observation, it appears that the species is generally uncommon, although concentrations occur in scattered localities where suitable habitat is available. Peripheral localities: *New Brunswick:* (**1**) Charlotte County (an old record from 1884). *Ontario:* (**2**) Pancake Bay; (**3**) Port Sydney; (**4**) St. Catharines; (**5**) 32 km west of London. *Quebec:* (**6**) Québec City; (**7**) Mount Orford; (**8**) Mont-Tremblant.

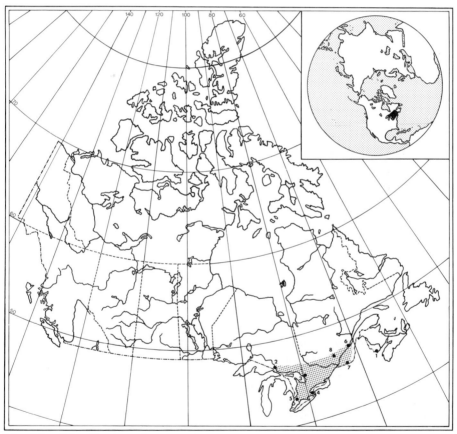

Map 20.   Distribution of *Parascalops breweri*

Systematics

The hairy-tailed mole is a monotypic species displaying little
geographic variation.

Biology

Originally an inhabitant of the temperate deciduous woodlands of
eastern North America, it is now found mainly in second-growth
hardwoods, forest edges, and old fields near hardwood stands. The
species is most abundant in light and moist, but well-drained soils
(sandy loams and sand), especially in friable woodland soils in
which organic matter and mineral soil are well mixed (mull) [10]. It
is less abundant in woodland soils where the humus forms a fibrous
mat separated from the mineral soil below (mor). Mull generally
supports an abundant and diverse invertebrate fauna and makes for
easy burrowing. The type of topsoil formed in any particular locality
is influenced by topography, conditions of the substrate, moisture,
and the type of vegetation. All these factors ultimately determine the
distribution and abundance of this mole in a given area within its
general range. Rockiness of the soil does not appear to be important,
but hard, dry soils are avoided, as are those that are wet or that have
a heavy clay content.

 The hairy-tailed mole digs an extensive system of surface tunnels
in the loose top layer of the soil and a less extensive one deeper down.
The tunnels of this mole measure approximately 3.7 cm wide by
2.5 cm high [1]. The regularly used tunnels are somewhat larger and
have smoother, well-packed walls than those constructed by the
mole in search of food. Deep tunnels are dug down to a depth of
56 cm, but most are between 25 to 45 cm. Shallow tunnels are often
indicated by the presence of surface ridges. However, in wooded
country, these are difficult to see. In loose soil or humus no ridges
are formed. Molehills, produced by soil that has been pushed up
during the construction of deeper tunnels, also indicate the presence
of this mole. The hills made by *Parascalops* are smaller than those
of other moles in their range, and usually have a diameter of 15 cm
and a height of 7.5 cm. Larger hills may be present where a nest
chamber has been excavated. In autumn, particularly in October
and early November, a greater number of hills are pushed up than at
any other time of year because of the mole's increased digging activity
to extend the deep tunnel system for the winter. After the soil freezes,
no new molehills appear. The nests built by this mole consist of
resting nests, breeding, and winter nests. Resting nests are merely
enlargements in a tunnel, measuring about 8 cm in diameter. Breeding nests are larger cavities of a roughly spherical shape, 15 or 16 cm
in diameter and some 30 cm below the surface, which contain a nest
of clean dry leaves. The winter nest consists of a bulkier mass of
dry vegetation (20 cm by 15 cm) and is situated well below the surface.
One winter nest was 41 cm below the surface of the soil and 21 cm
below the frost line [1].

 The hairy-tailed mole feeds on soil invertebrates [1, 8]. Its most-
important prey is earthworms (34% by volume), followed by larvae
and pupae of insects (29% by volume). In the latter category, beetle

Habitat

Food

160

larvae are most important. Adult insects, predominantly beetles and ants, are much less important (18% by volume); they are mostly eaten in spring and autumn when other food is less available. Other invertebrates such as millipedes, snails and slugs, and sow bugs appear to be of only minor importance in the diet of this mole. One 50 g hairy-tailed mole consumed 66 g of earthworms and insect larvae in 24 hours [4]. But if fed *ad libitum*, this species can consume a quantity of earthworms equivalent to more than 300% of its own body weight. This probably represents an upper limit and a captive mole can be maintained on much less. Nothing is known about how this mole satisfies its moisture requirements in the wild, but a captive mole was observed by me to drink frequently.

The hairy-tailed mole shares its tunnels with a number of other small mammals, such as short-tailed shrews, voles, deer mice, common shrews, jumping mice and, where its home range borders on wet habitats, also the star-nosed mole [1]. There does not appear to be any serious competition with any of these. It is possible that the short-tailed shrew preys on nestling moles, but so far the evidence is lacking. Fleas (*Nearctopsylla hygini laurentina* and *Ctenopthalmus* sp.), mites, and lice (*Euhaemotopinus abnormis*) have been collected from the hairy-tailed mole. Internal parasites found in the intestine and stomach of this species include acanthocephalid worms of the genus *Moliniformis* and undetermined nematodes [1, 6]. The major predators of the hairy-tailed mole are unknown. Remains of this mole have been reported as an infrequent item in fox droppings [9].

Associated Mammals

Parasites

Predators

Population structure and dynamics of this species have not been adequately studied. Estimated densities in suitable habitat vary approximately from 3 to 30 animals per hectare [1, 7]. The home range of an individual hairy-tailed mole in winter is estimated to cover an area of 15 to 24 m in diameter. In summer, when the animal uses its superficial tunnel system, the home range is probably much more extensive. The sexes appear to be equally numerous in the population. Trapping records show a greater number of males than females caught in the early part of the year, reflecting the greater activity and range of the male during the breeding season. On the basis of toothwear, four age-classes can be distinguished. One sample of 55 animals captured during the spring of the year (March, April) showed an age structure of 45.4% one-year-olds; 34.5% two-year-olds, 14.5% three-year-olds and 5.4% four-year-olds [1]. It is doubtful if any animals survive beyond five years.

Population

The hairy-tailed mole is active throughout the year [1]. Its circadian activity pattern is independent from the alternation of day and night, so that active hairy-tailed moles can be encountered at any time of the day [1, 7]. Adequate quantitative data on activity in this species have not yet been collected. A single captive mole I observed in November alternated periods of activity (feeding, drinking, digging, etc.) with periods of relative inactivity throughout the day, the former lasting an average of 1 hour and 27 minutes (13 observations) and the latter 2 hours and 54 minutes (12 observations). Like other moles, this species sleeps usually in an upright position with its head tucked under its body. The manner of locomotion and digging is similar to that reported for *Scalopus* and *Scapanus*. Like these, the hairy-tailed mole is unable to raise the anterior part of its body,

Behaviour

which is supported on the medial sides of the front feet and the chest. The animal moves through its tunnels with ease. With its hind feet extended in a semi-lateral position against the side walls of the burrow, the mole straddles the tunnel with both front and hind feet and progresses by moving two diagonally opposite feet at one time. The speed of this mole on the surface has been estimated at 4.6 m/30 sec. (approximately 0.5 km/hr.) [1]. It probably can move faster in its tunnels. The hairy-tailed mole is able to turn around in its narrow tunnel with ease because of the great flexibility of its spine. When the animal is digging, it braces itself against the walls of the burrow with its hind feet, which are extended laterally and at right angles to the body. The tail is usually held erect, touching the ceiling of the burrow, during digging. Whether the tail acts as an additional brace or as a tactile organ at that time is not certain. The hairy-tailed mole is capable of swimming [5], but probably does so rarely. The hairy-tailed mole responds defensively to an intruder by rapid thrusts of its heavily clawed front feet and by pushing quantities of earth toward or on the intruder.

Sight is poorly developed, although this mole may be able to discriminate between light and dark. The eyes are characterized by small size ($<$ 1 mm in diameter) and are similar to those of other fossorial moles. All structural elements are present, but the lens is composed of large polyhedral cells with nuclei. The hair around the ocular aperture can be spread out radially and the eyeball extruded [1]. This suggests that the eye still functions in some way, although how is unknown. It probably serves to indicate the light intensity outside the burrow to the animal, as the hairy-tailed mole apparently leaves its burrows at night on occasion to forage in the forest litter. Normally the eye aperture is closed and hidden by hair. The sense of smell appears to play a role in the animal's search for food and in sexual behaviour. Captive hairy-tailed moles appeared to be able to detect food as far as 5 or 6 cm away. When the animal is in search of food, its moist pink nose is in constant motion, moving up, down, and sideways and sniffing constantly. The sense of touch is also concentrated in this organ and comes into play at close range. Vibrissae are present on the snout and one pair on each side of the head, approximately 1 cm behind the eye. The forefeet have a fringe of stiff carpal vibrissae at least some of which may serve a tactile function. The position of the tail during certain movements (e.g. backing up) suggests that it too may function as a tactile organ, but this needs investigation. Hearing undoubtedly plays a role as well in food seeking and social behaviour, but little information is available. Captive moles react to high-pitch sounds, but seem to ignore low-frequency sound. The hairy-tailed mole itself appears to be a relatively silent animal. Harsh guttural squeaks have been reported from this species, while being held in the hand. I have heard rhythmic squeaks uttered at approximately 1 second intervals, while the mole was in a sleeping position, but in the process of waking. It also uttered weak high-pitched sounds while sniffing around.

Small prey is bitten and immediately swallowed whole. Large prey is bitten into pieces while held down with the front paws and swallowed in fairly large pieces after a brief mastication. The poor mastication is evident from examination of the stomach contents; small prey can be found whole, and the parts of larger prey are easily recognizable. The manner in which earthworms are consumed is rather stereotyped (pers. obs.). When first encountered, the worm is examined with the nose for a longer or shorter period. The mole then takes one end (both front and hind end are used) and begins to devour the worm. The front paws are brought underneath the mouth with the palms turned slightly out and forward, while the worm is held between the claws of the index and middle fingers. The mole then pulls the worm through its claws, chews off a piece, and swallows it. The process of short jerky pulls, chewing, and swallowing is repeated in quick succession until the whole worm is consumed. By pulling the worm through its claws the mole strips off the earth and slime from the outside and squeezes out the gut contents. The brownish-black scats, which are cylindrical in shape and approximately 15 cm long and 0.5 cm wide, are deposited outside the tunnels in small piles [1].

The hairy-tailed mole is a solitary creature for most of the year, except during the breeding season when males leave their tunnel systems to look for females [1]. In late summer and early autumn, adult males and females, as well as young, may be taken from the same surface tunnel and it appears therefore that they mix freely at this time. Intraspecific fighting, at least fighting serious enough to leave wounds or scars, is rare.

The hairy-tailed mole mates in late March and early April. The testes and accessory glands are greatly enlarged during this time. The testes measure 12×7 mm in March against the 3×2 mm during the resting phase. After the breeding season, the testes diminish in size, with a sharp decrease occurring in mid-May. They reach their minimum size in late summer. In the female, the vaginal orifice, which is covered by skin outside the reproductive season, opens up. By September, the surface skin will again completely close off the vaginal orifice. After copulation, the vagina is closed by a copulatory plug. The length of the gestation period that follows is not precisely known, but lies probably between 4 and 6 weeks. Only one litter is produced per year, averaging 4 young. The young are toothless and hairless when born, except for the short vibrissae and tactile hairs on the upper and lower lips and face. The eyes, covered by skin, show up as black spots 0.5 mm in diameter. The forelimb is shaped like that of the adult, but the claws are short and soft. The young probably remain in the nest for a period of about a month after birth [1].

The permanent dentition is completely erupted in June, and the young animals begin to take solid food. The young mature sexually at about 10 months of age and reach adult size and weight probably shortly before that time [1].

Reproduction and Ontogeny

References

[1] Eadie, W.R., 1939, [2] 1945, [3] 1947
[4] Fay, F.H., 1954
[5] Foote, L.E., 1941
[6] Hallett, J.C., 1978
[7] Hamilton, W.J., Jr., 1939, [8] 1941
[9] Hamilton, W.J., Jr., M.W. Hosley, and A.E. MacGregor, 1937
[10] Jameson, E.W., Jr., 1949

Genus *Scapanus* Pomel, 1848
(f. Gk *skapanē* a digging tool)

Stocky, robust moles with short, round, thick, fleshy, thinly haired tails. Nose thin and long, but less so than that of *Scalopus*; tip naked, nostrils crescent-shaped and superior; eyes minute, hidden in the fur; feet similar to those of *Scalopus*, but hind foot with one to three distinct plantar tubercles and no webs between the toes of fore- and hind feet; claws of the forefeet broad and flat. Fur dark, velvet-like with sheen; 8 mammae (4 pectoral, 2 abdominal, 2 inguinal).

Skull generally similar to that of *Scalopus*, frontal sinus somewhat swollen, auditory bullae complete, flattened external pterygoid region, basioccipital and basisphenoid inflated and cancellous. Mandible relatively heavy with well-developed angular process. Dental formula i 3/3, c 1/1, p 4/4, m 3/3, total of 44 teeth; I1 large, anterior convex, posterior flat as in *Scalopus*, I 2, 3 and C1 simple conical structures, P 1, 2, 3 similar to I 2, 3, P4 much larger with lingual cusp-like expansion, upper molars with W-shaped cusp pattern and lingual V-shaped shelf; i 2, c1. and p1, 2, 3 small and conical and lower molars with M-shaped cusp patterns.

The karyotype of one species in this genus (*S. latimanus*) has been determined (2N = 34, FN = 64). The genus *Scapanus* is confined to the Pacific rim of North America from southern California to southern British Columbia. There are three Recent species, two of which occur in Canada. Biochemical evidence suggests that *Scapanus'* nearest living relative in North America is *Parascalops* [1].

References

[1] Yates, T.L., and I.F. Greenbaum, 1982

Scapanus townsendii (Bachman)
(Named after collector J.K. Townsend)

Townsend Mole   **Taupe de Townsend**

1839 *Scalops townsendii* Bachman, J. Acad. Nat. Sci. Phila. 8(1):58
1848 *Scapanus tow(n)sendii* Pomel, Arch. Sc. Phys. Nat. Genève,
       sér. 4, vol. 9, p. 247
1885 *Scapanus townsendii* True, Proc. U.S. Nat. Mus. 7:607
Type locality: Vicinity of Vancouver, Clarke County, Washington

External Measurements and Weight

	TL	T	HF	W*	
N	6	6	6	3 ♂ ♂	6 ♀ ♀
X̄	203.3	36.2	26.7	147	117
SD	19.29	3.24	1.50		
CV	9.48	8.96	5.62		
OR	179–237	33–41	25–29		

*from Dalquest 1948

Cranial Measurements

	SL	CB	IOW
N	5	5	5
X̄	40.8	19.8	7.8
SD	1.03	0.39	0.11
CV	2.53	1.98	1.39
OR	39.9–42.2	19.3–20.2	7.7–7.9

Description (Colour Plate IV)

Description as under genus. In winter, this mole is almost black in
colour; in summer somewhat lighter. The tail and tip of the nose are
nearly hairless and pink in colour. Front feet nearly hairless and
whitish. Townsend mole can be distinguished from the very similar
coast mole (*S. orarius*) by its larger size (TL usually exceeds 175 mm,
HF > 24, skull > 37 mm). Young *S. townsendii* can be distinguished
by their relatively broader feet and heavier claws.

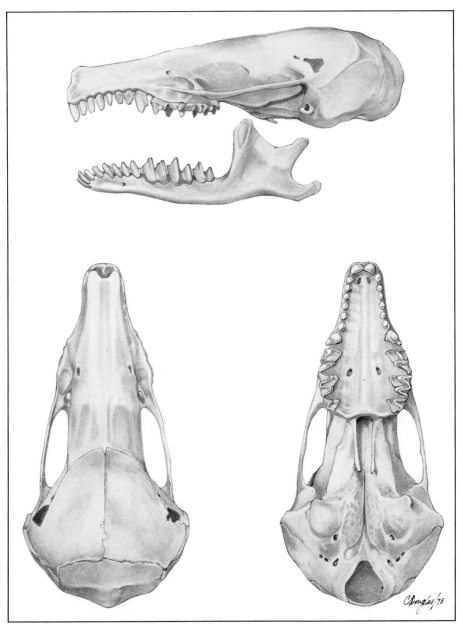

Figure 33.   Skull of *Scapanus townsendii*

Distribution

Townsend mole has an extremely limited distribution in Canada, occurring only in a small area of about 13 km² north of the international boundary near Huntingdon, British Columbia. The species' geographic range includes western Washington and Oregon and a thin strip in extreme northwestern California.

Systematics

S. townsendii has two subspecies. Only one, *S. t. townsendii*, is found in Canada.

Biology

Townsend mole prefers the deep loose soil of cultivated fields, and the open brushlands of the valley bottoms. When the gravel content of the soil is high, numbers of this mole are low.

Habitat

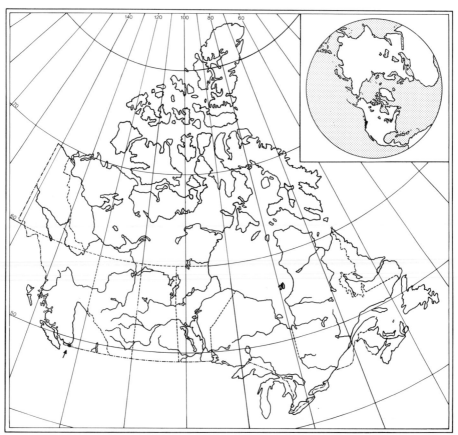

Map 21.   Distribution of *Scapanus townsendii*

As with other highly specialized fossorial moles, the tunnel system of Townsend mole consists of shallow surface tunnels and deep tunnels. The earth produced in digging the deep tunnels is thrust up to form numerous conspicuous molehills, which are larger than those of any other native mole [3]. The large amount of earth removed in constructing the nest cavity is deposited in a single large mound, with dimensions exceeding those of normal mounts (76 to 127 cm in diameter and 30 to 46 cm high), or as a cluster of normal-sized mounds in an area with a diameter of 1.8 to 3.0 m. The nest chamber has generally a somewhat spherical shape with a diameter of 23 cm and a height of 15 cm. A varying number of tunnels radiates laterally from the nest chamber, giving access to different parts of the tunnel system. Many nest cavities possess a so-called bolt hole, a tunnel that leads straight down and then turns upwards to join one of the upper-level burrows. The nest within the nest chamber consists of a two-layered ball of plant material, usually grass, although other plant material such as moss or leaves may be used also if available. The inner core, which makes up about 25 per cent of the total, consists of fine dry grass. The outer layer, which is about 10 cm thick, is composed of coarse green grass. Fresh green grass is added to the outside at intervals when the young are in the nest. The heat generated by the fermentation of this moist grass probably functions to prevent chilling of the young while the mother is away.

It feeds predominantly on earthworms, followed by insect larvae and pupae [4, 6]. Centipedes, slugs, and mature insects are consumed in smaller amounts. Some vegetable matter is also ingested.

Food

Population density in the most heavily populated pastures may be as high as 12 moles per hectare [3]. The home range of an individual mole of this species is relatively small. In one study, the mean of the greatest distance between points of capture for 14 moles, captured three or more times, was 40.5 m [2]. Once established in a tunnel system, the animal rarely makes long movements to new habitat.

Population

Little is known of the activity pattern and behaviour of this mole. Some authors believe this mole to be predominantly nocturnal [1], but quantitative observations are lacking.

Behaviour

Townsend mole breeds in February [5]. A single litter is produced in late March. The number of young in a litter varies from 1 to 4 with a mean of 2.87 [3]. Litters of 3 and 2 young respectively occur most frequently. The newly born young are hairless and weigh around 5 g. They mature rapidly and within 30 days they are fully furred and weigh 60 to 80 g. At or shortly after this stage, the young leave the nest. Dispersal of the young from the maternal tunnel system occurs mainly in May and June [2]. Observations on 44 young gave a range of dispersal distances of 13 to 85.6 m in 4 to 6 months. Judging from the occurrence of the remains of juveniles in owl pellets during this time, some of the dispersal takes place above ground at night. The animals are extremely reluctant to leave their burrows during daylight. The young animals are probably capable of reproducing themselves in the breeding season following their births.

Reproduction and Ontogeny

References

[1] Cowan, I. McT., and C.J. Guiguet, 1965
[2] Giger, R.D., 1973
[3] Kuhn, L.W., W.Q. Wick, and R.J. Pedersen, 1966
[4] Moore, A.W., 1933, [5] 1939
[6] Wight, H.M., 1928

Scapanus orarius True
(f. L *orarius* belonging to the coast)

Coast Mole	**Taupe du Pacifique**
(Pacific Coast Mole)	

1896 *Scapanus orarius* True, Proc. U.S. Nat. Mus. 19:52
Type locality: Shoalwater Bay, Pacific County, Washington

External Measurements and Weight

	TL	T	HF	W*	
				74 ♂ ♂	30 ♀ ♀
N	25	25	25		
X̄	162.5	33.0	21.68	74.3	69.8
SD	5.30	2.39	1.19	—	—
CV	3.26	7.24	5.48	—	—
OR	154–173	28–37	20–24	64–91	61–79

*From Glendenning 1959

Cranial Measurements

	SL	DB	IOW
N	23	22	23
X̄	34.3	16.4	7.7
SD	0.74	0.33	0.18
CV	21.4	2.00	2.28
OR	32.4–35.3	15.7–16.8	7.3–8.0

Description (Colour Plate IV)

The coast mole is almost identical to *S. townsendii*, but differs from it in being noticeably smaller.

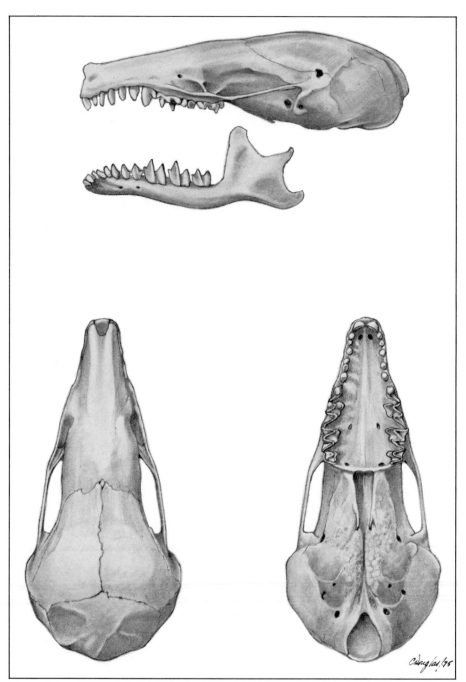

Figure 34.   Skull of *Scapanus orarius*

Distribution

The coast mole has a more-extensive distribution in Canada than its larger relative. It is found in the drainage basin of the lower Fraser River from Vancouver east at least up to Boston Bar. The species has not been found on the north shore of Burrard Inlet, and east of Vancouver it occurs along the north shore of the Fraser to Agassiz. Peripheral localities: *British Columbia:* (**1**) Vancouver; (**2**) Hope.

In the United States, the range extends south to California on the coastal slopes and inland as far east as western Idaho.

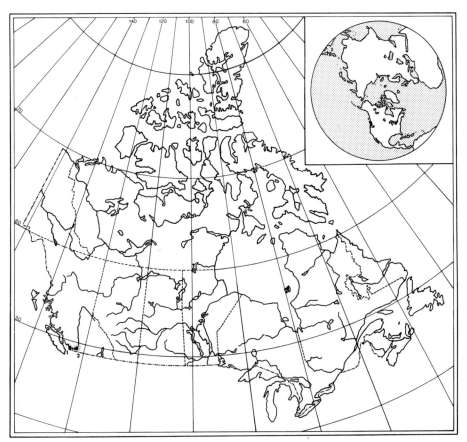

Map 22. Distribution of *Scapanus orarius*

Systematics

Two subspecies are recognized, of which only one, *S. o. orarius*, occurs in Canada.

Biology

The coast mole is most abundant in cultivated soil and pastures and occurs in lower densities in dry sandy ridges and wooded hillsides [2, 4].

Habitat

It lives in a wider range of habitats and a greater variety of soil types, including those with a high-gravel content, than *S. townsendii*. The coast mole prefers better-drained soils than its larger relative and is absent from land subject to flooding. It also occurs in dense deciduous woods, brush, and even in coniferous forest, although it is absent in highly acidic soils. The coast mole is also found at higher altitudes, up to 300 m, than the Townsend mole. The two species appear, therefore, to have decidedly different habitat preferences.

The mounds of the coast mole are smaller than those of the Townsend mole, being about 30 cm in diameter and 15 cm high and are more widely spaced. An average hill contains some 1000 cm³ of earth excavated from nearly 2 m of tunnel. The tunnels have a diameter of approximately 5 cm and tend to lie deeper than those of *S. townsendii*, ranging in depth from 8 to 90 cm below the surface. There are fewer surface ridges than in the tunnel system of the Townsend mole. At regular intervals, the tunnels have chambers (10 cm long by 8 cm wide), the function of which is unknown. In woodlands, or areas with loose soil, molehills are infrequent because the mole simply compacts the loose soil. Between October and March, when most of the deep tunnels are dug, one mole may push up 200 to 400 hills, resulting in the excavation of between 400 and 500 m of tunnel [4].

Breeding nests are about 15 cm below the surface and are not marked by an extra-large mound of earth, as is the case in some species of mole. The nest cavity is approximately 20 cm across, is lined with coarse grass, and has several entrances [4].

The kinds and relative proportions of food eaten by the coast mole are similar to those of the Townsend mole [4, 5, 6]. Earthworms constitute the bulk of the food consumed (more than 90 per cent), followed by slugs, insect larvae, and adult insects. Small quantities of plant material (bulbs, grain, peas, potatoes) have also been reported from some areas. Captive moles of this species consumed nearly twice their own weight in earthworms every day. It has been estimated that one adult mole can consume approximately 55,000 earthworms in a year. This mole may obtain sufficient moisture from its prey under normal conditions, but deep tunnels, one reported to penetrate more than 2 m down, suggest that subsoil water is used also [3].

Food

Ectoparasites reported for this species include mites and fleas, (*Corypsylla ornata* Fox and *Epitedia scapani* (Wagner)) [6, 7]. Unidentified cestodes have been reported from the duodenum.

Parasites

It is not known to what extent populations of this species are controlled by natural predation, but it is probably small. Man's

Predators

agricultural activity has probably had a positive effect on the distribution and abundance of this species in British Columbia because of the increase in soil fertility, which led to an increase in the numbers of earthworms. In settled areas, this mole may become a pest because of its hills and its tunnelling activity, which damages seedlings and provides access to roots, bulbs, and corms so that voles (*Microtus*) may enter and damage these. Control can be achieved by trapping and use of repellents.

Population densities vary greatly ranging from 1 mole per 0.10 ha to 1 mole per 14 ha. Four groups can be recognized in the population: young of the year (40 to 60 g); one-year-old adults (65 to 70 g), two-year-old adults (71 to 75 g); aged adults (> 75 g). Populations appear to be fairly stable, the proportion of animals less than one-year-old (55 per cent) and adults over one-year-old (45 per cent) was constant during a ten-year period according to one study. The maximum longevity is probably four to five years [4]. Population

The coast mole is believed to be active throughout the day and night like most other moles. The presence of its skull in owl pellets testifies to the fact that this species occasionally moves on the surface at night. Observations on the activity, behaviour, the population structure, and dynamics of this species are few or lacking. Behaviour

Males with enlarged testes have been found from late January onwards and breeding takes place from January to early March. The young are born in late March and early April. Yearling females usually have 2, two-year-olds 3, and older females 4 young [4]. Reproduction and Ontogeny

References

[1] Cowan, I. McT., and C.J. Guiguet, 1965
[2] Dalquest, W.W., 1948
[3] Glendenning, R., 1953, [4] 1959
[5] Moore, A.W., 1933
[6] Whitaker, J.O., Jr., C. Maser, and R.J. Pedersen, 1979
[7] Yates, T.L., D.B. Pence, and G.K. Launchbaugh, 1979

Genus *Condylura* Illiger, 1811
(f. Gk *kondulos* condyle, the knob of a joint + Gk *oura* tail)

A mole with a relatively long tail, as long as the body without the head, and a naked disk with 22 tentacle-like processes surrounding the round nostrils, which are situated on the anterior surface of the nasal disk. The annulated scaled tail is sparsely haired, thick and fleshy, constricted at its base, and tapering gradually toward the tip. In winter, the tail becomes greatly enlarged. The eyes are small, but relatively larger than those of our other moles. The auricular orifice is relatively large. The legs are short; the feet large, scaled and thinly furred on top, and naked below. The hand is as broad as long, with long broad and flattened claws (narrower than those of *Scalopus*, *Scapanus*, or *Parascalops*). The first, second, third, and fourth digits have three, flattened, triangular processes on the distal palmar edge. The hind feet are long and narrow, broadening distally. There is a large, flattened, triangular, plantar tubercle near the base of the first digit and five smaller tubercles on the sole. The claws are slender and laterally compressed. There are 8 mammae (4 pectoral, 2 abdominal and 2 inguinal). The nearly black fur, which is somewhat lighter ventrally, is dense, long and soft, but not velvet-like as in the more-fossorial moles because some of the guard hairs are distinctly longer than the underfur.

The skull is high compared to that of other moles, and has a long narrow rostrum and thin zygomatic arches. The auditory bullae are incomplete and the pyterygoid is not much inflated. The mandible is slender with a thin angular process. The dental formula is i 3/3, c 1/1, p 4/4, m 3/3, with a total of 44 teeth. The milk dentition, except the first upper and lower premolar, is resorbed some time after birth without erupting.

I1 large, spatulate and projecting anteriad and visible when the skull is viewed dorsally. I2 is minute and I3 is large and canine-like; C1 conical and small; P1, 2 and 3, small, triangular, and laterally compressed; P4 much larger and possessing a lingual cusp. The cusps of the upper molars form a W pattern and have an indistinctly tricuspidate inner margin. In the lower jaw, i1 is flat and projects forward, i2 and i3 are similar but smaller, c1 long and curved with a posterior basal accessory cusp. The lower premolars are small and laterally compressed and each has a small anterior cusp and a posterior cusp-like talon. The cusps of the lower molars have an M-shaped pattern. The living species has a karyotype of 2N = 34 and FN = 64 [2].

The genus contains a single living species from the Recent and Pleistocene of eastern North America. Two fossil species, *C. kowalskii* and *C. izabellae*, have been described from the Middle and Late Pliocene of Poland [1].

Reference

[1] Skoczen, S., 1976
[2] Yates, T.L., and D.L. Schmidly, 1975

Condylura cristata (Linnaeus)
(f. L *cristatus* crested)

Star-nosed Mole   **Condylure à nez étoilé**

1758 *(Sorex) cristatus* Linnaeus, Syst. Nat., 10th ed., vol. 1, p. 53
1819 *Condylura cristata* Desmarest, J. Physique, de Chimie, d'Hist.
     Nat. et des Arts 89:232
Type locality: Eastern Pennsylvania

External Measurements and Weight

	TL	T	HF	W
N	73	73	74	13
X̄	190.9	76.8	27.7	48.3
SD	13.56	6.57	2.61	6.78
CV	7.10	8.55	9.41	14.04
OR	162–238	64–92	15–32	31.5–55.2

Cranial Measurements

	SL	CB	IOW
N	33	34	36
X̄	33.6	13.4	6.1
SD	0.78	0.31	0.21
CV	2.34	2.29	3.44
OR	31.8–35.1	12.8–14.1	5.5–6.6

Description (Colour Plate IV)

See the description of the genus. Because of its obvious and unique
characters, the star-nosed mole cannot be confused with any other
mole.

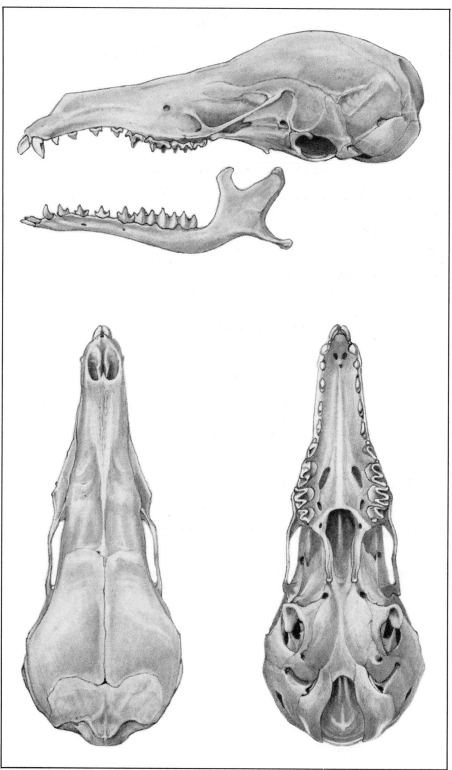

Figure 35.   Skull of *Condylura cristata*

Distribution

The star-nosed mole has the most-extensive distribution of any of the Canadian moles and occurs farther north. It is distributed throughout the mainland of eastern Canada from the Atlantic region, including Cape Breton Island, in the east to Manitoba in the west. Peripheral localities: *Manitoba;* (**1**) Island Lake; (**2**) Mukutawa River; (**3**) Riding Mountain; (**4**) Winnipeg; (**5**) 4 km north of Piney. *New Brunswick:* (**6**) Bathurst; (**7**) Albert. *Newfoundland (Labrador);* (**8**) Hamilton Inlet; (**9**) south end of Wightman Lake. *Nova Scotia:* (**10**) Margaree Valley; (**11**) Canaan. *Ontario:* (**12**) Big Trout Lake; (**13**) Fort Albany; (**14**) Port Stanley; (**15**) St. Joseph Island. *Quebec:* (**16**) Papp's Cove, Lake Guillaume-Dèlisle (formerly Richmond Gulf); (**17**) Moisie Bay; (**18**) Trois-Pistoles.

In the United States this mole is found in the northeastern states, in the mountains south to South Carolina and from the Great Lakes states west to North Dakota. An isolated population occurs in Georgia.

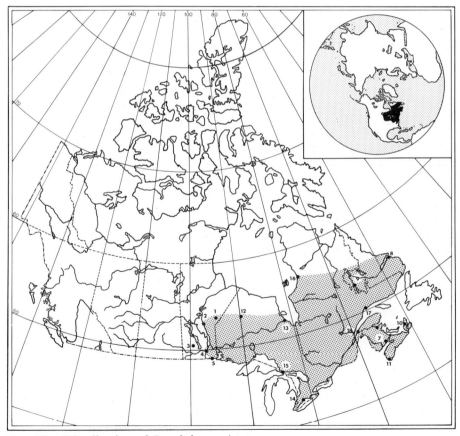

Map 23.   Distribution of *Condylura cristata.*

179

Systematics

Aside from a gradual decrease in size from north to south, the star-nosed mole exhibits little geographic variation and only two subspecies are currently recognized.

C. c. cristata (Linnaeus) 1758, Syst. Nat., 10th ed., vol. 1, p. 53 (*nigra* Smith is a synonym).
For measurements see those of the species. The typical form is the more-widespread subspecies. Distribution: Eastern Canada.

C.c. parva Paradiso, 1959, Proc. Biol. Soc. Wash. 72:103.
TL 158–170 (N = 8); T 56–63 (N = 10); HF 24–26 (N = 10);
SL 30.8–32.4.
Distribution: According to Petersen and Yates [5], this smaller form occurs in southern Ontario, southeastern Manitoba, and adjacent parts of Ontario.

Biology

This mole prefers wet places with soils ranging from clay loam to sand or muck [4, 6]. The species is most abundant along small streams, but is also found in wet fields and sometimes in well-drained sites. The tunnels made by this mole usually are approximately 4 cm wide and are found from 3 to 60 cm below the surface [6, 7]. When digging immediately below the surface, the star-nosed mole pushes up shallow ridges. Excess earth from deeper tunnels is pushed out, forming molehills that may be quite large. Surface runways are also used by this species, and in some areas, this mole produces little conspicuous evidence, in the form of molehills and ridges, to betray its presence. Nearly all burrow systems have branches opening at or below the water level of adjacent streams or ponds. In swampy ground, tunnels may be below the water-table [4]. The nest chamber, which is about 13 cm wide and 10 cm high [6, 7], is situated in a dry place. The nest contained in it is composed of dry leaves or grass, whatever is most readily available. Breeding nests are larger than resting nests. *[margin: Habitat]*

Available information indicates that star-nosed moles living near open water do most of their hunting along the bottoms of streams and other small water bodies [4]. In the winter they may be entirely dependent on benthic prey. In one study aquatic invertebrates predominated in the diet [4], with aquatic annelids (aquatic oligochaetes, leeches) and aquatic insects (caddis fly larvae, midge larvae, dytiscid larvae, Plecoptera, etc.) being most important. Crustacea and molluscs seem to be eaten less frequently. Small fish are eaten occasionally. Terrestrial insects (white grubs) and terrestrial annelids, on the other hand, were less important in the diet of this mole and only account for a small fraction of the total bulk of the food consumed (12 per cent in one study), except in areas where no open water is available [6, 7]. Known predators of the star-nosed mole include hawks (*Buteo jamaicensis*), owls (*Bubo virginianus*, *Otus asio*, and *Tyto alba*), and skunks [4, 5]. It is also frequently caught by domestic cats. *Condylura* is infected by a number of ecto- and endoparasites [4, 11]. The former include mites (*Androlaelaps* sp.) and fleas *[margin: Food]* *[margin: Predators]* *[margin: Parasites]*

(*Ctenophthalmus* sp. and less frequently *Ceratophyllus*), the latter include unidentified cestodes and intestinal and subcutaneous nematodes.

Population

Nearly nothing is known of the population structure and dynamics of this species. Because of its choice of habitat, the distribution of this mole in any particular area tends to be patchy. Even along streams the abundance of this species appears to be concentrated at irregular intervals. This clumped distributional pattern makes it difficult to express population densities in terms of numbers per unit area. Densities of 25 and 41 animals per hectare have been reported from two areas of swamp land [4].

Behaviour

Condylura is active throughout the day and night and [4], as in other moles investigated, the total time spent sleeping is about 43 per cent [1]. The fact that this mole tends to concentrate in relatively small areas, where it shares tunnels and runways with its conspecifics, suggests that it is quite social. The star-nosed mole is less fossorial than other native moles except *Neurotrichus*. Like the latter, *Condylura* has large hind feet and a long tail, which enable it to assume a position in which the anterior part of the body is raised off the ground. The highly specialized fossorial moles are incapable of doing this. The palms of the hand are turned out and are not placed flat on the ground when the animal walks or rests. During digging, the forepaws are pressed close to the snout, which is drawn back with the tentacles brought together to protect this sensitive organ. The animal braces itself by extending its hind feet at right angles to the body and laterally against the walls of the tunnel. The front paws then make rapid alternate, or sometimes synchronous, strokes sideways and backwards. The star-nosed mole swims and dives well [3, 4, 7]. It has been observed, and also caught, swimming under the ice. In swimming, as in walking, the diagonally opposed front and hind limb are moved at the same time. The forelimbs strike alternately in rapid succession, while the hind feet are kicked back one after the other [4]. The tail is not used in propelling the animal through the water, although it wiggles somewhat from side to side. Hunting is done on or near the bottom, where the mole roots around in the bottom sediment. It finds its prey with the aid of the tactile organs in the nasal tentacles [9]. The tentacles are reported to move when the animal is searching, except for the two median tentacles, which point forward. The nasal organ is well adapted for rooting in soft bottom deposits, but poorly adapted for probing in soil, for which the pointed noses of the highly fossorial moles are much better. When the mole is feeding, the tentacles are drawn together. Small prey, such as chironomid larvae, are ingested whole with quantities of organic and mineral matter. Larger prey may also be swallowed whole. Leeches as long as 5 cm have been found, although usually bitten into several pieces [4]. The front feet are used in holding large prey. Grooming consists entirely of scratching and combing which are elicited by the activity of ectoparasites or by wet fur after swimming. In the latter situation the mole presumably fluffs the fur and speeds up drying. This mole is said to deposit its faeces in a special place. The star-nosed mole does not vocalize to any great extent. It is reported to squeak once in a while when picked up and young ones will emit shrill cries when touched [10]. Wheezing noises coinciding with each inhalation have been reported from a sleeping mole. The sense of touch appears to be the most highly developed of the senses. It is concentrated in the nose and in areas marked by tactile hairs on the feet and head. The specialized nasal organ, the large size of the maxillary ramus of the trigeminal nerve, and the large diameter of the infraorbital canal through which it runs, indicate that the sense of touch is better developed in this species than in our other moles. In underwater hunting, the animal probably depends solely on this sense in finding its prey. Hearing is apparently well developed, but its role in the animal's life is not understood. The internal ear is less specialized than in the highly specialized fossorial genera. Observations indicate that the sense of smell is only moderately developed, which is supported by the relatively small size and slight swelling of the turbinals in this species. The secretion of scent suggests that the sense of smell plays a role in the social behavior of this mole. Vision plays only a very subordinate role, if any. The eye, although reduced, is complete in all its functional parts. When the mole is on the surface, it is capable of parting the hair around the eye so as to expose it. The eye may function better in this species, as it spends more time above ground, but it seems unlikely that the animal can distinguish much more than variations in light intensities [4].

Breeding occurs mainly in March and April [2]. Males reach breeding condition in mid-February and mature sperm is present by late February (central New York State). The sex organs return to a non-breeding state in late May or early June, but some animals remain in breeding condition until mid-June. Embryos are found from mid-March to July (Ontario), but most pregnant females are taken in April (New York). The 2 to 7 young (an average of 5) are born from late March to early August. Gestation and lactation period are not exactly known. The newborn young are hairless, except for 6 mystacial vibrissae, and are pale pink in colour. They are about 49 mm long and weigh about 1.5 g. The eyes are closed but visible as dark swelling. The external auditory orifice is closed. The nasal processes are present, but are not free and are pressed against the snout and lips. The young grow rapidly and by the time they weigh between 15 and 20 g they are covered with fine black hair. At 31 to 33 g they are fully furred and able to move around. At or shortly after this time they are weaned and able to exist on their own. By late summer the young moles are approximately the same size and weight as the adults, but they can be identified by their unworn dentition. Both sexes are capable of reproduction in the spring following their birth.

Reproduction and Ontogeny

References

[1] Allison, T., and H. Van Twyver, 1970

[2] Eadie, W.R., and W.J. Hamilton Jr., 1956

[3] Fisher, A.K., 1885

[4] Hamilton, W.J., Jr., 1931

[5] Petersen, K.E., and T.L. Yates, 1980

[6] Rust, C.C., 1966

[7] Schmidt, F.J.W., 1931

[8] Simpson, S.E., 1923

[9] Van Vleck, D.B., 1965

[10] Wiegert, R.G., 1961

[11] Yates, T.L., D.B. Pence, and G.K. Launchbaugh, 1979

GLOSSARY

Abdominal
(L *abdomen* belly)
Pertaining to structures, organs, or parts of organs situated in, on, or in vicinity of the abdomen.

Acrocentric
(Gk *akros* tip; *kentron* centre)
Rod-shaped chromosome with centromere at one end.

Agonistic
(Gk *agōnistikos* f. *agōnistēs* combatant)
Agonistic behaviour is a general term for the different forms of aggressive behaviour found in animals.

Alisphenoid
(L *ala* wing; Gk *sphen* wedge; *eidos* form)
Wing-like portion of sphenoid forming part of cranium.

Allopatric
(Gk *allos* other; *patra* native land)
Having separate and mutually exclusive areas of geographical distribution.

Alveolus
(L small pit)
Tooth socket.

Ambient temperature
(L *ambire* to go around)
Temperature of the surrounding.

Amnion
(Gk *amnion* foetal membrane)
A foetal membrane.

Angular process
(L *angulus* corner)
A membrane bone of the lower jaw projecting back and down or inwards at the posterior ventral portion of the mandible.

Anteriad
(L *anterior* former)
Nearer head end.

Autosome
(Gk *autos* self; *sōma* body)
Chromosome that is not a sex chromosome.

Beringia
Unglaciated area in Alaska, the Yukon and District of Mackenzie during the Illinoian and Wisconsin glaciation. Separated from the rest of North America by the Laurentide and Cordilleran ice sheet and connected with northeast Asia by the Bering Land Bridge.

Bicornate
(L *bis* twice; *cornu* horn)
With two horn-like processes.

Boreal Forest
Continuous belt of primary coniferous forest stretching from Newfoundland and Labrador to the Rocky Mountains and Alaska.

Bulla (auditory)
(L *bulla* bubble)
Rounded, inflated bone encasing the inner ear.

Canine (caniniform)
(L *caninus* pertaining to dog)
Dog- or eye-tooth.
Carnivorous
(L *caro* flesh; *vorare* to devour)
Flesh-eating.
Carpal
(L *carpus* wrist)
A wrist bone; pertaining to the wrist.
Cataplectic (cataplexy)
(Gk *kataplēxis* stupefaction)
Temporary paralysis or hypnotic state in animals when shamming death.
Cenozoic
(Gk *kainos* recent; *zōē* life)
Geological era from Mesozoic to Recent; age of mammals, i.e. from Eocene to Holocene epoch.
Cerebellum
(L *cerebrum* brain)
Outgrowth of anterior end of dorsal surface of hind brain of vertebrates, concerned in coordination of complex muscular movements.
Cerebral hemisphere
Paired outgrowth of front end of fore brain of vertebrates.
Chorion, n.; chorionic, adj.
(Gk *khorion* skin)
An embryonic membrane external to, and enclosing the amnion.
Cingulum
(L *cingulum* girdle)
Ridge around the base of the crown of the tooth.
Circadian
(L *circum* around; *dies* day)
Pertaining to the 24-hour period of night and day.
Class
(L *classis* division)
A taxonomic category, a division of a phylum; divided into orders.
Clavicle
(L. *clavicula* small key)
Collar bone.
Coleoptera
(Gk *koleos* sheath; *pteron* wing)
Beetles, an order of the class Insecta.
Conspecific
(L *conspecies* of the same particular kind)
Belonging to the same species.
Coronoid process
(Gk *korōnis* crook-beaked; *eidos* form)
Dorsal projection of the posterior part of the mandible.

Corpus callosum
(L *corpus* body; *callosus* hard)
The broad transverse band of white fibres connecting the cerebral hemispheres.
Cranial breadth
The greatest distance across the braincase.
Cretaceous
(L *creta* chalk)
The last period of the Mesozoic era, lasting approximately from 135 to 70 million years ago.
Cursorial
(L *currere* to run)
Having limbs adapted for running.
Cutaneous
(L *cutis* skin)
Pertaining to skin.

Data (plural), datum (sing.)
(L *dare* to give)
Things known or given, facts.
Diffuse (placenta)
A non-deciduate (i.e. there is no loss of the lining of the uterus at birth) placenta in which the villi (i.e. processes through which nourishment passes to the embryo) are scattered on the embryonic side of the placenta.
Dilambdodont
(Gk *dis*, twice; Λ, lambda; *odous* tooth)
Applied to molar teeth with W-shaped transverse ridges.
Diphyodont
(Gk *diphues* twofold; *odous* tooth)
Having deciduous (milk) and permanent sets of teeth.
Diploid
(Gk *diplous* double; *eidos* form)
Having a double set of chromosomes, the typical number of chromosomes of a species.
Diptera
(Gk *dis* twice; *pteron* wing)
Flies. Order of insects having one pair of wings.
Discoidal (placenta)
A deciduate (i.e. the uterine epithelium is destroyed by the embryonic side of the placenta) placenta with a close relationship between maternal and embryonic circulations usually of discoidal shape.
Distal
(L *distare* to stand apart)
Farthest from the midline of the animal, or farthest from the point of attachment.
Dorsad
(L *dorsum* back; *ad* to)
Towards the back.

Dorsoventral
(L *dorsum* back; *venter* belly)
Pertaining to space or structures between the dorsal and ventral surface.

Echolocation
(L fr. Gk *ekho* echo; L *locare* to place)
Location of objects by means of echos usually of supersonic sounds.
Ecotone
(Gk *oikos* household; *tonos* brace)
A transition between two communities.
Elaterid
(Gk *elater* driver)
Belonging to the family Elateridae, click beetles.
Endotheliochorial
(Combination of endothelium, the inner lining of blood vessels, and chorion)
The type of implantation in which the embryonic tissue erodes the epithelium of the uterine wall, bringing the embryonic epithelium in contact with the endothelium of maternal blood vessels.
Epitheliochorial
(Combination of epithelium and chorion)
Type of implantation in which the embryonic tissue is in intimate contact with the epithelium of the uterus but does not erode it.
Eutheria
(Gk *eu* well; *thēr* wild beast)
Placental mammals.
External temporal fossa
Shallow depression on the outside of the coronoid process.

Fecundity
(L *fecunditas* fruitfulness)
Capacity of a species to multiply rapidly.
Fenestra
(L *fenestra* window)
An opening in a bone or between two bones.
Fibula
(L *fibula* buckle)
Splint bone on the outer side of the leg.
Foramen ovale
(L *foramen* opening; *ovum* egg)
Openings in the alisphenoid bone on each side of the skull through which branches of the trigeminal nerve pass.
Fossorial
(L *fossor* digger)
Adapted for digging.

Genal (vibrissa)
(L *gena* cheek)
Pertaining to the cheek.

Glenoid fossa
(Gk *glēnē* socket; *eidos* form; L *fossa* ditch)
Depression on the squamosal bone for articulation of the mandible.

Haemochorial
(Gk *haima* blood; *khorion* skin)
Type of implantation in which epithelium, connective tissue and endothelium of the maternal blood vessels in the uterine wall are eroded by embryonic tissue that is in direct contact with the maternal blood.

Hallux
(L *hallux* great toe)
First digit of the hind limb.

Hepialid
Belonging to the family Hepialidae. Ghost moths. Their larvae bore in the roots of various trees.

Heterodont
(Gk *heteros* other; *odous* tooth)
Having teeth differentiated for different functions.

Hindfoot length
Length from the heel to the tip of the claw on the longest toe.

Holarctic
(Gk *holos* whole; *arktos* bear)
Zoogeographical region including the northern part of the Old and New World.

Home range
Area over which an adult animal normally travels to perform the functions of life.

Homologous
(Gk *homologos* agreeing)
Pertaining to resemblance of structures inherited from a common ancestor.

Incisor
(L *incisus* cut into)
Teeth in the premaxillae and their opposites in the mandible.

Infraclass
Taxonomic category between subclass and cohort.

Infraorbital canal
Canal leading from orbit through the maxilla to the side of the rostrum, through which blood vessels and nerves pass.

Inguinal
(L *inguen* groin)
In the region of the groin.

Insectivorous
(L *insectum* cut into; *vorare* to devour)
Insect-eating.

Interorbital width
The least width between the orbits.

Isotherm
(Gk *isos* equal; *thermē* heat)
Line connecting points of same mean temperatures.

Kansan Glacial stage
Major division of the Pleistocene time in North America. The second
of four major glaciations occurred during this stage.
Karyotype
(Gk *karuon* nucleus; *tupos* pattern)
Chromosome complement (size, shape, and number) of a somatic
cell.
Keratinous
(Gk *keras* horn)
Horny.

Labial
(L *labium* lip)
Nearest the lip.
Lacrimal foramen
(L *lacrima* tear)
Opening of the tear duct that pierces the lacrimal bone and passes
into the nasal cavity.
Lateral gland
Skin gland on the flank.
Lepidopterous
(Gk *lepis* scale; *pteron* wing)
Pertaining to insects of the order Lepidoptera, butterflies, and moths.
Lingual
(L *lingua* tongue)
Nearest the tongue.
Longevity
(L *longus* long; *aevum* age)
Life span.

Mamma
(L *mamma* breast)
Milk-secreting organ.
Mammalia
Class of animals having mammae for nourishing their young.
Marsupial
(L *marsupium* pouch)
A mammal belonging to the infraclass metatheria, among others,
characterized by the young being born in a very undeveloped state
and usually continuing its development in a pouch.
Mastication
(L *masticare* to chew)
Process of chewing food.
Maxillary width
The greatest width between the maxillary processes.
Mean
Arithmetic mean, the sum of a particular variate of each animal in
a sample divided by the number of animals in the sample.
Medial
(L *medium* middle)
In the middle.

Mental
(L *mentum* chin)
Pertaining to the chin.
Mesostyle
(Gk *mesos* middle; *stulos* pillar)
The outer, middle cusp of the first and second upper molars.
Metacentric
(Gk *meta* among; *kentron* centre)
Applied to chromosomes having the centromere at or near the middle.
Metastyle
(Gk *meta* after; *stulos* pillar)
The last outer cusp of the upper premolars and molars.
Metatheria
(Gk *meta* beyond; *thēr* wild beast)
Infraclass of the class Mammalia comprising all marsupials.
Miocene
(Gk *meion* less; *kainos* recent)
Tertiary geological epoch, between Oligocene and Pliocene, lasting
from approximately 25,000,000 to 12,000,000 years B.P.
Mode
The value in the frequency distribution represented by the greatest
number of individuals.
Molar
(L *molere* to grind)
Teeth adapted for grinding or crushing; they are not preceded by
milk-teeth.
Monophyodont
(Gk *monos* single; *phuein* to produce)
Having only one set of teeth.
Morphology
(Gk *morphē* form; *logos* discourse)
The science of form and structure in organisms.
Mucopolysaccharide
Compound of polysaccharides (i.e. complex carbohydrates) with
mucoprotein.
Mystacial (vibrissae)
(Gk *mustax* moustache)
On the side of the snout.

Nearctic
(Gk *neos* new; *arktos* bear)
Zoogeographical region comprising North America including
northern Mexico and Greenland.
Neotropical
(Gk *neos* new; *tropikos* tropic)
Zoogeographical region including southern Mexico, Central and
South America, and the West Indies.
Nymph
(Gk *numphē* chrysalis)
Young stage of an insect resembling the adult in nearly all respects,
but differing in size, being sexually immature, wingless, or having
undeveloped wings.

Observed range (OR)
The difference between largest and smallest values observed in a sample.
Olfactory
(L *olfacere* to smell)
Pertaining to the sense of smell.
Oligocene
(Gk *oligos* few; *kainos* recent)
A Tertiary geological epoch between the Eocene and Miocene, lasting from approximately 34,000,000 to 25,000,000 years B.P.
Omnivorous
(L *omnis* all; *vorare* to devour)
Eating both animal and vegetable matter.
Orbit
(L *orbita* circuit)
Bony cavity in the skull that contains the eye.
Order
(L *ordo* order)
Taxonomic category ranking below class and above family.

Palearctic
(Gk *palaios* old; *arktos* bear)
Zoogeographical region including Europe, North Africa, western Asia, Siberia, and northern China.
Palmar
(L *palma* palm of hand)
Pertaining to the palm of the hand.
Pectoral
(L *pectus* breast)
Pertaining to the chest.
Pentadactyl
(Gk *pente* five; *daktulos* finger)
Having five digits on all four limbs.
Pericentric inversion
(Gk *peri* around; *kentron* centre)
Breakage of a chromosome in two places on either side of the centromere, followed by 180° rotation and fusion of the segment between the breaks.
Peritoneal
(Gk *periteinein* to stretch around)
Pertaining to the peritoneum, a membrane lining the abdominal cavity and the organs within.
Piloerection
(L *pilus* hair; *erigere* to raise up)
Raising of hair.
Pinna
(L *pinna* feather)
Outer ear.
Piscivorous
(L *piscis* fish; *vorare* to devour)
Fish-eating.

Placenta
(L *placenta* flat cake)
Organ consisting of embryonic and maternal tissues in close contact, through which the embryo is nourished.

Plantar
(L *planta* sole of foot)
Pertaining to the sole of the foot.

Plantigrade
(L *planta* sole of foot; *gradus* step)
Walking with the entire sole touching the ground.

Pleistocene
(Gk *pleistos* most; *kainos* recent)
Geological era that lasted from approximately 3,000,000 years B.P. to 10,000 years B.P., characterized by four major ice-ages.

Pliocene
(Gk *pleion* more; *kainos* recent)
The last epoch of the Tertiary period, lasting from approximately 12,000,000 years B.P., to 3,000,000 years B.P.

Pollex
(Gk *pollex* thumb)
Thumb or first or innermost digit of the forelimb.

Postglenoid process (apophysis)
(L *post* after; Gk *glēnē* socket)
Process behind the glenoid fossa.

Postmandibular canal
(L *post* after; *mandibulum* jaw)
An opening in the posterior lingual side of the mandible opening into the internal temporal fossa.

Postorbital bar
(L *post* after; *orbita* circuit)
A bony bar behind the orbit.

Premolar
(L *prae* before; *mola* mill)
Teeth between the canine and the molars.

Protoconid
(Gk *prōtos* first; *kōnos* cone; *eidos* form)
External cusp of lower molar.

Prototheria
(Gk *prōtos* first; *thēr* wild beast)
Subclass of the class Mammalia including the egg-laying mammals.

Proximal
(L *proximus* next)
Nearest centre or midline of body or nearest point of attachment.

Pterygoid
(Gk *pterux* wing; *eidos* form)
A bone in the base of the cranium

Radius
(L *radius* ray)
A bone of the forelimb between humerus and carpals.

Recent
(L *recens* recent)
Geological period from about 10,000 years B.P. to the present (also called Holocene).
Rhinarium
(Gk *rhis* nose)
The area surrounding the nostrils.
Rostrum
(L *rostrum* beak)
Part of the cranium anterior to the orbits.

Sangamon
Interglacial stage preceding the last glaciation (Wisconsin).
Scrotum
(L *scrotum* skin)
External sac containing the testicles.
Seral vegetation
(L *serere* to put in a row)
A plant community before reaching a state of relative equilibrium (climax).
Sex ratio
Number of males per hundred females.
Skull length
The distance between the most posterior part of the cranium and the tip of the premaxillae.
Species
(L *species* particular kind)
Groups of actually or potentially interbreeding natural populations that are reproductively isolated from other such groups.
Spermatogenesis
(Gk *sperma* seed; *genesis* origin)
Sperm formation.
Standard deviation
A measure of dispersion or variability given by the square root of the sum of the squared deviations from the mean divided by the number of observations.
Subclass
Taxonomic category between class and infraclass.
Subequal
(L *sub* under)
Approximately or nearly equal.
Subnivean
(L *sub* under; *nivea* snow)
Under the snow.
Submetacentric
(L *sub* under; Gk *meta* among; *kentron* centre)
Nearly metacentric.
Subspecies
(L *sub* under; *species* a particular kind)
A geographical subdivision of a species that differs taxonomically from other subdivisions of the same species.

Subtelocentric
(L *sub* under; Gk *telos* end; *kentron* centre)
Nearly telocentric.
Supercilliary
(L *super* over; *cilia* eyelids) Pertaining to the region above the eye or eyebrows.
Syndactyly
(Gk *sun* with; *daktulos* finger)
Condition in which two or more digits are fused.
Synonym
(Gk *sun* with; *onuma* name)
Each of two or more scientific names for the same taxon.
Synoptic (classification)
A brief summary classification.
Systematics
(Gk *sustēma* system)
The science dealing with the diversity of organisms.

Tail length
The length from the base of the tail to the tip of the tail vertebrae.
Taxon (pl. taxa)
(Gk *taxis* arrangement)
A taxonomic group that is sufficiently distinct to be named and to be ranked in a definite category.
Taxonomy
(Gk *taxis* arrangement; *nomos* laws)
The theory and practice of classifying organisms.
Telocentric
(Gk *telos* end; *kentron* centre)
Chromosome with the centromere at one end.
Temporal
(L *tempora* temples)
Pertaining to the region of the temples.
Territory
(L *territorium* domain)
That part of an animal's home range that is actively defended.
Theria
(Gk *thēr* wild beast)
Subclass of the class Mammalia comprising the marsupials (Metatheria) and placental mammals (Eutheria).
Thermoregulation (Thermoregulate)
(Gk *thermē* heat)
The regulation of an animal's body temperature.
Tibia
(L *tibia* shin)
Shinbone, the larger bone between knee and ankle.
Total length (TL)
The distance from the tip of the nose to the tip of the tail (last verebra).
Tritubercular
(L *tres* three; *tuberculum* small hump)
Molar teeth with three cusps.

Tuberculo-sectorial
(L *tuberculum* small hump; *sector* cutter)
Molars adapted for crushing and cutting.
Tympanic
(Gk *tumpanon* drum)
Ring-shaped bone surrounding the eardrum in shrews; in other
mammals, it may expand inwards to form part of the bulla.

Ulna
(L *ulna* elbow)
A long bone of the forelimb, parallel to and longer than the radius.
Ultrasonic
(L *ultra* beyond; *sonare* to sound)
Sound beyond the upper limit of human hearing.
Unguiculate
(L *unguis* claw)
Clawed.
Unicuspid
(L *unus* one; *cuspis* point of spear)
Small, one-cusped teeth.

Variate
(L *variare* to change)
A continuous or discontinuous variable that takes a numerical value.
Vasoconstriction
(L *vas* vessel; *constringere* to draw tight)
The constriction of blood vessels.
Vibrissa
(L *vibrissa* nostril hair)
Hair growing on the face of mammals that functions as a tactile
organ.

Zygomatic arch
(Gk *zugoma* yoke)
Arch of bone, outside of the skull formed by the zygomatic process
of the squamosal and the cheekbone (jugal).

BIBLIOGRAPHY

Allison, T., and H. Van Twyver
(1970). Sleep in moles, *Scalopus aquaticus* and *Condylura cristata*. Expl. Neurol. 27(3):564–78.
Allison, T., S.D. Gerber, S.M. Breedlove, and G.L. Dryden
(1977). A behavioral and polygraphic study of sleep in the shrews *Suncus murinus, Blarina brevicauda* and *Cryptotis parva*. Behav. Biol. 20(3):354–66.
Anderson, R.M.
(1939). Mammals of the province of Quebec. Ann. Report Provancher Soc. Nat. Hist. 1938:50:114.
(1946). Catalogue of Canadian Recent mammals, Nat. Mus. Can. Bull. 102.
Anthony, H.E., and G.G. Goodwin
(1924). A new species of shrew from the Gaspé Peninsula. Am. Mus. Novit. 109:1–2.
Arlton, A.V.
(1936). An ecological study of the mole. J. Mammal. 17(4):355–59.

Banfield, A.W.F.
(1974). The mammals of Canada. University of Toronto Press.
Barbehenn, K.R.
(1958). Spatial and population relationship between *Microtus* and *Blarina*. Ecology 39:293–304.
Barrett, G.W.
(1969). Bioenergetics of a captive least shrew, *Cryptotis parva*. J. Mammal. 50:629–30.
Beck, W.H.
(1958). A guide to Saskatchewan mammals. Spec. Publ. Sask. Nat. Hist. Soc. I.
Bee, J.W., and E.R. Hall
(1956). Mammals of northern Alaska. Univ. Kans. Mus. Nat. Hist. Misc. Publ. 8.
Bernard, R., R. Cayouette, C. Delisle, P. DesMeules, L. Lemieux, and G. Moisan
(1967). Noms français des Mammifères du Canada. Les carnets de Zoologie 27(2):25–30.
Blair, W.F.
(1940). Notes on home ranges and populations of the short-tailed shrew. Ecology 21(2):284–88.
Blossom, P.M.
(1932). A pair of long-tailed shrews (*Sorex cinereus cinereus*) in captivity. J. Mammal. 13(2):136–43.
Broadbrooks, H.E.
(1952). Nest and behavior of a short-tailed shrew, *Cryptotis parva*. J. Mammal. 33(2):241–43.
Brocke, R.H.
(1970). Ecological inferences from oxygen consumption data of the possum. Ecol. Soc. Am. Bull. 51:29.

Brown, R.J.
(1974). A comparative study of the chromosomes of three species of shrews. *Sorex bendirii, Sorex trowbridgii,* and *Sorex vagrans.* Wasmann J. Biol. 32(2):303–26.
Buchler, E.R.
(1976). The use of echolocation by the wandering shrew (*Sorex vagrans*). Anim. Behav. 24:858–73.
Buckner, C.H.
(1957). Population studies on small mammals of southeastern Manitoba. J. Mammal. 38(4):87–97.
(1964). Metabolism, food capacity and feeding behavior in four species of shrews. Can. J. Zool. 42:259–79.
(1966). Populations and ecological relationships of shrews in tamarack bogs of southeastern Manitoba. J. Mammal. 47(2):181–94.
(1970). Direct observation of shrew predation on insects and fish. Blue Jay 28(4):171–72.
Butler, P.M.
(1956). The skull of *Ictops* and the classification of the Insectivora. Proc. Zool. Soc. Lond. 126:453–81.

Cabrera, A.
(1925). Genera mammalium—Insectivora, Galeopithecia, Mus. Nac. de Ciencias Naturales, Madrid.
Calder, W.A.
(1969). Temperature relations and underwater endurance of the smallest homeothermic diver, the water shrew. Comp. Biochem. Physiol. 30:1075–1082.
Cameron, A.W.
(1958). Mammals of the islands in the Gulf of St. Lawrence. Nat. Mus. Can. Bull. 154.
Carl, G.C., and C.J. Guiguet
(1972). Alien animals in British Columbia. B.C. Prov. Mus. Handb. 14.
Christian, J.J.
(1950). Behavior of the mole (*Scalopus*) and the shrew (*Blarina*). J. Mammal. 31(3):281–87.
(1969). Maturation and breeding of *Blarina brevicauda* in winter. J. Mammal. 50(2):272–76.
Clemens, W.A.
(1968). Origin and early evolution of marsupials. Evolution 22:1–18.
Clothier, R.R.
(1951). Taxonomy of the *Sorex vagrans-obscurus* group in western Montana. Proc. Mont. Acad. Sci. 10:11–12.
(1955). Contribution to the life history of *Sorex vagrans* in Montana. J. Mammal. 36(2):214–21.
Clough, G.C.
(1963). Biology of the arctic shrew, *Sorex arcticus.* Am. Midl. Nat. 69(1):69–81.

Conaway, C.H.

(1952). Life history of the water shrew (*Sorex palustris navigator*). Am. Midl. Nat. 48(1):219-48.

(1958). Maintenance, reproduction and growth of the least shrew in captivity. J. Mammal. 39(4):507-12.

(1959). The reproductive cycle of the eastern mole. J. Mammal. 40(2):180-94.

(1960). The water walker. Nat. Hist. 69(6):21-25.

Cowan, I. McTaggart, and C.J. Guiguet

(1965). The mammals of British Columbia. B.C. Prov. Mus. Handb. 11. 3rd ed.

Criddle, S.

(1973). The granivorous habits of shrews. Can. Field-Nat. 87(1):69-70.

Crowcroft, W.P.

(1957). The life of the shrew. London: Max Reinhardt.

Dalquest, W.W.

(1941). Ecologic relationships of four small mammals in western Washington. J. Mammal. 22(2):170-73.

(1948). Mammals of Washington. Univ. Kans. Mus. Nat. Hist. Publ. 2:1-444.

Dalquest, W.W., and D.R. Orcutt

(1942). The biology of the least shrew-mole. *Neürotrichus gibbsii minor*. Am. Midl. Nat. 27(2):387-401.

Dalton, M., and B.A. Sabo

(1980). A preliminary report on the natural history of the Gaspé shrew. The Atlantic Center for the Environment.

Dapson, R.W.

(1968a). Growth patterns in a post-juvenile population of short-tailed shrews (*Blarina brevicauda*). Am. Midl. Nat. 79:118-29.

(1968b). Reproduction and age structure in a population of short-tailed shrews *Blarina brevicauda*. J. Mammal. 49:205-14.

Davis, W.B. and L. Joeris

(1945). Notes on the life-history of the little short-tailed shrew. J. Mammal. 26:136-38.

DeByle, N.V.

(1965). Short-tailed shrew attacks garter snake. J. Mammal. 46:329.

De Vos, A.

(1957). Peak populations of the masked shrew in northern Ontario. J. Mammal. 38:256-58.

(1964). Range changes of mammals in the Great Lakes region. Am. Midl. Nat. 71:210-31.

Diersing, V.E.

(1980). Systematics and evolution of the pygmy shrews (subgenus *Microsorex*) of North America. J. Mammal 61:76-101.

Dionne, C.E.

(1902). Les mammifères de la province de Québec. Québec: Dussault et Proulx.

Dötsch, C., and W. von Koenigswald

(1978). Zur Rotfärbung von Soricidenzähnen, Z. Säugetierkd. 46:65-70.

Doucet, G.J. and J.R. Bider
(1974). The effects of weather on the activity of the masked shrew.
J. Mammal. 55:348-63.
Doutt, J.K.
(1954). The swimming of the opossum *Didelphis marsupialis
virginiana*. J. Mammal. 35:581-83.
Dusi, J.L.
(1951). The nest of a short-tailed shrew. J. Mammal. 32:115.

Eadie, W.R.
(1939). A contribution to the biology of *Parascalops breweri*.
J. Mammal. 20:150-73.
(1945). The pelvic girdle of *Parascalops*. J. Mammal. 26:94-95.
(1947). The accessory reproductive glands of *Parascalops* with notes
on homologies. Anat. Rec. 97:239-52.
(1949). Predation on *Sorex* by *Blarina*. J. Mammal. 39:308-09.
(1951). A comparative study of the male accessory genital glands of
Neürotrichus. J. Mammal. 32:36-43.
(1952). Shrew predation and vole populations on a localized area.
J. Mammal. 33:185-89.
Eadie, W.R., and W.J. Hamilton, Jr.
(1956). Notes on reproduction in the star-nosed mole. J. Mammal.
37:223-31.

Fay, F.H.
(1954). Quantitative experiments on the food consumption of
Parascalops breweri. J. Mammal. 35:107-09.
Findley, J.S.
(1955). Speciation of the wandering shrew. Univ. Kans. Publ. Mus.
Nat. Hist. 9:1-68.
Findley, J.S., and J.K. Jones, Jr.
(1956). Molt of the short-tailed shrew *Blarina brevicauda*. Am. Midl.
Nat. 56:246-49.
Fisher, A.K.
(1885). The star-nosed mole amphibious. Am. Nat. Extra 19:895.
Fitch, H.S., and H.W. Shirer
(1970). A radiotelemetric study of spatial relationships in the
opossum. Am. Midl. Nat. 85:170-86.
Foote, L.E.
(1941). A swimming hairy-tailed mole. J. Mammal. 22:452.
Forsyth, D.J.
(1976). A field study of growth and development of nestling masked
shrews (*Sorex cinereus*). J. Mammal. 57:708-21.
Foster, J.B.
(1965). The evolution of the mammals of the Queen Charlotte
Islands, British Columbia. Occas. Pap. B.C. Prov. Mus. 14.
Fowle, C.D. and R.Y Edwards
(1955). An unusual abundance of short-tailed shrews, *Blarina
brevicauda*. J. Mammal. 36(1):36-41.

Francq, E.N.
(1969). Behavioral aspects of feigned death in the opossum *Didelphis marsupialis*. Am. Midl. Nat. 81:556-68.
(1970). Electrocardiograms of the opossum, *Didelphis marsupialis*, during feigned death. J. Mammal. 51:395.

Gardner, A.L.
(1973). The systematics of the genus *Didelphis* (Marsupialia: Didelphidae) in North and Middle America. The Museum Texas Tech Univ., Spec. Publ. 4.
Gashwiler, J.S.
(1976). Notes on the reproduction of Trowbridge shrews in western Oregon. Murrelet 57(3):58-62.
Genoways, H.H. and J.R. Choate
(1972). A multivariate analysis of systematic relationships among populations of the short-tailed shrew (genus *Blarina*) in Nebraska. Syst. Zool. 21:106-16.
George, S.B., H.H. Genoways, J.R. Choate, and R.J. Baker
(1982). Karyotypic relationships within the short-tailed shrews, Genus *Blarina*. J. Mamm. 63(4):639-45.
Giger, R.D.
(1973). Movements and homing in Townsend's mole near Tillamook, Oregon. J. Mammal. 54:648-59.
Gillette, L.N.
(1980). Movement patterns of radio-tagged opossums in Wisconsin. Am. Midl. Nat. 104(1):1-12
Glendenning, R.
(1953). Does the Scheffer mole drink? Can. Field. Nat. 67:138-39.
(1959). Biology and control of the coast mole, *Scapanus orarius orarius* True, in British Columbia. Can. J. Anim. Sci. 39:34-44.
Godfrey, G.K.
(1979). Gestation period in the common shrew, *Sorex coronatus (araneus) fretalis*. J. Zool. Lond. 189:548-51.
Goodwin, G.G.
(1924). Mammals of the Gaspé Peninsula, Quebec. J. Mammal. 5:246-57.
(1929). Mammals of the Cascapedia Valley, Quebec. J. Mammal. 10:239-46.
Goodwin, M.K.
(1979). Notes on caravan and play behavior in young captive *Sorex cinereus*. J. Mammal. 60:411-13.
Gould, E.
(1969). Communication in three genera of shrews (*Soricidae*); *Suncus*, *Blarina* and *Cryptotis*. Commun. Behav. Biol. Part A Orig. Artic. 3:11-31.
Gould, E., N.C. Negus, and A. Novick
(1964). Evidence for echolocation in shrews. J. Exp. Zool. 156:19-38.
Grassé, P.P.
(1955). Traité de Zoologie. Tome XVII, Mammifères, Fascicule II, Paris: Masson et Cie.

Hall, E.R., and K.R. Kelson
(1959). The mammals of North America. Vol. I. New York: Ronald Press.

Hallett, J.C.
(1978). *Parascalops breweri*. Mamm. Species 98:1-4.

Hamilton, W.J., Jr.
(1929). Breeding habits of the short-tailed shrew, *Blarina brevicauda*. J. Mammal. 10:125-34.

(1930). The food of the Soricidae. J. Mammal. 11:26-39.

(1931). Habits of the star-nosed mole, *Condylura cristata*. J. Mammal. 12:345-55.

(1934). Habits of *Cryptotis parva* in New York. J. Mammal. 15:154-55.

(1939). Activity of Brewer's mole (*Parascalops breweri*). J. Mammal. 20:308-09.

(1940a). The molt of *Blarina brevicauda*. J. Mammal. 21:457-58.

(1940b). The biology of the smoky shrew (*Sorex fumeus fumeus* Miller). Zoologica (NY) 25:473-92.

(1941). The food of small forest mammals in eastern United States. J. Mammal. 22:250-63.

(1944). The biology of the little short-tailed shrew, *Cryptotis parva*. J. Mammal. 25:1-7.

(1953). The food of the opossum in New York state. J. Wildl. Manage. 15:258-64.

(1958). Life history and economic relations of the opossum (*Didelphis marsupialis virginiana*) in New York State. Mem. Cornell Univ. Ag. Exp. Sta. 354: 1-48.

Hamilton, W.J., Jr., and W.J. Hamilton III
(1954). The food of some small mammals from the Gaspé Peninsula, P.Q. Can. Field-Nat. 68:108-09.

Hamilton, W.J., Jr., M.W. Hosley, and A.E. MacGregor
(1937). Late summer and early fall foods of the red fox in central Massachusetts. J. Mammal. 18:366-67.

Harper, F.
(1956). The mammals of Keewatin. Mus. Nat. Hist. Univ. Kansas Misc. Publ. 12:1-94.

Hartman, C.G.
(1952). Possums, Austin: University of Texas Press.

Harvey, M.J.
(1976). Home range movements, and diel activity of the eastern mole, *Scalopus aquaticus*. Am. Midl. Nat. 95:436-45.

Hatt, R.T.
(1938). Feeding habits of the least shrew. J. Mammal. 19:247-48.

Hawes, M.L.
(1976). Odor as a possible isolating mechanism in sympatric species of shrews (*Sorex vagrans* and *Sorex obscurus*). J. Mammal. 57:404-06.

(1977). Home range, territoriality and ecological separation in sympatric shrews, *Sorex vagrans* and *Sorex obscurus*. J. Mammal. 58:354-67.

Hennings, D., and R.S. Hoffmann
(1977). A review of the taxonomy of the *Sorex vagrans* species complex from western North America. Occas. Pap. Mus. Nat. Hist. Univ. Kans. 68.
Hisaw, F.L.
(1923*a*). Feeding habits of moles. J. Mammal. 4:9–20.
(1923*b*). Observations on the burrowing habits of moles (*Scalopus aquaticus machrinoides*). J. Mammal. 4:79–88.
Hoffmann, R.S.
(1971). Relationships of certain Holarctic shrews, genus *Sorex*. Z. Säugetierkd. 36:193–200.
Hoffmann, R.S., and R.S. Peterson
(1967). Systematics and zoogeography of *Sorex* in the Bering Strait area. Syst. Zool. 16:127–36.
Hopkins, D.
(1977). Nest-building behavior in the immature Virginia opossum (*Didelphis virginiana*). Mammalia 41(3):361–62.
Horváth, O.
(1965). Arboreal predation on bird's nest by masked shrew. J. Mammal. 46:495.
Hunsaker, D.
(1977). The biology of marsupials. New York: Academic Press.
Hutchison, J.H.
(1968). Fossil Talpidae (Insectivora, Mammalia) from the later Tertiary of Oregon. Bull. Mus. Nat. Hist. Univ. Oreg. 11:1–117.
Hutterer R., and T. Hürter
(1981). Adaptive Haarstrukturen bei Wasserspitzmäusen (Insectivora, Soricinae). Z. Säugetierkd. 46:1–11.

Ingram, W.M.
(1942). Snail associates of *Blarina brevicauda talpoides* (Say). J. Mammal. 23:255–56.

Jackson, H.H.T.
(1915). A review of the American moles. N. Am. Fauna 38.
(1928). A taxonomic review of the American long-tailed shrews. (Genera *Sorex* and *Microsorex*). N. Am. Fauna 51.
Jameson, E.W., Jr.
(1949). Some factors influencing the local distribution and abundance of woodland small mammals in central New York. J. Mammal. 30:221–35.
(1950). The external parasites of the short-tailed shrew, *Blarina brevicauda* (Say). J. Mammal. 31:138–45.
(1955). Observations on the biology of *Sorex trowbridgii* in the Sierra Nevada, California. J. Mammal. 36:339–45.
Junge, J.A., and R.S. Hoffmann
(1981). An annotated key to the long-tailed shrews (Genus *Sorex*) of the United States and Canada, with notes on middle American *Sorex*. Univ. Kans. Occ. Pap. 94:1–48.

Keast, A., F.C. Erk and B. Glass (eds.)
(1972). Evolution, mammals and southern continents. Albany: State University of New York Press.

Kirkland, G.L., Jr.
(1977). A re-examination of the subspecific status of the Maryland shrew, *Sorex cinereus fontinalis* Hollister. Proc. P. Acad. Sci. 51:43–46.

(1981). *Sorex dispar* and *Sorex gaspensis*. Mammal. Species 155.

Kirkland, G.L., Jr., and D.F. Schmidt
(1982). Abundance, habitat, reproduction and morphology of forest-dwelling small mammals of Nova Scotia and southeastern New Brunswick. Can. Field-Nat. 96:156–62.

Kirkland, G.L., Jr., D.F. Schmidt and C.J. Kirkland
(1979). First record of the long-tailed shrew (*Sorex dispar*) in New Brunswick. Can. Field-Nat. 93:195–98.

Kirkland, G.L., Jr. and M.H. Van Deusen
(1979). The shrews of the *Sorex dispar* group: *Sorex dispar* Batchelder and *Sorex gaspensis* Anthony and Goodwin. American Museum Novitates 2675.

Kirsch, J.A.W.
(1968). Prodromus of the comparative serology of Marsupialia. Nature 217:418–20.

(1977). The comparative serology of Marsupialia, and a classification of marsupials. Aust. J. Zool. Suppl. Ser. 52.

Kivett, V.K., and O.B. Mock
(1980). Reproductive behavior in the least shrew (*Cryptotis parva*) with special reference to the aural glandular region of the female. Am. Midl. Nat. 103:339–45.

Klugh, A.B.
(1921). Notes on the habits of *Blarina brevicauda*. J. Mammal. 2:35.

Kritzman, E.B.
(1971). Minimole acts like a shrew. Pacific Search 5:7.

(1972). A captive shrew-mole and her litter. Murrelet 53:47–49.

Kuhn, L.W., W.Q. Wick, and R.J. Pedersen
(1966). Breeding nests of Townsend's mole in Oregon. J. Mammal. 47:239–49.

Lampman, B.H.
(1947). A note on the predaceous habit of the water shrew. J. Mammal. 28:181.

Lawrence, B.
(1946). Brief comparison of the short-tailed shrew and reptile poisons. J. Mammal. 26:393–96.

Layne, J.M.
(1951). The use of the tail by an opossum. J. Mammal. 32:464–65.

Long, C.A.
(1972*a*). Taxonomic revision of the mammalian genus *Microsorex* Coues. Trans. Kans. Acad. Sci. 74:181–96.

(1972*b*). Notes on habitat preference and reproduction in pigmy shrews, *Microsorex*. Can. Field-Nat. 86(2):155–60.

(1974). *Microsorex hoyi* and *Microsorex thompsoni*. Mamm. Species 33:1–4.

Lund, D.
(1975). A chromosome analysis of the short-tailed shrew *Blarina carolinensis*. Mamm. Chrom. Newsl. 16(4):160–61.

Macleod, C.F.
(1960). The introduction of the masked shrew into Newfoundland. Bimonthly Progress Rept., Forest Biol. Div., Res. Br., Dept. Agr. 16(2):1.
Macpherson, A.H.
(1965). The origin of diversity in mammals of the Canadian arctic tundra. Syst. Zool. 14:153–73.
Mann, P.M., and R.H. Stinson
(1957). Activity of the short-tailed shrew. Can. J. Zool. 35:171–78.
Martell, A.M., and A.M. Pearson
(1978). The small mammals of the Mackenzie Delta Region, Northwest Territories, Canada. Arctic 31(4):475–88.
Martin, I.G.
(1981). Venom of the short-tailed shrew (*Blarina brevicauda*) as an insect immobilizing agent. J. Mammal. 62:189–92.
Martin, R.A.
(1967). Notes on the male reproductive tract of *Nectogale* and other soricid insectivores. J. Mammal. 48:664–66.
Martin, R.L.
(1966). Redescription of the type locality of *Sorex dispar*. J. Mammal. 47:130–31.
Martinsen, D.L.
(1969). Energetics and activity patterns of short-tailed shrews (*Blarina*) on restricted diets. Ecology 50:505–10.
McCarley, W.H.
(1959). An unusually large nest of *Cryptotis parva*. J. Mammal. 40:243.
McDowell, S.B., Jr.
(1958). The Greater Antillean insectivores. Bull. Am. Mus. Nat. Hist. 115:113–214.
McManus, J.J.
(1967). Observations on sexual behavior of the opossum. J. Mammal. 48:486–87.
(1969). Temperature regulation in the opossum, *Didelphis marsupialis virginiana*. J. Mammal. 50:550–58.
(1970). Behavior of captive opossums *Didelphis marsupialis virginiana*. Am. Midl. Nat. 84:144–69.
(1971). Activity of captive *Didelphis marsupialis*. J. Mammal. 52:846–48.
(1974). *Didelphis virginiana*. Mamm. Species 40.
Meylan, A.
(1967). Formules chromosomiques et polymorphisme Robertsonien chez *Blarina brevicauda* (Say) (Mammalia, Insectivora). Can. J. Zool. 45:1119–27.
Meylan A., and J. Hausser
(1973). Les chromosomes des *Sorex* du groupe *araneus-arcticus* (Mammalia, Insectivora). Z. Säugetierkd. 38:143–58.
Mock, O.B.
(1970). Reproduction in the least shrew (*Cryptotis parva*) in captivity. Ph.D. Thesis, Univ. Mo. (Diss. Abstr. Intern. 31(8B) 1971).

Moore, A.W.
(1933). Food habits of Townsend and coast moles. J. Mammal. 14(1):36-40.
(1939). Notes on the Townsend mole. J. Mammal. 20:499-501.
(1942). Shrews as a check on Douglas fir regeneration. J. Mammal. 23:37-41.
Moore, J.C.
(1949). Notes on the shrew, *Sorex cinereus*, in the southern Appalachians. Ecology 30:234-37.
Morris, R.F.
(1948). The land mammals of New Brunswick. J. Mammal. 29(2):165-76.
Morrison, P.R., and O.P. Pearson
(1946). The metabolism of a very small mammal. Science 104:287-89.
Morrison, P.R., M. Pierce, and F.A. Ryder
(1957). Food consumption and body weight in the masked and short-tailed shrews. Am. Midl. Nat. 57:493-501.

Newman, J.R.
(1976). Population dynamics of the wandering shrew *Sorex vagrans*. Wasmann J. Biol. 34:235-50.
Northcott, T.
(1974). The land mammals of insular Newfoundland. Wildlife Division, Department of Tourism.
Norton, A.C., A.V. Beran, and J.A. Misrahy
(1964). Electroencephalograph during "feigned" sleep in the opossum. Nature 204:162-63.
Nussbaum, R.A., and C. Maser
(1969). Observations of *Sorex palustris* preying on *Dicamptodon ensatus*. Murrelet 50:23-24.

Okhotina, M.V.
(1977). Palaearctic shrews of the subgenus *Otisorex*: Biotopic preference, population number, taxonomic revision and distribution history. Acta Theriol. 22(11):191-206.
Olive, J.R.
(1950). Some parasites of the prairie mole, *Scalopus aquaticus machrinus* (Rafinesque). Ohio J. Sci. 50:263-66.
Olsen, R.W.
(1969). Agonistic behavior of the short-tailed shrew (*Blarina brevicauda*). J. Mammal. 50:494-500.
O'Reilly, R.A., Jr.
(1949). Shrew preying on ribbon snake. J. Mammal. 30:309.

Pattie, D.L.
(1969). Behavior of captive marsh shrews (*Sorex bendirii*). Murrelet 50:27-32.
(1973). *Sorex bendirii* Merriam 1884. Mamm. Species 27:1-2.

Pearson, O.P.

(1942). On the cause and nature of a poisonous action produced by the bite of a shrew (*Blarina brevicauda*). J. Mammal. 23:159–66.

(1944). Reproduction in the shrew (*Blarina brevicauda* Say). Am. J. Anat. 75:39–93.

(1945). Longevity of the short-tailed shrew. Am. Midl. Nat. 34:531–46.

(1946). Scent glands of the short-tailed shrew. Anat. Rec. 94:615–29.

(1956). A toxic substance from the salivary glands of a mammal (short-tailed shrew). Venoms 44:55–58.

Petersen, K.E., and T.L. Yates

(1980). *Condylura cristata*. Mamm. Spec. 129.

Peterson, R.L.

(1966). The mammals of eastern Canada. Toronto: Oxford University Press.

Peterson, R.L., and S.C. Downing

(1956). Distribution records of the opossum in Ontario. J. Mammal. 37:431–35.

Peterson, R.S. and A. Symansky

(1963). First record of the Gaspé shrew from New Brunswick. J. Mammal. 44:278–79.

Pfeiffer, C.J., and G.H. Gass

(1963). Note on the longevity and habits of captive *Cryptotis parva*. J. Mammal. 44:427–28.

Pine, R.H.

(1975). Star-nosed mole eaten by bull frog. Mammalia 39:713–14

Platt, W.J.

(1976). The social organization and territoriality of short-tailed shrew (*Blarina brevicauda*) populations in old-field habitats. Anim. Behav. 24:305–18.

Pray, L.

(1921). Opossum carries leaves with its tail. J. Mammal. 2:109–10.

Prince, L.A.

(1940). Notes on the habits of the pigmy shrew (*Microsorex hoyi*) in captivity. Can. Field-Nat. 54(1):97–100.

Pruitt, W.O., Jr.

(1953). An analysis of some physical factors affecting the local distribution of the short-tailed shrew *Blarina brevicauda* in the northern part of the lower peninsula of Michigan. Misc. Publ. Mus. Zool. Univ. Mich. 79:1–93.

(1954a). Aging in the masked shrew *Sorex cinereus cinereus* Kerr. J. Mammal. 35:35–39.

(1954b). Notes on a litter of young masked shrews. J. Mammal. 35:109–10.

(1957). A survey of the mammalian family Soricidae (shrews). Säugetierkd. Mitt. 5:18–27.

Quay, W.B.

(1951). Observation on mammals of the Seward Peninsula, Alaska. J. Mammal. 32:88–89.

Racey, K.
(1929). Observations on *Neürotrichus gibbsii gibbsii*. Murrelet 10:61–62.
Reed, C.A.
(1944). Behavior of a shrew-mole in captivity. J. Mammal. 25:196–98.
Repenning, C.A.
(1967). Subfamilies and genera of the Soricidae. U.S. Geol. Surv. Prof. Paper 565.
Reynolds, H.C.
(1952). Studies on reproduction in the opossum (*Didelphis virginiana virginiana*). Univ. Calif. Publ. Zool. 52:223–84.
Richardson, John
(1829). Fauna boreali-americana. Part 1, The quadrupeds. London: John Murray.
Richardson, J.H.
(1973). Locomotory and feeding activity of the shrews, *Blarina brevicauda* and *Suncus murinus*. Am. Midl. Nat. 90:224–27.
Richmond, N.D., and W.C. Grimm
(1950). Ecology and distribution of the shrew *Sorex dispar* in Pennsylvania. Ecology 31:278–82.
Ride, W.D.L.
(1970). A guide to the native mammals of Australia. Melbourne: Oxford Univ. Press.
Rongstad, O.J.
(1965). Short-tailed shrew attacks young snowshoe hare. J. Mammal. 46:328–29.
Rood, J.P.
(1958). Habits of the short-tailed shrew in captivity. J. Mammal. 39:499–507.
Roscoe, B., and C. Majka
(1976). First records of the rock vole (*Microtus chrotorrhinus*) and the Gaspé shrew (*Sorex gaspensis*) from Nova Scotia and a second record of the Thompson's pygmy shrew (*Microsorex thompsoni*) from Cape Breton Island. Can. Field-Nat. 90(4):497–98.
Rust, A.K.
(1978). Activity rhythms in the shrews, *Sorex sinuosus* Grinnell and *Sorex trowbridgii* Baird. Am. Midl. Nat. 99(2):369–82.
Rust, C.C.
(1966). Notes on the star-nosed mole (*Condylura cristata*). J. Mammal. 47:538.

Scheffer, T.H.
(1949). Ecological comparisons of three genera of moles. Trans. Kans. Acad. Sci. 52:30–37.
Schmidt, F.J.W.
(1931). Mammals of western Clark County, Wisconsin. J. Mammal. 12:99–117.
Scott, T.G.
(1939). Number of fetuses in the Hoy pigmy shrew. J. Mammal. 20(2):251.
Seton, E.T.
(1909). Life histories of northern mammals. 2 vols. New York: Charles Scribner's Sons.

Short, H.L.
(1961). Fall breeding activity of a young shrew. J. Mammal. 42:95.
Simpson, G.G.
(1945). The principles of classification and a classification of mammals. Bull. Am. Mus. Nat. Hist. 85.
Simpson, S.E.
(1923). The nest and young of the star-nosed mole (*Condylura cristata*). J. Mammal. 4:167–71.
Skoczen, S.
(1976). Condylurini Dobson, 1883 (Insectivora, Mammalia) in the Pliocene of Poland. Acta Zool. Cracoviensia. 218:292–313.
(1980). Scaptonychini Van Valen, 1967, Urotrichini and Scalopini Dobson 1883 (Insectivora, Mammalia) in the Pliocene and Pleistocene of Poland. Acta Zool. Cracoviensia 24:411–48.
Slaughter, R.H.
(1968). Earliest known marsupials. Science 162:254–55.
Slipp, J.W.
(1942). Nest and young of the Olympic dusky shrew. J. Mammal. 23:211–12.
Smith, L.
(1941). Observation on nest building behavior of the opossum. J. Mammal. 22:201–02.
Smith, R.W.
(1940). The land mammals of Nova Scotia. Am. Midl. Nat. 24:213–41.
Snyder, L.L.
(1929). *Cryptotis parva*, a new shrew to the Canadian list. J. Mammal. 10:79–80.
Soper, J.D.
(1961). The mammals of Manitoba. Can. Field-Nat. 75(4):171–219.
(1964). The mammals of Alberta. Edmonton: Government of Alberta.
Sorensen, M.W.
(1962). Some aspects of water shrew behavior. Am. Midl. Nat. 68:445–62.
Stonehouse, B., and D. Gilmore (eds.)
(1977). The biology of marsupials. Baltimore: University Park Press.
Svihla, A.
(1934). The mountain water shrew. Murrelet 15:44–45.

Taube, C.M.
(1947). Food habits of Michigan opossums. J. Wildl. Manage. 11:97–103.
Terry, C.J.
(1978). Food habits of three sympatric species of Insectivora in western Washington. Can. Field-Nat. 92(1):38–44.
(1981). Habitat differentiation among three species of *Sorex* and *Neurotrichus gibbsi* in Washington. Am. Midl. Nat. 106:119–25.

Tomasi, T.E.
(1978). Function of venom in the short-tailed shrew, *Blarina brevicauda*. J. Mammal. 59:852–54.
(1979). Echolocation by the short-tailed shrew, *Blarina brevicauda*. J. Mammal. 60(4):751–59.
Tyndale-Biscoe, H.
(1973). Life of marsupials. London: Arnold.

Van Valen, L.
(1967). New Paleocene Insectivores and Insectivore Classification. Bull. Am. Mus. Nat. Hist. 135:219–84.
Van Vleck, D.B.
(1965). The anatomy of the nasal rays of *Condylura cristata*. J. Mammal. 46:248–53.
van Zyll de Jong, C.G.
(1976a). A comparison between woodland and tundra forms of the common shrew (*Sorex cinereus*). Can. J. Zool. 54:963–73.
(1976b). Are there two species of pygmy shrews (*Microsorex*)? Can. Field-Nat. 90:485–87.
(1980). Systematic relationships of prairie and woodland forms of the common shrew, *Sorex cinereus* Kerr, in the northern zone of contact. J. Mamm. 61:66–75.
(1982a). Relationships of Amphiberingian shrews of the *Sorex cinereus* group. Can. J. Zool. 60:1580–87.
(1982b). An additional morphological character useful in distinguishing two similar shrews, *Sorex monticolus* and *Sorex vagrans*. Can. Field-Nat. 96 (3):349–50.
Verts, B.J.
(1963). Movements and populations of opossums in a cultivated area. J. Wildl. Manage. 27:127–29.
Vickery, W.L., and J.R. Bider
(1978). The effect of weather on *Sorex cinereus* activity. Can. J. Zool. 56(2):291–97.
Vogel, P., and B. Köpchen
(1978). Special hair structures in Soricidae (Mammalia Insectivora) and their taxonomic interpretation. Zoomorphologie 89:47–56.

Walker, E.P.
(1975). Mammals of the world. 3rd ed. Vol 1. Baltimore: Johns Hopkins Press.
Warren, G.L.
(1970). Introduction of the masked shrew to improve control of forest insects in Newfoundland. Proc. Tall Timbers Conf. Ecol. Anim. Control Habitat Manage. 2:185–202.
Weber, M.
(1928). Die Säugetiere. Band II. Zweite Auflage, Nachdruck 1967. Amsterdam: A. Asher & Co.
Whitaker, J.O., Jr., C. Maser, and R.J. Pedersen
(1979). Food and ectoparasitic mites of Oregon moles. Northwest Sci. 53:268–73.
Whitaker, J.O., Jr., and R.E. Mumford
(1972). Food and ectoparasites of Indiana shrews. J. Mammal. 53:329–35.

Whitaker, J.O., Jr. and D.D. Pascal, Jr.
(1971). External parasites of the arctic shrew (*Sorex arcticus*) taken in Minnesota. J. Mammal. 52:202.

Whitaker, J.O., Jr., and L.L. Schmeltz
(1973). Food and external parasites of the eastern mole, *Scalopus aquaticus*, from Indiana. Indiana Acad. Sci. 83:478–81.

Wiegert, R.G.
(1961). Nest construction and oxygen consumption of *Condylura*. J. Mammal. 42:528–29.

Wight, H.M.
(1928). Food habits of Townsend's mole *Scapanus townsendi* (Bachman). J. Mammal. 9:19–23.

Wrigley, R.E., J.E. Dubois, and H.W.R. Copland
(1979). Habitat, abundance and distribution of six species of shrews in Manitoba. J. Mammal. 60(3):505–20.

Yates, A.T., and T.G. Newell
(1969). Social organization of shelter seeking behavior within a group of opossums (*Didelphis virginiana*). Am. Zool. 9:572–73.

Yates, T.L.
(1978). The systematics and evolution of North American moles (Insectivora: Talpidae). Ph.D. dissertation, Texas Tech. University.

Yates, T.L., and I.F. Greenbaum
(1982). Biochemical systematics of North American moles (Insectivora: Talpidae). J. Mamm. 63:368–74.

Yates, T.L., D.B. Pence and G.K. Launchbaugh
(1979). Ectoparasites from seven species of North American moles (Insectivora: Talpidae). J. Med. Entomol. 16:166–68.

Yates, T.L., and D.L. Schmidly
(1975). Karyotype of the eastern mole *Scalopus aquaticus* with comments on the karyology of the family Talpidae. J. Mammal. 56:902–05.

(1977). Systematics of *Scalopus aquaticus* (Linnaeus) in Texas and adjacent states. Occas. Papers, Texas Tech Univ. 45.

Youngman, P.M.
(1975). Mammals of the Yukon Territory. Natl. Mus. Nat. Sci. (Ottawa) Publ. Zool. 10.

Yudin, B.S.
(1969). Taxonomy of some species of shrews (Soricidae) from Palearctic and Nearctic. Acta Theriol. 14:21–34.

(1973). On characteristics of the transarctic pigmy shrew (*Sorex cinereus* Kerr, 1794) from northeast Siberia and Kamchatka. (In Russian). The fauna of Siberia, part 2. Proc. Biol. Inst. Acad. Sci. U.S.S.R. (Novosibirisk) 16:269–79.